CW01021435

THE SERIES OF
THE LOGIA OF ISRAEL

Vol. I. EZEKIEL, *A Cosmic Drama*

Vol. II. ISAIAH, *A Cosmic and Messianic Drama*

To be followed by other volumes

THE ORDER OF THE CROSS
10 DE VERE GARDENS
KENSINGTON, LONDON W.8.

ISAIAH

A COSMIC
AND
MESSIANIC DRAMA

By J. TODD FERRIER

VOL. II

OF

THE LOGIA OF ISRAEL

First published in 1934
Second Edition   1949

PRINTED BY THE REPLIKA PROCESS
IN GREAT BRITAIN BY
LUND HUMPHRIES
LONDON · BRADFORD

DEDICATION

TO all my spiritual Children who have suffered world-oppression and great inward Travail throughout the ages since this Cosmic Revelation was first given, and especially to those mystical Fishermen of Galilee who toiled all night and caught nothing, that they may all be comforted and illumined and borne up on the Eternal Strength to Angelic Realizations and Ministries; and that the promised Day-break may be witnessed by them in this recovered Message of Isaiah, together with the Vision of their LORD walking upon the troubled waters and commanding these to be still as HE sheds HIS Peace; and that all may again hear HIS tender Voice saying to them, but with added intensity of meaning because of the accomplishment of the Oblation:—

"Children, have ye naught to eat that ye sorrow so? Come! Dine with ME: Take ye this Bread of Life, and be ye nourished."

DEDICATORY PRAYER

O Most Holy One, my Father-Mother!
The motion of my Being is unto Thee
In Praise, Worship, and Adoration.

$$* \quad * \quad * \quad * \quad * \quad *$$

Upon the Oblatory of Thine Altar
Within the Sanctuary where Thy Presence abides,
Thy Servant would, in deep humility,
Lay this tribute of Thy Love and Wisdom
In the recovered Message of Thy Messianic Messenger.

$$* \quad * \quad * \quad * \quad * \quad *$$

O Lord, God of Sabaoth! How glorious Thou art!
May the Revelation of Thyself in the Holy Passion,
Bring back the whole House of Israel to a state
Of remembrance of Thee and all Thy Goodness.
And may they once more become as
The Sacred Ark of Thy Presence moving through
The Wilderness of this world, shedding the glory of Thy
Resplendence in Thy Love and Wisdom.

I

NOTE TO SECOND EDITION

THIS Edition contains certain new elements, the chief of which are the five passages of Logia which now appear on pages 98, 126, 148, 170 and 190. These were part of the original MS., went to the printers and were set, proofed and paged, but were evidently inadvertently omitted from the make-up. They were discovered among the Author's papers and are now included in their right places.

A Synopsis of the part-titles and contents has been upgathered into the preliminary pages. The Foreword to the Text and Notes will be found on page 311.

A Glossary of terms and quotations selected from the original, enabling the Reader and Student to find and correlate many of the thematic sayings and writings, especially those which are definitionary in character, will be found at the end of the volume.

THE TRUSTEES.

CONTENTS

PART ONE

PART TWO

PART THREE

CONTENTS

PART FOUR

PART FIVE

PART SIX

CONTENTS

PART SEVEN

PART EIGHT

PART NINE

CONTENTS

PART TEN

PART ELEVEN

PART TWELVE

PART THIRTEEN

PART FOURTEEN

PITY COMPASSION LOVE

SELF-ABANDONMENT

SELF-SACRIFICE

SELF-DENIAL

REDEMPTION

REGENERATION

ILLUMINATION

The Order of the Cross

SPIRITUAL
AIMS AND IDEALS

THE Order is an informal Brother-hood and Fellowship, having for its service in life the cultivation of the Spirit of Love towards all Souls: Helping the weak and defending the defenceless and oppressed; Abstaining from hurting the creatures, eschewing bloodshed and flesh eating, and living upon the pure foods so abundantly provided by nature; Walking in the Mystic Way of Life, whose Path leads to the realization of the Christhood; And sending forth the Mystic Teachings unto all who may be able to receive them — those sacred interpretations of the Soul, the Christhood, and the Divine Love and Wisdom, for which the Order of the Cross stands.

SERVICE DEVOTION PURITY

THE BOOK OF ISAIAH

PART ONE

THE UNITY OF DIVINE REVELATION

*Showing that all true Revelation is from the One
Source, whether it comes through Moses,
Isaiah, the Master known as Jesus,
or another; there is no contradiction between the messages
through Seers and
Prophets, but one
Purpose in and
through
all.*

B

CONTENTS

Most Glorious One, our Father-Mother! We would Praise Thee.

Thou art indeed, even unto us Thy Children, the Light-Ineffable, the Life Transcendent, and the Love whose Deeps are unfathomable.

Thou art ever the same in Thy Nature and Ways, Eternal and Unchangeable.

We know now when Thou revealest Thyself; for Thy Revelations bear within them the Light of Thy Glory and the Likeness of Thy Love.

How honoured we are that Thou shouldest unveil Thy Radiance unto us, and show us Thy Glory!

In all our Ways we would Image Thee, showing forth in our likeness to Thee, the beauty of Thy Holiness and the tenderness of Thy Love.

May we dwell within Thy Sanctuary in the consciousness of Thine overshadowing, and know ourselves so encompassed and upheld from Thee, that Thy Love in its exquisite lowliness as well as in the might of its sublime Majesty, may be made manifest through us, and our service for Thee be the interpretation of Thy Holy Will.

Unto this end we would dedicate ourselves anew to Thee.

Amen and Amen.

THE UNITY OF DIVINE REVELATION

ALL true Revelation has one source. It may proceed from that source through many realms, states and degrees of manifestation, but it is from the one Divine Centre. As the FATHER-MOTHER is the Magnetic Pole that holds the Universe in Eternal Unity, all Revelation must necessarily partake of HIS Nature and reflect the glory of HIS Mystery expressed in the terms, Love and Wisdom. And it must needs be that, however varied the Revelation, and however great or less it may be in the degree of its intensity, yet there must be, from the centre to the circumference of that which is revealed, Divine Unity. There could not be any contradiction in that which the FATHER-MOTHER revealed, although in the Revelation of HIMSELF and HIS works, Truth may have to be aspected and partially veiled. But even then, as the further unveilings of the Truth proceeded, there would be found no contradiction between the greater and that which was given forth in less degree.

Perhaps it would help the reader to follow me with clearer understanding in this unveiling if, first of all, I dealt with two great aspects of this Mystery wherein there will be recognized Divine oneness; and then showed that there would be a reflection of those two aspects on another kingdom wherein there might seem to be something contradictory; and then witnessed to the sublime purpose lying behind all Revelation.

THE UNCHANGEABLE ETERNAL ONE

In the Old Scriptures we read of the Everlasting GOD. HE is ever the Eternal LORD of Being, the Unchangeable

5

ONE, the same throughout all ages. Such a state postulated of the Divine LORD is to be understood in no mono-
tonous sense, but rather that in HIS Nature HE is ever ONE
and the same. HIS Purpose is one with HIS Nature, though
the mediation of HIS Love and Wisdom unto the fulfilment
of HIS Purpose and the realization of HIMSELF in the manifold expositions of HIS creation, varies. Through HIS
mediation HE causes to come forth into manifestation
infinite degrees of life, experience, vision, realization; all
of them leading on to the sublime climax for which every
Human Soul has been created, evolved, fashioned,
enriched, and borne along on the motion of the Eternal
Law from degree to degree, unto the realization within
itself of HIS Sacred Mystery.

Thus GOD is spoken of as the Unchangeable ONE; though
in creation there is an eternal process of manifestation in
embodiments implying many changes. But in all this
there is no change of the Divine Purpose. That is ever the
same. As HE is from everlasting to everlasting, so is HIS
holy Will to bless and give. The ages testify of this
sublime oneness.

In the New Testament Scriptures we read that "Jesus
Christ is the same yesterday, to-day and for ever." If that
be so, then HE is one with the Eternal Mystery, the
FATHER-MOTHER, Who is Unchangeable. Here is a revelation of Divine Unity between the Absolute Universal
and the Particular, between the Eternal Mystery Who fills
all creation, Whom we speak of as THE ONE, and one of
HIS sublime embodiments and revelations.

The FATHER-MOTHER's children find it difficult to think
of HIM in the Universal sense (and it is difficult until a Soul
gets there through growth and evolution and ascension);
yet it is the great Purpose of the ministry of the FATHER-
MOTHER unto all HIS children that they should ascend into

6

such a state of consciousness as would enable them to
think of HIM as the same in the Universal as in the
Particular, the Unchangeable ONE amidst all the manifestations in HIS glorious Universe. And then when focus-
sed into what seems to be an individual expression of
HIMSELF as given forth in the terms Jesus Christ the LORD,
HE is still accounted the same yesterday, to-day and
for ever. Yesterday here means the past; to-day is one with
the past; and to-morrow is to indicate that there could be
no change evermore, and that the embodiment known as
Jesus Christ the LORD is of the very nature of the Eternal,
Unchangeable, Absolute Mystery.

We will see, presently, how beautiful is this Revelation
of the FATHER-MOTHER unto HIS children. But, first of
all, we will look at what seems to be a contradiction in HIS
Unchangeable Nature as that is set forth in the Old
Scriptures; for these latter do represent HIM as a most
variable quality and quantity, and have caused unspeakable tragedy by the conception of GOD which they reveal.

APPARENT CONTRADICTIONS

In those Old Scriptures it is recorded that GOD gave
HIS Law and HIS Testimony unto the Children of Israel
through Moses. Then in the New Testament Scriptures
we read, "The Law was given by Moses, but Grace and
Truth came in Jesus Christ." By a strange misapprehen-
sion of the truth herein expressed in both instances, and
which has led to unspeakable tragedy, there has been an
application of the expression "The Law of GOD was given
by Moses" to something that was quite unlike the real
Teachings of Moses and the Ways of the Divine Love and
Wisdom. For that Law is represented as causing great
affliction, pain and travail. When we turn to the Christian
Scriptures as set forth in the Pauline writings, and in less
degree in some other parts of the New Testament, and find

7

the interpretations given to these all through the ages by theological schools, especially concerning the Law of Moses and the Teachings of Jesus Christ, we are informed that the Law of GOD set forth by Moses was something that mankind had to be delivered from, and that the deliverance had to be effected through Jesus Christ. It is most obviously implied that the Law could not save anyone, and that by Grace alone was mankind saved, because Grace was different from and yet much more than the Law.

Here the confusion of truth with error is lamentable. The Law given by Moses, and the Grace of GOD in Jesus Christ, are one. Without the Law there could not be any Jesus Christ states. The Grace that makes even a Son of GOD hold the high estate and office of Jesus Christ the LORD, is the resultant of the operation within such an one of the Law of the LORD.

*　　*　　*　　*　　*　　*

For, consider this: Moses was a Messenger. He was not only a Messenger as you would understand that term as relating to one who came in the human form to speak to the children of men. He was a great Messenger unto a special People, called in the Scriptures, "The Elect Nation." They were "A Chosen People." They had been specially chosen by the Heavens to come to this world to minister to other children of the FATHER-MOTHER who were in less degrees of spiritual attainment. As a Messenger, Moses had to minister to this People who had been elected to visit the Earth and interpret spiritual things unto the children of men who were in less degrees of spiritual estate. And the great mission that Moses had unto this Elect People, was of a dual nature and in a dual capacity, and in order to bring back to their remembrance through their recovered consciousness, *the Law of the Lord.*

The Law of the LORD is not to be confounded with beliefs and ceremonial. Ceremonial laws may be instituted for communal, religious and national purposes. But these must not at any time be confounded with the Law of the LORD. This latter is said to be perfect, converting or restoring the Soul. But ceremonial in itself does not bring anyone to the right vision, nor convert to the true way of life, unless a right use be made of it. If it be rightly understood in its use, it may become a venue through which the Soul seeks to approach HIM Who is the LORD. Such is the only value of ceremonial. It could thus become an aid to the Soul by which to reach forward and upward unto HIM.

But the Law of the LORD as set forth in the Old Scriptures, as these have been interpreted through the ages, has been confounded with the ceremonial law of Jewry and the Decalogue, or Ten Commandments. Yet the Ten Commandments which are believed to contain the Law as given by Moses, and which are recited in the Churches so frequently, are as unlike the Laws that Moses unveiled to Israel as the dusk at eventide or the hour before the dawn is unlike the splendour of the day. The phrases which are supposed to have been given as commandments in the ten words, were Jewish accommodations. The Jewish people needed direction. As a race their outlook on life and their spiritual realizations were so infantile, that they required laws that would act upon them to guard them against the temptation of yielding to the evil conditions which obtained and prevailed in the world, and thus become an incentive to them to seek unto the finding of the more spiritual, the more inward, and the diviner things of the Soul.

9

The Law of the Lord that converts the Soul and restores it to perfect equilibrium, is none other than the motion of the Holy Spirit within the Being; for that Spirit gives to the Soul perfect balancing power. *His Law is one. It makes for unity.* It is the Law of His perfect Love operating in the universal life; the individual life; the great worlds and the little worlds; amidst the Gods and the Sons of the Gods; and in the heart of every one of His children who will respond to its motion. For there is no other way of attainment than by the path of the Law of the Lord. It is the path that Love reveals. There is no other road by which a Soul can attain.

Thus spake He who came as the exposition of Grace and Truth—"Love ye one another. Even as I have loved you, so love ye one another." And the Saying is burdened with truth of Divine immensity, that there is no attainment in any other way than by the path of Divine Love. It is the Law of the Lord. Its dual aspect is that which brings it to the Soul's realization. The first is the realization of the Divine Law of Love. The second is the opening up of the Heavens of the Soul unto the understanding of the Mystery of Being. For no one can climb unto the Heavens by the path of the mind. The mind may be illumined; but the illumination must also be from the Inner Heavens. And it will be so in the degree in which the Soul attains through walking in the path of Love, even unto the realization of the Presence. For the dual aspect of the Law of the Lord is the Revelation of His Wisdom; not in an objective aspect of it only, but in the subjective understanding which leads unto the realization of it.

The Law of Moses and Jesus Christ

Such was the Law that came by Moses. It contained the Grace and Truth which came in Jesus Christ. But Jesus Christ (even if you think of those terms as related very specially to the Servant who was the Messenger of the Most High), even as the Messenger of the FATHER-MOTHER coming with Grace and Truth, did not come to do away with the Law of the LORD. When a Soul realizes the Law of the LORD within itself, it transcends all the limitations of materiality. It issues from bondage and becomes a free Soul. It has the freedom of the City of GOD. Did Jesus Christ come to do away with the Law of the LORD given through Moses? Did He come to negative through His manifestation and ministry that which had been given to Moses to transmit unto the Children of Israel, and to accomplish in and through them? Nay, verily! There was Divine Unity between the two Messengers, and also between the Messages which the two Messengers had to give.

There is no inheritance of Grace other than that which the operations of the Law of GOD within the Being, bring. There can be no realization of the Grace of Jesus Christ, except in that realization which is the resultant of the operation of the Law of Love within the Being. For, if Jesus be GOD's manifestation of what a child of Love should be, then that child's realization of Divine Grace is the resultant of the operations of the Divine Law within him. Moses brought back to Israel the vision of that Law of Life. Through the understanding of that Law there again opened up within the vision of Israel, that Mystery which was operative at the heart of each one, whose motion caused an expansion of consciousness, and through that expansion, a deeper and fuller understanding of the Mystery of GOD as Universal Being. It is even thus we come to understand ourselves through the operation of the Law of GOD within us; nor can we know and understand HIS embodiments in the Universe except through the realization of HIS Law within ourselves.

For the Law is HIMSELF in us. If it were not so, we could never understand HIM. For only the God within us can apprehend GOD the Absolute ONE, the Overshadowing ONE. Only that which is of GOD can enable us to apprehend the like qualities.

It is thus, because we are of HIM, that we can ascend the heights of the Heavens even unto the realization of HIMSELF. For the realization of HIM is a great verity. The Eternal Potency is in us, and it is the transcendent experience into which all Souls are to come as the apex of their evolution. Nay, more. Surely all who are able in part to receive this Message, will come to realize HIM in such fulness through the Divine apex of their Being, which was once their radiant centre, being again made radiant from HIM through HIS Overshadowing of the magnetic pole.

GRACE AND TRUTH

Thus it may be seen that there is no difference between Moses and Christ. There is no contradiction in their Messages when rightly understood. There never has been. The Message of Moses was that of the FATHER-MOTHER concerning Spiritual Law; the Law of Universal Being; Divine Law expressed Celestially in HIS Universe; that Law also accommodated within each Soul; the Law of HIS Love as the Spiritual and Divine force in the realm of consciousness, whose operations make for the expansion, the deepening, and the ascension of the Being.

There could be no contradiction between any Message brought by a Divine Messenger in the far past, or at the present time, and that which the Master gave during the Manifestation. The Grace of Jesus Christ is the exquisite beauty of Love in manifestation. A Soul full of Grace is garmented from GOD. Grace flows from the lips through the words spoken. Grace flows through the auric radiations, so that the paths of such a Soul, in the language of the Old Scriptures, "drop fatness"—they make rich wheresoever the footsteps tread. Through every action of such an one the riches of the Grace of the FATHER-MOTHER are bestowed. For no one can love divinely without shedding Love. No one can know the Divine Love and be in attitude to another, in conduct in the world, and in service unto men and women, as if he or she did not know it. A Soul full of Divine Love could not be as a nonentity where Love was concerned. It is well to remember that Love is not something to be captured by the mind as a belief in it, but a living force to be realized and made manifest. When the Being is filled with the Law of Divine Love, and moved by the operation of that Law, such an one becomes the bond-servant of His LORD. Such is not the bondage that the world knows; it is the sacrificial attitude of the Being in response to the sweet, Divine constraint of the FATHER-MOTHER.

*   *   *   *   *   *

Grace and Truth always have come in Christ. The Western world limits the appearing of Christ to some nineteen hundred years ago. In historical Christianity Christ and the Master were and are one and the same. But Christ was in Moses, and in the teaching of Moses. Christ was operating on the realms whence proceeded the Message that Moses communicated unto Israel. Christ is the same yesterday, to-day and for ever. He is Eternal. He is always impersonal, even when individual in the ADONAI. There could not be any difference between the estates of Jesushood and Christhood lived a thousand ages past, and the Jesushood and Christhood that the Master is said to have revealed and manifested, or the Jesushood and the Christhood that we are all now asked to realize and embody in life and service.

13

In Jesus, GOD is the Unchangeable Love. Thus Jesus becomes the same yesterday, to-day, and for-ever. He is always compassionate, gracious, beautiful, and lovely, the true exposition of the LORD of Love and Wisdom. And the LORD of Love and Wisdom is our FATHER-MOTHER.

All Truth comes through Christ. He makes all things clear. But the Truth of which the Christ speaks, is not different from the Truth which Moses brought back to Israel. The Master, great ages before He came for the Manifestation, was the bearer of Revelation unto the Children of Israel. He came to seek unto the finding of them, and the bearing of them back through the Revelation He had to give. He was one of them, for He was their Elder Brother. The Message He brought in the days of the Manifestation was one with the Message of the great ages. It had relation to Life and Realization, Manifestation and Service. That which was new in His Message, which He brought to such as could receive it in the days of the Manifestation, concerned itself with things that were indicated in preceding ages only to Israel through the Messenger and the Prophets. Those things were related to the Oblation. This latter became one of the greatest mysteries held by the Messenger and those to whom He revealed it, as of the secrets of GOD. It was not revealed until the second Naros B.C.

But this new Revelation did not reveal any change in Purpose of the FATHER-MOTHER. It rather confirmed the eternal quality of that Purpose. When the Divine World purposed to alter its form of ministries and those of the Solar World, unto this Earth, and to effect the Planet's redemption by means of the Oblation, the Gods did not change one iota the Eternal Purpose. They only added to the means by which that Purpose was to be triumphantly fulfilled—a great work which will be accomplished bye and bye. In the meantime, so far as the ministry within the Planetary Heavens is concerned, that Purpose has been fulfilled and realized.

No Contradiction in Divine Revelation

Behold, then, the unity of the varied ministries of the Divine Love and Wisdom in all ages, and the Unchangeable Nature of our FATHER-MOTHER. HIS Purpose is ever the same. Think of this when you are in the changing world. Remember it day by day. Try to hold the thought when you are tempted and tried; when the enemy whispers in your ear such things as might cause you to doubt the goodness of GOD, because everything around you seems to be a contradiction of HIS Presence in the world. Be established in your trust in HIM, and never think HE is changeable. At all times remember that HE is the Unchangeable ONE.

*   *   *   *   *   *

In this relationship I would say a word to all. Do not ask GOD for impossible things. Do not request HIM to do for you what you are able but unwilling to do for yourself. Do not entreat HIM for that which, if HE gave it to you, you could not receive because you are not in the state to receive it rightly. Remember always that HE is Unchangeable.

The many prayers of people do not change HIM. It is good to pray. Prayer is the Being's motion to HIM. The Soul cannot get anywhere upward without prayer. But prayer is no vain utterance. It is the Soul's spiral breathing motion to HIM. It is the Soul's desire to know HIM; to realize HIM; to be filled from HIM; to have HIS qualities more and more manifested; to live in the vision of HIM always. HIS Purpose is eternally the same.

So we do not change HIM. But HE teaches us to pray. Because, prayer is the natural opening out of our Being to HIM, the true expansion of our desire, the deepening of our consciousness and the exaltation of our vision. We fulfil HIS Law in the motion of prayer. HE changes and exalts us through the fulfilment of that Law. By means of it, HE accomplishes HIS Purpose in and through us. Yet HE is always just the same to us. In every way HE remains the Unchangeable ONE. If we are ever tempted to utter some of those wonderful sayings found in the Psalter, such as—"LORD, why hast THOU cast me off from THEE? Wilt THOU be merciful no more?"—recall to remembrance that HE never casts anyone off, and HIS mercy doth not fail. For HIS mercy is the tenderness of HIS Love in its healing inflow. Therefore we have no occasion at any time to doubt HIM. All our prayers should be the Soul-expressions of children who understand the beauty of HIS Love and the glory of HIS Wisdom, the fidelity of HIS Purpose and the unshakable nature of HIS goodness, together with the immeasurable capacity of that Love to give to HIS children unto the uttermost.

It is a remarkable thing that in the real mystical teachings found in both the Old Testament and the New Testament, there is no contradiction. Any difference that may appear on the surface will be found to relate to the degrees of the Revelations given, the Kingdom to which they belong, and the Plane of realization on which the recipient receives them. The mystical Scriptures in both Testaments are like scattered jewels found amongst strange soil which, instead of adding to their revealing beauty, dims their inherent light and oft-times quite veils their message. And some of the most precious gems of Divine Revelation have been broken and the fragments scattered, so that the service intended by the Revelation

contained in any one of these cannot be rendered. The
Old Testament contains many precious gems buried
amidst the changed histories and biographies found in
Jewish story. Even whole books have undergone such a
process of elimination of true Revelation, with addenda
added of many things foreign to such Revelation, and the
materialization of such gems of Revelation as were
retained, through personal, national and racial application, until the Revelation has been lost. Thus the books
have become other than they originally were.

THE FIVE BOOKS OF MOSES

We have a most startling illustration of this in the five
Books specially attributed to Moses—Genesis, Exodus,
Leviticus, Numbers and Deuteronomy. Of the five Books,
Genesis is most like the original, though it also has been
so changed that most of its contents are related to outer
history rather than to Celestial drama and Planetary
tragedy.

The Book of Genesis is mostly Celestial, Solar and
Planetary. It is like a Masonic repository. It is full of
things whose meanings are hidden. Its fragments of
apparent history cover great ages, and these are chiefly
related to dramatic situations after what is termed The
Fall. The Open Sesame can be given alone from the
Divine World, by which its many dramas may be un-
ravelled and the truth of them revealed. The names
Adam, Enoch, Noah, Abraham, Isaac, Jacob, Melchisedek are names of sacred lore concerning things Divine,
Celestial, and Planetary.

Of the Book of Exodus similar things may be said.
That book is apparently a history of the Jewish people in
Egypt, and the delivery of the nation from bondage, and,
in part, their journeyings through the wilderness of Sin

and the giving unto them of the Law from Mount Sinai, together with the most elaborate priestly ceremonial and barbaric sacrificial ritual and acts for the pleasing of GOD, the Eternal Love and Wisdom, and the forgiveness of the sins of the people. But the original Book of Exodus was that of Moses, the Messenger unto Israel whilst they were in states of bondage to the elemental conditions which arose within this world; and the recovery for them and transmission unto them by Moses through their Elders, of the Laws of the Divine Love and Wisdom; together with the restoration unto them by means of Revelation, of the vast knowledge which they once had of Angelic and Celestial symbolism in relation to the worship of the Most High ONE; the path of the Soul in its ascension; and the sublimity of the spirit of sacrifice in the worship of the Eternal.

*   *   *   *   *   *

The original Book of Leviticus was a Record containing most profound teaching concerning Priesthood in its various orders; the Spiritual and Divine significance of Temples, Altars and Vestments, and the inner significance of Sacrifice as the Soul's oblation was offered from the outer court to the innermost Sanctuary. It embraced in its teaching the various orders and degrees of sacrifice, beginning with the consecration of the body and all its powers unto the service of the Most High; leading on to those offerings expressive of the devotion of the mind that is full of exquisitely beautiful purpose, lowly in ambition but exalted in desire; then into the court of the heart with its sacred altar, its sweet savour of most pure incense wherein all that the heart stands for was made consecrate in and through the motion of its love with all its magnetic streams, for the service of its LORD; and still upward and inward to that altar of sacrifice wherein the Soul came into the consciousness of that most holy Mystery of which the Ark with its Mercy Seat spake, at which stage in the ascension of Being, the Soul laid itself upon the Mercy Seat overshadowed by the Cherubim, in perfect oblatory sacrifice unto the LORD; and then, these initiatory sacrifices were crowned by that supreme act wherein the Will, which is the electro-magnetic force at the centre of the substance of every Soul, and by which all souls are related to the Eternal Light, Life and Love, became one in sublimest sacrifice with the Divine Purpose, so that the whole Being lived and moved and had Divine consciousness in the Eternal Presence.

When the Logia spoken by the Master on the Priesthood of the Soul, the Priesthood of Israel, and the Priesthood of the One sent, together with that of the Priesthood of Melchisedek—treasures which were stolen from the Brotherhood, fragments of which are found in the Epistolary Letters, especially in that of the Epistle to the Hebrews—are regathered and interpreted, it will then be possible also to re-state the Divine contents of the original book of Leviticus.

* * * * * *

The original Book of Numbers had profound teaching concerning the Law of Balance. It was a Celestial Book. The numbering of the Children of Israel was not the counting of a people, but the knowledge which that People once held of the value of numbers and geometrical formations. The Book of Numbers as it related to the drama of the Solar system, revealed its Celestial balance and formation. That included all the members of the system. But it also contained teaching which may be expressed in axiomatic terms and postulates, indicating the structure of the Universe, the formation of systems, how the Law of perfect balance obtained throughout the Universe, and also how a disturbance in one system affected all in some degree, and in greater degree affected the system where the cause of the disturbance took place. It was a book full of Divine Revelation of Celestial import. The Revelation was broken up into fragments, which may be found scattered throughout the book—of which more bye and bye.

* * * * * *

The Book of Deuteronomy purports to be a re-promulgation of the Law. There are recorded in it three special addresses by Moses to those Children of Israel who had been born in the wilderness and who had not heard the original promulgation. It also gives the closing scenes of the life of Moses, and the call of Joshua to lead the people. The first address by Moses is an exhortation to the Children of Israel to remember the Law of the LORD and to be obedient to the Divine Command. The second address is given as an exposition of the Ten Commandments. The third address purported to be a solemn renewal of the Covenant, with many curses upon all who should fail to observe the Law and the Testimony. The original book, however, had to do with the repromulgation of the Law from Gilgal to Shechem, just as the first promulgation of the Law given in Exodus was from Sinai. Now, Sinai was the Mountain that represented that altitude of consciousness from which the Mystery of the Law of Life as expressed in the superstructure of the Soul, and the Law of Universal Being as revealed in the Celestial Universe, could be received from the Divine Hand through HIS Messenger, and apprehended and realized by the Soul. Whereas, Gilgal represented the Circle, and was of the nature of Golgotha or Calvary. It embraced the Planetary Heavens whose circuli took in a radius from the lower Angelic Heavens to the

Planetary outer planes where the most fallen states prevailed. And this second promulgation of the Law was of a prophetic order, indicating that the Law of GOD must be restored fully within all the Children of Israel who were the Ancient Sons of GOD, and within the children who did not know the Law in its higher and more inward aspects, in so far as it related to fidelity, purity, honour and truth, so that they might in due course be also led to the understanding of the Law of the LORD in its deeper meanings.

THE DIVINE PURPOSE IN ALL REVELATION

The height, depth and expansiveness of Revelation varies, but it is always in harmony with the Divine Purpose and concerns some further fulfilment of it. New orders and forms of ministry are prefaced by Revelation. The Revelation proclaims the coming of these new orders and forms of ministry and the nature of them.

It was thus with the Oblation. During the period represented by the historical Moses, according to the Old Scriptures, it was not even projected; but there are a number of references to it in the books of Numbers, Joshua and the Judges. It is found covertly indicated in some of Balaam's prophecies found in the book of Numbers, and there are elements of it in the story of Samson as told in the book of Judges. The latter story was originally a Solar myth connected with the Oblation, and full of Divine significance. It was given as a revelation of what the Divine Love and Wisdom purposed, and the nature of the ministry that would have to be rendered unto the fulfilment of that Purpose ere the great mystery of evil could be unearthed and overthrown. For the path of the Oblation was one that was to accomplish the destruction of the House of the false Dagon; for the latter was the temple representing the great perversion, inversion and subversion of the Truth.

Then when we turn to the real book of the Oblation as set forth in the prophetic writings of Isaiah, we find a Divine Unity between such indications of the Divine Purpose as previously set forth, and the path of the Oblation revealed in the book of Isaiah.

The story of Israel as the Children of Zion, and of the City of Zion as the City of Light wherein the ancient Christhood once dwelt, and out from which they came to minister unto the children of this world; the travail of Israel and the revelation of what they once were as the Children of Zion; the return of Israel; the exquisite structure of the Temple of their redeemed state and regenerated attributes; the glory of their oncoming in the Return, and the resplendence with which the Earth would become clothed as the result; the triumph of the Divine Love over every opposing force and militating influence, and, as a resultant, a redeemed world; Jerusalem restored; Zion once more the City of the Sun, the vehicle through which the Divine glory would shed itself upon the life of the world—all these most precious gems have their glory unveiled and revealed in Isaiah. And the unveiling and revealing are interpretive of revelations concerning Israel; Zion; the needs of the world in its fallen state; and the Redemption and Regeneration indicated in earlier Scriptures.

THE BOOK OF ISAIAH

PART TWO

•

THE PROPHECY

*Being a Revelation of Cosmic Nature
relating to the Drama of a Messianic
Manifestation, Divine Burden-
bearing, Planetary Redemption
and the Regeneration of
the House of Israel—
the Community of
the Sons of
God.*

CONTENTS

O Lord, God of Sabaoth! Most Holy and Adorable Source of all Being, before Whom Cherubim bow in Adoration, and Seraphim minister of Thy Sacred Fire!

Though we be but as little Children amid the splendours of Thy vast Universe, yet would we aspire and ascend to share in the Song of wondrous Praise before Thy Throne sung by all the Heavenly Hosts.

According to the degree of our Realization of Thine Overshadowing of us, we would be uplifted to where the Vision of Thy Glory may be beheld, before which the Eternals abide and move at Thy command unto the fulfilment of Thy Holy Purpose. Before Thy High Altar we would bow adoringly, and cry out from Thy Deeps within us, even as the Seraphim do in antiphonal song.

Holy! Holy! Holy! Lord God of Hosts:
Thy Glory is revealed within all Thy Heavens;
And even the Earth-spheres Thou didst fashion to make manifest Thy Holy Mystery.

And we would also hear Thy Voice calling us from between the Cherubim, even though its command should shake us from the Threshold to the Foundations of our Being.

May Thy Sacred Fire touch us by the hand of Thy Seraph; and may our response to Thy Call be that of those who have been honoured to know Thee, and whose delight is found in the fulfilment of Thy Holy Purpose, and the accomplishment of Thy Glorious Will.

We would be Thine, even unto the uttermost of our Being. As Thou hast endowed us, so would we that all our gifts lay upon Thine Oblatory for the Service of Thee.

Amen and Amen.

THE PROPHECY OF ISAIAH

AMONGST the prophetic Books of the Old Testament that of Isaiah may be said truly to occupy a unique place. It is more read than the other prophets; and there is something strangely appealing in its language and motion. It may not be better understood than Ezekiel, though its form and style appear to be simpler; yet there is that within its contents which arrests, holds and moves the devout student and even the scholar.

And this is true of the parts of the Book which are attributed to two quite different authors and periods; for, except to the scholar, there seems little difference between the mystical part of the message set forth in the first thirty-nine chapters, and that proclaimed with which the fortieth chapter opens, and which fills the remainder of the Book.

CHARACTERISTICS OF THE BOOK

But the real Book of Isaiah is one. Many addenda were added to it. These are found mixed with the true Book and its message. They are accretions of many ages introduced by scribes and redactors for racial and religious purposes. These addenda form a large portion of the book as it is found to-day in the Old Testament. Even many parts of the real prophecy have been changed in the original documents; and the translators have failed lamentably to apprehend the inner meaning of the prophecy, and consequently have misunderstood and misinterpreted many of the terms used by the Prophet;

27

for many of these were like Masonic signs and mysterious cryptograms, holding great secrets.

The Secrets of GOD in all Revelation are couched in the terms used. In this way the Revelation is also protected as well as revealed. It is guarded against those who are not in a state to receive its Secrets, and who might make use of the knowledge to their own destruction and the hurt of many; and it is revealed through its terms to the initiated in the hour of the unveiling of their intuition.

The Book of Isaiah has for its message The Burden of the Spirit of the LORD. It is the Burden of the Oblation. As the Book of Ezekiel reveals the mystery of the Planetary constitution and its past glory; the betrayal of the Planetary Directors; the fall of the Princes or Rulers of Tyrus, Sidonia and Egypt; the desolation wrought in the land; the sufferings of Judah and the travail of Israel as an outcome of the great change; and then the resurrection of the House of Israel, followed later by that of the House of Judah; and then the coming into manifestation of the Priesthood of the Ancients who were of the Christhood—so the Prophecy of Isaiah sets forth the Divine Way of the restoration. It is a Book recording the sore travail of Israel resulting from the betrayal which brought about the fall of Judah and the desolation of Ierusalem. It reveals what it has meant to this world to lose the glorious Christhood manifestation associated with the Children of Zion; and all the humiliation, pain and sorrow which have been the lot of the real Israel. It portrays the path of the Oblation, the need for its Burden, and the call of the Servant of the LORD who was to be the Divine Love's vehicle for the Redemption of Judah and the Regeneration of Israel. It describes the *Return*, first of "the Servant of the LORD" from the land where the Oblation had to be borne, and then the release of all Israel.

Because of the Burden of the Oblation and the glorious resultant, the Prophet sings the Song of a great hope for the future of the Children of Zion and Ierusalem when all of them would be redeemed and restored. And in this connection it is made quite clear that in the Redemption, the Princes of Tyrus, Sidonia and Egypt are to share; and that even Lucifer—the one-time glorious and radiant Star of the morning who was drawn down in the planetary Descent to the hell-states created by those who effected the betrayal—shall once more be restored to his former estate.

Through such a complete and perfect healing and restoration of Elements and Hierarchy, all the kingdoms of this world shall again become the Kingdoms of our LORD and HIS Christ. The ancient Theocracy shall be restored, and Christ shall reign.

THE VISION OF ADONAI

The Book opens with the transcendent vision found in the sixth chapter wherein there is an unveiling of ADONAI as He reigns within the Sanctuary of Being in the Divine Kingdom. It brings us face to face with the Eternal Mystery, and we behold the Seraphic ministries to and from the Divine. We are taken into the Inner Temple where we witness the Call of the Servant of the LORD, and His appointment to be the Redeemer of the Houses of Israel and Judah by means of the Oblation.

The vision is full of dramatic situations. Though in form and language the incidents and addresses in the vision, down from the ADONAI Himself through the Seraphim to the Prophet, seem to be impressed with a human and personal estate, yet the drama enacted is essentially and altogether cosmic. It is a cosmic vision of the ADONAI. The ministries rendered by the Seraphim are of cosmic nature. The realization by the Prophet of the nature and exaltation of the vision, is within the cosmic realms. The ministry of the Seraph unto the Prophet partakes of cosmic elements and potency. The address of the ADONAI unto the Assembly of the Sons of GOD is from the innermost Divine Kingdom, and, therefore, exceeds in majesty and glory such an address as might have been given through the Solar World. And the mystery implied in the Prophet's recognition of the Divine World question—"Who will go for us? Whom shall we send?" transcends anything of a merely personal or mental order; for he is looking upon the KING of all the Kings, and the LORD of all. He is hearkening to the intonations of a Voice he well knows. His whole Being feels bowed down with the consciousness of his unworthiness to stand in such a Presence witnessing such a cosmic unveiling, and hearing that Voice which may be said to find its echo in the Seven Thunders.

*   *   *   *   *   *

It was no ordinary clairvoyant vision, nor a passing experience begotten of Soul-vision which every great initiate has on his way as he ascends from kingdom to kingdom and realm to realm. It was an actual experience within the Divine Kingdom itself, for the one who was named Isaiah. The occasion was most momentous. It was verily an Assembly of the Divine Hierarchy at which many of the Sons of GOD were present, amongst whom Isaiah found himself.

The momentous occasion arose as the result of the conditions into which this Planet had gone down. The Earth had witnessed ages of travail. Tragedy upon tragedy had succeeded each other in the outworking of the results of that great betrayal which had brought down this world, with its hierarchical system and all its children. Solar ministries beyond telling, and, indeed, such as may not yet be fully revealed, had been rendered for many ages in the hope that this Planetary home might be saved. But, owing to the impoverished spiritual state of the Planet and the weakened condition of all her children, the Solar ministries required for the assured restoration of the Planet could not be rendered with sufficient intensity, because the spiritual states of the children of the Earth were so low that such an intensive ministry would have caused them to have been annihilated as Souls, and disintegrated.

THE MOMENTOUS OCCASION

The Divine World, whose ministries are always contingent though ever permeated with unchangeable Love and marvellous and unshakable Wisdom, had to find some other way of recovering the Planet and all her children, and of restoring her various Hierarchies to their unfallen estate. It was for such a purpose that the Assembly of the Gods had been called, at which so many of the Sons of GOD were present, especially those who would have to be most intimately concerned with the outcarrying of the Divine Purpose.

It was in the midst of such an Assembly that Isaiah found himself the object of special interest. It was in the hour of transcendent worship by such an Assembly, and in response to the Divine request, that he laid his Being on the Altar of Oblation for service unto the Divine on behalf of all this system, but very specially for the recovery and redemption of this world. And in connection with that recovery there was to be a ministry having for its object the finding of those Sons of GOD who once formed the ancient Christhood in this world, and who had been the revealers and interpreters unto the children of men for long ages. For those had all become involved in the terrible débâcle resulting from the betrayal of the Planet's

Hierarchy, and the going down of the whole Planetary Household.

The significance of the question said to have been asked by ADONAI of the Gods and the Sons of GOD, will now bear a real meaning for the reader and student of these Mysteries; and the reply by Isaiah may give a passing glimpse of the sublimity of Divine Soul-sacrifice for the LORD'S service, when the whole Being is laid upon the Altar of Oblation. And, as the result of such an event, the question that would not unnaturally arise in the mind of the earnest student would concern itself with the story of Isaiah, who and what he was.

THE STATUS OF THE PROPHET

No one who had not attained to the estate of a Son of the Gods could have witnessed such a sublime, Divine spectacle. The measure of a Soul's potency when operating within the Divine Kingdom, is commensurate with the degree of such an one's capacity to behold, realize, and receive from the Divine. To endure such a vision in itself implies that Isaiah had oft-times stood upon the threshold of the Divine World and witnessed dramas of transcendent order. To have had the power to respond to such a call as was given to him implied a very high degree of Divine realization. To have had the capacity to understand the Message given concerning the Divine purpose in relation to the Oblation, signifies in itself that Isaiah had not only Planetary cosmic consciousness, but such a consciousness of cosmic requirements as would give him a place in the Sun, and within its Divine Kingdom; and even beyond that glorious Body.

Therefore, in a special sense it must needs be recognized for the full understanding of his Message, that he had attained to the estate wherein he was crowned A SON OF GOD.

32

Such a conception of the nature of the attainment and estate of the Prophet, exalts him above all merely individual, national and racial limitations of office, and emphasizes the cosmic·character of the Revelation given through him. His name itself is significant. It was not his personal name, nor the name by which he was known in the Assembly of the Sons of GOD. For his real name denoted his spiritual estate, and the ministry unto which he had been appointed from the Divine World. The term Isaiah was not related to him as a person, nor as an individual, but to the nature of the Office he was called upon to fill as the Servant of the LORD. His Message was concerned with the burden of YAHWEH in relation to the whole of this system, and especially to this world. And as the Prophet, who was also a Son of GOD, had been chosen to become the vehicle of such a Divine Message, so had he, in his very Being, to carry the burden of YAHWEH as the Servant of His LORD. In this way he became absolutely identified with the Message he had to proclaim and the burden that was yet to be borne.

THE SERVANT'S IDENTIFICATION WITH ISRAEL

This identification of one who was a Son of GOD in estate, with the Message of YAHWEH unto HIS people Israel; also unto the LORD's vicegerent, Ya-akob-El; the Planetary Hierarchies; and even unto the Planet-Soul Judah; explains so much of the nature of the Text of his prophecy. For he was most intimately related to Israel and Ya-akob-El and the members of the Hierarchy, and also to the Planet-Soul Judah. And this identification as a Son of GOD with his people Israel; the redemption of the household of Ya-akob-El; the restoration of the land of Judah; and the return of Israel from the bondage of a Planetary captivity, to that Celestial land wherein the whole household of Israel could again realize the regnancy of the LORD CHRIST, and become once more the vehicle of Divine Theocracy; will help the reader also to understand how Isaiah had to become one with the Oblation which he so graphically describes as seen in vision. He enters into the land where it would have to be accomplished, and follows the path which would have to be trodden in the bearing of the Burden of YAHWEH.

* * * * *

The exalted estate of consciousness into which Isaiah had entered, enabled him, through the Divine lovingkindness and mercy, to look out upon the travail of this distraught world; to behold its intense darkness and its awful states of spiritual impoverishment, and yet sing songs of undying hope; to portray in exquisite diction the coming of that Redemption by means of the Oblation, followed by the Regeneration of Israel through the purification of the Heavens of the Earth, to issue in a grand and glorious ascension of the whole household of Israel. As a further grand resultant there is anticipated the healing of all peoples; the redemption of the Planetary elements; the full restoration of the whole household of Judah when it would be reclothed, as in the ancient days, with the glory of that blessed life of which the Ierusalem which was from above, spake. For such are the closing cadences of the real Message—the Message brought by the Servant of the LORD who beheld the coming of the manifestation of the Christhood, and sang of the arising of the Sons of GOD into the realm of the Light resplendent and the Vision glorious.

THE MESSIANIC MESSAGE

The Book is essentially Messianic. It is really a cosmic drama. There are five main acts with changing scenes in which there is the proclamation of the coming of the Messiah and the manner of His coming. That is followed

by a portrayal of the characteristics that would be associated with the Manifestation, emphasizing the revelatory
nature of the life manifested and the Message given from
the Divine World. Then there is the Messiah's identification with the suffering household of Israel, the nature of
the Burden to be borne unto the restoration of Israel
and the healing of this world. That is followed by a great
appeal to Israel to rise out of the Planetary conditions
and become once more the City of GOD, the dwellers
whose household is built upon the Hill of Zion. And
then, as the grand finale, the last act concerns itself with
the effect of such a Return upon the cities of Judah and
all their inhabitants.

*   *   *   *   *   *

It is clearly revealed that the Servant of the LORD bore
a most intimate relationship to the whole House of Israel;
and that the Elders of Israel, or the members who formed
the Hierarchy for the Christhood manifestation when the
Sons of GOD came to this world, were his Brethren.
In a remarkable way, this intimate relationship is also
brought out in the Book. And since Isaiah was the
Messianic Prophet foretelling the coming of the Servant
of the LORD for the Manifestation, and the bearing of the
Burden of YAHWEH as the vehicle of the ELOHIM, it is not
surprising to find many sayings in the Logia spoken by
the Master in the days of the Manifestation, revealing the
Messiah's relationship to the whole House of Israel,
such as may be found set forth in the allegories of the
Shepherd and the Sheepfold.

It will thus be seen that, however far afield Biblical
Scholars may be in their understanding of the Manifestation, the Oblation, and the relation of these to Israel,
they have, nevertheless, sensed something of the truth

when they have regarded the book of Isaiah as containing
Messianic prophecy, and sayings whose nature were akin
to the teachings of the Gospels.

* * * * * *

The wonder of it all reveals anew the holy Passion of
that ONE Whose Love never wearies in its ministry, nor
withholds in its giving; Who never hasteneth in a world-
sense to accomplish HIS Will, and yet resteth not day nor
night, but worketh through great ages unto the fulfilment
of HIS Purpose and the accomplishment of HIS holy Will.

Here is a vision of that Love revealed in its infinite
patience, its sublime majesty, its inexpressible tenderness,
and its profound gentleness.

Here we witness the unveiling of the Divine Counsels
and the Revelation of the Divine Purpose to effect the
recovery of Israel and the healing of this world by means
of a Divine Christhood Manifestation, followed by the
Divine Travail of the Oblation unto the purification of
the Planetary Heavens.

And this Divine drama in the Heavens in the Presence
of the glorious ONE, and the Gods in Assembly as actors,
shared in by the Sons of GOD as witnesses, and the
Servant of the LORD as the chosen vehicle of the Message
and the Burden, being enacted more than a Naros[1]
before the Manifestation was to be made and the Burden
of the Oblation undertaken and borne by the Servant of
the LORD, reveals the exquisite beauty of that Love which
hasteneth not yet tarrieth not in its eternal purpose and
sublime ministries.

---

[1] The Naros was a prophetic day covering over 600 years
of the Earth's revolution. For great ages it belonged to the
Secrets of GOD in the Mysteries. The three hours on the Cross,
and the three days from the Gethsemane to the Resurrection,
were related to the Naronic Mystery.

THE BOOK OF ISAIAH

PART THREE

THE WORD OF THE LORD

*Wherein is unveiled Who the Word is, how
the Word comes to a Soul, the status of
Isaiah, the nature of the Theophany,
the subject matter of the Revelation,
the path of the Oblation, the Zion
of the Ancients, the Restoration of Zion and the
Regeneration of the
whole House of
Israel.*

CONTENTS

O Wondrous Father-Mother, the Source and Sustenance of Thy glorious Universe! Thy Word is our Meat and our Drink.

Through the Word Thou dost communicate unto us of Thy Sublime Mystery.

He is the Living-Bread of Thy Holy Wisdom broken unto Thy Children as the Shew-Bread within Thy Courts, to aid them in their approach to Thee that they may become enriched and strengthened, and so prepared to enter into the Most Holy Place and partake of Thy Word as He is mediated there as the Heavenly Manna, the Sacramental Bread of Thine Host contained within the Tabernacle of Being.

More and more fitted and worthy may we become to partake of Thy Holy Mystery.

Thou hast also, through Thy Word, given unto us of the Eternal Aqua Vitæ flowing from the Fountain of Thy Being, and thus made us sharers of Thy Holy Life-Stream.

And Thou hast gifted unto us the power to change such a Holy Mystery of Living Waters into the Blood of the Lamb, the Wine of Thy Chalice which dwells within the Tabernacle with Thy Sacred Manna.

O Most Holy and Most Lovely One! Thy Children would live before Thee as those who know the Secret of living in Thee, whose lives are embodiments of Thee through Praise, Worship and Adoration, and whose whole motion of Being is evermore in the Service of Thee.

Unto this end evermore abide with us.

Amen and Amen.

THE WORD OF THE LORD

WHEN the Word of the LORD speaks, it is with the voice of ADONAI.

When the Word of the LORD comes to a Prophet, it is the vision of the ADONAI that breaks upon the magnetic plane of the Prophet's Being.

The revelation which comes to the Prophet through the voice and vision of ADONAI, concerns itself only with those things which are related to the Divine Will and Purpose as these are to be revealed and embodied in ministry.

In the vision and through the call, the Prophet realizes in such fulness the sacred Mystery of the Divine Immanence, that he is able to re-intonate the voice in the Message, and outline and portray the Holy Divine Purpose.

Such a consciousness through vision and inward realization of the ETERNAL ONE, gives to the Prophet the status of a Son of the Gods, and enables him to be the vehicle of the holy Passion of ADONAI.

* * * * *

The Word of the LORD that came to the Prophet concerned itself with the Angel of the Planet, Ya-akob-El; with Lucifer, the seventh Angel of the Planetary Hierarchy of administration; with the Planet-Soul whose name was Judah; and, in addition to these, it was also deeply concerned with the recovery of the lost Sons of GOD who were denizens upon the planes of this world, and who were known as Ancient Israel.

Therefore, the Prophet foretells the Messianic Advent; a Divine Manifestation of a dual nature; and then the ultimate finding, restoration and regeneration of all Israel.

That these tremendous ministries are associated with the Divine Purpose is revealed in the prophetic message. And there is also portrayed as a resultant of the Oblation, the great liberation from Babylonian captivity of ancient Israel, through Cyrus the Servant of the LORD. And there is indicated as a further resultant of such sublime Planetary and Solar ministry, the trek homeward of the Sons of GOD to the Holy City of Zion, the one-time ancient estate of their Christhood; with the glorious fruitage of all their travail and their labour in the restoration of the whole Planetary Household when the Earth shall become again a concrete and active reflection of the Jerusalem which is above.

THE HOUSE OF YA-AKOB-EL

The House of Jacob was not simply a human household, but was related to the Kingdom of the Planetary Angel. Into his House are upgathered those children who are of the House of the Planet-Soul Judah, as they pass through the Twelve Houses or degrees of Spiritual realization within the House of Jacob or Ya-akob-El. When the great Descent and Fall of the Planet took place, the Planetary Angel found himself most deeply involved.

There is a profound mystery hidden in the name Ya-akob-El. He was the descendant of Abraham and Isaac. His name was Ja-akob. The story of Jacob in the Old Testament is a human adaptation of the Celestial story of the Planetary Angel. He held the high position of Divine Vicegerency in this Planet's system. In a Spiritual, Celestial, and even Divine sense, he was appointed Lord of this world.

It is well to remember that all the Lords and Kings

42

appointed of GOD in the Celestial realms, relate their kingship and regnancy unto the FATHER-MOTHER. For the higher Souls rise in consciousness the less they think of themselves in a personal and individual way. The nearer to HIM Souls reach in their inward state, vision and realization, the more GOD becomes unto them, in them, and through them, *all in all*. And this is true of all Celestial and Divine Sons who retain their first estate. All the potency inherent in them, all the riches gathered by them, and all the power of administration attained by them, they lay at the feet of HIM Who so endowed them.

A clear understanding of this will throw light upon many things associated with the Planet-Soul, the Planetary Hierarchy, and the Angel of the Planet. It will help the reader to understand how it comes to pass that the measure of such a consciousness of GOD realized by the Planet-Soul, the members of the Hierarchy, and the Divine Vicegerent, will also be the measure within them of the sorrow and the travail begotten of the conditions of a fallen world. The one must be commensurate with the other.

* * * * * *

After the great Descent, Ya-akob-El, the Planetary Angel, could have been withdrawn from this system and appointed to another. But that is not the way of the Eternal Love. The CREATOR of the Universe of glorious embodiments and majestic Suns, meets the new need of those who are HIS vicegerents and administrators, and who are confronted with difficulties too great to be met and rectified by the obtaining administration orders and ministries. The new conditions were met by new kinds of ministry.

Thus it came to pass that in the prophetic Message, the Prophet has to speak unto the House of Ya-akob-El, and also unto the House of Israel through the Vicegerents, informing them of the holy purpose of the

ADONAI. And it is also shown how much Ya-akob-El, as the great Patriarch of the Planet and the administrator through the Celestial Hierarchy of the Planet's kingdoms, was dependent upon the response to his commands within the Planet's Hierarchy.

But that Hierarchy was also brought down into bondage; for the Angel of the seventh sphere was most especially affected. The seventh sphere represented the outer Celestial plane of the Planet. That Angel was a brilliant star. In the constitution of his Being he is still glorious, apart from the sorrowful experiences he has had to pass through and from which he is not yet altogether delivered. He is that Angel who has oft-times been spoken of as Satan, and sometimes referred to, though confusedly, as Saturn. He was indeed the real Lucifer, the brilliant plenipotentiary of GOD on the seventh Celestial plane for the administration of the Planetary life in relation to the generation, growth, and evolutionary processes in the bringing forth, the education and the exaltation of the human races of this world.

Therefore the Message is also unto Lucifer. The part of Isaiah's logia referring to him will be found in the Text. From that statement it will be understood how the Great Love reveals HIMSELF in a way which is all-conquering. It will be shown that the Planet's Hierarchies of both an earthly and celestial order, will be fully restored; and also that the lower or intermediary Hierarchy, through which the great Descent became fully accomplished, will share in the perfect redemption.

THE MESSIANIC MESSAGE

The Message begins with the Patriarch, the Divine representative of the Planet, GOD's Elect One, and passes on to the Celestial Hierarchy of the Planet—of which Lucifer was a noble and most active member—giving

44

to these the great promise that their ancient estate will be restored to them through the restoration of all Israel and the redemption of the Planet's Household. The Message which was given to the Prophet to chronicle upon the outer planes, was one given elsewhere than upon the planes of this world. But it had to be transmitted to the Sons of GOD, or Children of Israel, who were functioning upon this Planet, and serving her elder children. The hope raised in the very Being of Ya-akob-El, and the light flashed into the realm of Lucifer who was then in deep shadow notwithstanding his inherent radiance, were concerned with the Messianic Advent. For the whole Message is Messianic. It speaks of the coming of YAHWEH in and through HIS Servant. But here it should be clearly understood, so that there should be no confusion in the mind, that the coming of YAHWEH through HIS Servant is not simply the coming of a man who claims to be the Messiah. The Servant is one chosen by the Divine World to be the vehicle of YAHWEH. He is the Servant of the LORD. In consciousness and estate he is a Divine Being; and he has Divine fulness in realization. His relationships extend through Celestial realms, for he must have attained to be a Son of the Gods. And in the manifestation through which the Message of YAHWEH shall be proclaimed, he shall reveal the true nature and estate of Angelic Love.

Thus the Servant of the LORD becomes identified with the Messianic Message, and is GOD's Messiah; yet only as HIS vehicle. He is not simply a man, though the message must needs be spoken through the human vehicle. He is not merely a Human Soul chosen as a channel of communication. He is one who is so much a part of the Message that he knows it in realization. He is the centre of the Divine vibratory action contained in the Message,

and becomes one with it in the nature of its revelation
and the life of its manifestation.

It is thus that the Servant of the LORD who is called
to be such a vehicle, must have risen into the estates of
consciousness wherein is greatly realized by him, the
overshadowing and indwelling ONE. He is a Soul who
has become one, in the motion of his spirit, with the
Breaths of the Eternities, so that their Lifestream
can flow through his Being.

* * * * * *

The Messianic Advent was concerned with the Manifestation of the Christhood in and through the Servant;
then the Manifestation was to be crowned by the Planet's
Redemption. That "Advent" is heralded for the first
time by the Servant of the LORD. It is couched in the
transcendent vision and call wherein the Servant is
appointed to be the vehicle of YAHWEH. In the proclamation there is the revelation of the world's need,
followed by the consecration of the Servant of the LORD
as the Burden-bearer. The opening of the Heavens to
Isaiah is not only the story of the Prophet having a
transcendent vision. It is, rather, the story of a Soul
raised into consciousness of Messiahship, wherein he
realizes the Divine Presence in such fulness that he is one
with the Messianic Message, and becomes altogether
the Servant of the LORD as a Divine vehicle.

THE SERVANT OF THE LORD

It is impressive to note how often the phrase occurs—
"The Servant of the LORD." On these planes when we
are serving for the Divine, it is exhilarating to think of
ourselves as servants of the LORD. It is a most blessed
thing to be in HIS service, and in all the motion of our
Being to have the consciousness that we are absolutely

His. And to be His servants surely means for us, that He must be all and in all to us, and within us, and through us. In such a state there is no room for self-regard, nor merely human or earth-bound ambition, nor a craving to be great and to have power on the Earth beneath or in the Heavens above. To be His servant is to act in a way that makes our action the interpretation of His own motion in us and through us, the rendering of a service freed absolutely from all self-regard, from all desire for reward of any kind whatever, even from the craving to have our powers increased that we may be conscious of yet greater power. For the more power we acquire in Him, the less conscious shall we be of having any power whatever of our own. This may seem a contradiction, but it is in absolute harmony with the Eternal Law of Divine Being.

Therefore, to be His servant is just to be His perfect vehicle. He made us. He brought us out of the Great Deep. He fashioned us. He enriched us. He endowed us. He gave to us the garments of His own glory. Therefore, our Being is His. A Son is His to call; to use as He willeth; to reveal through; to speak through; and even to travail through, if travail be required.

There are significant indications of the Messianic Advent given in that astonishing vision wherein the Prophet saw the Heavens open unto him and heard the call of the Divine. He had often seen the Heavens open. But in that transcendent hour there was a new aspect of the Holy Mystery presented to him. There was experienced a call to an order of ministry burdened with most grave responsibilities. The Message he gives is rich in Divine revealings. After the call to new ministry, there is a gradual revelation of how the Messianic Advent is to take place. There is a clear indication of what we now name the Manifestation. That is prophetically set forth as the coming of CYRUS the Divine Liberator.

A Divine Manifestation is not simply the appearing of a great personality upon these planes as Servant of the LORD. The Manifestation is in the estate or inheritance through attainment of the Being who is Servant. Though the personal equation must be attuned to the Inner Worlds, yet the embodiment through the vehicles is the Manifestation of Divine estate. It is the revelation of the radiance of the Divine LORD. The Love of the Eternal ONE and the Light of the Divine World, are revealed in the measure in which these have been realized by the Servant.

There is set forth in the original prophecy, some wonderful Logia concerned with the Manifestation, its threefold nature, its Divine constitution, its Celestial relationships, and its Angelic breaths. These Logia reveal the Divine Messianic power and life, thought and glory, to be expressed unto Israel in concrete form in a Divine Christhood through the Servant of the LORD. Because Israel knew such in the Celestial Heavens long ages ago when they dwelt within their own system, and they themselves were the appointed manifestors of the Messianic life in the glorious days of this land of Judah, the Messiah was to come to them as to those who could understand.

It was for this reason that, when the Manifestation was given through the Master, it was unveiled within a small area of Palestine to a few members of ancient Israel whose homes were there. There were great reasons for this. Of all peoples only they could recognize a Manifestation. For they were of the Ancient Christhood who had been sent to this world. But it was hoped that many more would be found to whom the light could be passed on, the full Message given, the Sacred Flame enkindled, and the Divine Vision more and more fully unveiled; whilst the manner of the giving of it might guard it from being wrecked by the enemy.

GOD'S GIFT TO THE WORLD

And then, as if that were not sufficient for the purpose, the Divine LORD revealed unto the Prophet, the Passion of HIS Own Love under the form of the Oblation, because HE knew that the Messianic revelation in itself was not sufficient for the full recovery of Israel; that the inimical conditions were too greatly against them for all the members of the Household to come back into their ancient Christhood, unless they were taken right up out of the conditions upon the planes of the Planet, raised to the Lower Angelic Kingdom and gradually restored again to the Christhood.

To have taken them right out of the world and brought to an end their service in it, would have become disastrous for the Planet. The world and its children would have gone down still further into the great darkness. For the Sons of GOD have been the preserving salt upon the earth. As the Children of Zion they have given their life-blood, the Divine magnetic streams in them, to keep alive in the world the Sacred Flame. They have done this great thing without knowing it. They have known only that they have been burden-bearers and sufferers. Therefore, in the prophetic unveiling it is revealed how the Divine LORD in the Manifestation for the Messianic revelation, would follow that Manifestation with the further ministry of the Divine Passion through Lives which would not be lives of Manifestation, but of deep travail. All the burden-bearing was to be a further revelation of the Travail of the Great Love. It would not simply be the travail of the Servant whom the Great Love used as a vehicle. Though the Servant would share the pain of the Travail, yet the actual Burden would be borne by the LORD of Glory. And what could be the travail begotten in the Soul of Him who was the LORD's vehicle, compared with that intensity of sorrow, grief and pain of the Divine Heart as HE bore the karmic Burden of Judah, the Planet-Soul, unto the healing of all her states within the Planet's Heavens, issuing in the restoration of Lucifer, the one-time radiant Angel of the seventh sphere, and the re-exaltation of the whole kingdom of the Celestial Hierarchy over whom Ya-akob-El presided?

It was thus the Divine and Celestial Hierarchies of the Planetary administration were to minister unto the healing of the Occult World, which belonged to the sphere of the third or lower Hierarchy. It was thus that the restoration of the intermediary administrators was to be effected, so that they could again receive from the Celestial Kings and Shepherds. And in order that every obstacle should be removed from the return of Israel and the restoration of the House of Judah, the Divine Passion in the Oblation, or Sin-Offering, became the second part of the Manifestation, and was the concrete revelation of the Divine Love, and the exposition of the Messianic Advent.

The Passion of the LORD through HIS Servant, was GOD's gift to the world unto its healing.

THE SEARCH FOR ISRAEL

In an amazing way all this work of the Divine Love and Wisdom is portrayed in the Prophet's Message. And it centres in and gathers around the ideal of the finding and restoration of the whole Household of Israel. Through the Manifestation of the Messianic glory, Israel was to be found again. Through the Message of the Christhood revealed in the Manifestation, followed by that of the

Divine Passion, Israel was not only to be found, but also to be fully restored.

Nor was this to be done in a personal way only. For many who would fain account themselves of Israel, did not belong to that noble company of the Ancients who, in other ages, were members of the Christhood and bore upon themselves the Insignia of Zion. It was to find these Sons of GOD through their heart's love in its Divine willinghood, and the one-time noble ambition of their mind, culminating in the realization within the Sanctuary of their Being of their ancient inheritance, that the Manifestation was to be made and the Oblation borne. For the finding of them through their love would mean Divine response to the sublime vision. To liberate them from bondage and capture their will for the Divine, would be prophetic of their future burden-bearing as they shared the redemption of the human race. To find them in their mind restored to heavenly vision and Divine ambition only, would be to increase the spiritual dynamic force in the world for its perfect healing. And to find them in their Being through their realization once more of the overshadowing and indwelling Presence, would be to restore them to that high estate of Christ-regnancy which they knew when they were in very deed the Kings of the Orient and the Shepherds upon the Planes ministering to their flocks, and, as the Children of Zion the holy City of the Sun, transmitting to those under their care the Light of the sacred Mysteries as that Light could be received.

*   *   *   *   *   *

It will thus be seen how essentially the Message of Isaiah was concerned with the finding of Israel. So much depended upon its accomplishment. In that finding and restoration to Christhood, were involved the healing, redemption and restoration of Jerusalem, the

Planetary Household; the ministries that would effectually accomplish the healing of the fallen Astral and Occult realms; the full restoration of Lucifer; the re-establishment in perfect harmonious ministry of the Planet's Celestial Hierarchy; and the making of the regnancy of Ya-akob-El, the Planetary Angel, King and High Priest, truly Theocratic.

It will also be seen from all this unveiling, that the finding of Israel had a great meaning for the whole of the system, and that the revelation of what had to be accomplished had a tremendous significance for Ya-akob-El and Lucifer, and indeed for the whole of the Planet's Hierarchies. And, also, that the coming of the Messiah in and through the Divine motion of the Solar Hierarchy, under the special guise of the Servant of the LORD who was to be Ambassador, Days-Man and Redeemer, would be unto the ultimate restoration of the whole system.

Such was the purpose of the Great Love revealed in the Message given to Isaiah. It is resplendent with the glory of the Eternal Light, as the recovered Logia bear witness.

ISRAEL'S LIBERATION FROM BABYLON

The deliverance of Israel from the mystical Babylonian captivity and the restoration of the ancient Christhood through their regeneration, was to be accomplished under Cyrus, the Anointed One. Historians think of Cyrus as one who was at the head of an earthly kingdom, who shared with Darius the Medo-Persian regnancy. But whatever strain of historical truth there may be in the regnancy of a Cyrus during the Medo-Persian period, the Cyrus who was spoken of in the Message of Isaiah was no earthly king, but the chosen Servant of the LORD of Love. The name itself has a Divine significance philologically and mystically. For Cyrus was known as

Kurush and Kurios. These terms are Divine names, and are representative of the Messianic Advent. Cyrus is GOD's Christ in regnancy. He is the vehicle of the Advent in the Manifestation, and then in the Travail of the Divine Love's Passion. He is the vehicle of the ETERNAL CHRIST for revelation, the visible and concrete exposition of Christhood for the finding of Israel in the midst of Babylon.

The ancient Babylonian city that took the name of the Sun, was great, after its order; but, as its name signifies, it was full of confusion. It was a city of many tongues, mystically understood. Within it the Tower of Babel had its place. In the midst of it Israel found themselves in bondage to the influences of Assyria and Egypt. For the mystical state of Assyria was the Babylonian concept of life, and the expression of that through the higher understanding; and the mystical land of Egypt had relation to the body with its attributes. Israel was in such bondage to these that there had to be a mighty deliverance; for the bondage was accentuated through the condition of the Occult World owing to the graven images and idols fashioned in the Intermediary Spheres by those who did not like spiritual and Divine things.

The Children of Israel were, therefore, in a strange land for great ages, suffering hardship and loss. Indeed, when, as Children of the Sun, they might have been taken away, their captivity had to be prolonged for the sake of this world. They had to be retained as a preserving quality in it until the purpose of the Divine Love and Wisdom could be realized through the Manifestation and the Oblation. Through the coming of Cyrus and the breaking again upon the mind of Israel, of the Messianic vision revealing the life which once they knew and the radiance in which they once dwelt, it was anticipated by the

Divine World that their response would be such that they would become fully restored.

* * * * *

In this day it may be seen how the Holy ONE of Israel, the GOD of Sabaoth, is finding them. It is not any man, nor any woman, nor any church, nor any philosophical or religious system, but the LORD of Love Who is finding them. Those who worship at the shrine of men and women, churches and seminaries, philosophical and religious cults, have not yet learned the meaning of the Divine Purpose, nor the ways of GOD in the great deeps of the outworking of HIS Mystery. The Ancients of Israel are finding that Vision of ADONAI as HE unveils HIMSELF in the inner Sanctuary of each one, and sheds the resplendence of HIS glory. They are re-discovering HIM in the Soul's own Sacred Flame which burns within its lamp as its power is increased as the Breaths of the Inner World fan it till the Flame becomes mighty in its potency and all the Sanctuary is illumined by the Presence, from the High Altar to the outer Gate. They are finding the Messiah in the Presence within them, the Paraclete or Holy Guest, as they are redeemed back to Divine consciousness through the redeeming power of the Message, and their rehabilitation to the estate of their ancient inheritance. Through the acceptance of the Message to-day they are realizing the liberation that Cyrus, GOD's Anointed One, has brought to them. And in response to the call of that Message, they are trekking back again to the land or high spiritual estate of ancient Israel.

THE LAND OF ISRAEL

Their return, however, has naught to do with that false Zionism which is associated with the return of the Jews to Palestine and the re-establishing of them there. Concerning this latter movement we might well ask this question—Would the Jewish people be any happier now if they were re-established in Palestine, than they were two thousand years ago? It is very doubtful whether any great good would be achieved by such a return. Herein it is necessary to emphasize with all the power that words can convey, that the return of Israel to the land of Zion has naught to do with the outward trek of Jewry to Palestine, and that the Children of Israel, who were also the Children of Zion, were emphatically a distinct people from the Jewish nation, though for fifteen hundred years many of them dwelt amidst the Syrian hills and southern Palestine.

How tragically sad it is that the most sacred Mysteries should have been so terribly perverted! They were materialized to such an extent that they ceased to have any spiritual import, and their associations with Jewry and their interpretations by the priesthood, gave most sad misrepresentation of the holy purpose of the Eternal ONE. The real Zionist movement was, is, and must ever be, soulic. It is a racial processional of Spiritual, Celestial and Divine significance. It concerns solely those Souls who were designated the Children of Zion; and they were so designated because they had the status of Solar citizenship. Their life's ministry was a Solar manifestation upon the Earth planes. The LORD was ever their Sun. HE gave unto them the glory of HIS Grace. In them HIS holy Awe dwelt.

The land of Israel is, therefore, the land where the Sons of GOD held their ancient Inheritance. It was an Inheritance that was full of Solar radiance. The possession of that radiance marked the high degree of their attainment. In these days as they arise and return, that radiance will again become manifest through them. They will carry that radiance with them wherever they go; for it is begotten of the motion of the Divine Love-Principle, and is that Love's iridescency. They will take their love with them unto the uttermost parts, and shed its glory through all their service. When once they have again attained the possession of their ancient Inheritance, they will have the power to descend without loss in order to minister to those in lowly estate, taking their love with them and shedding its glory around them. Their love will enable them to stoop to the less degrees of life where ministry is called for, without knowing that they have stooped; for perfect love gives unto the uttermost, and the consciousness of its giving never obtrudes itself.

These Children of Zion were great in their stooping in the ancient times. They became even as the children of the Earth when they entered into lowly estate. But they were great within themselves; yet without knowing it. Those who dream that they are great because they stoop, have assuredly not reached the goal of Divine Inheritance held by the ancient Children of Zion when they were the segregated communities of the Sons of GOD in this world. Those who would pride themselves in their strength and acclaim the greatness of their love in its stooping, have haunting them, though they know it not, the same deep, dark, long shadow which fell so tragically upon the kingdom of Lucifer.

* * * * * *

The promised land of Israel is the land of the Covenant and the Testimony. The Covenant is GOD's Shekinah within the Being; and the Testimony is the Ark of HIS Indwelling. The land of Israel to which the Sons of GOD are all trekking as to their homeland, is the country of Divine Realization. Those who dwell in that country make manifest the love that obtains amongst the Angels whose breaths are fragrant and full of healing for everyone.

56

For such a possession brings back to the consciousness the Zionist's relationship to all living creatures over whom Divine Pity is to spread its wings. The Being's memory retains the consciousness of inter-relation to all Souls unto whom Divine Compassion is to flow from it. Yea, the Inheritance of that glorious country makes the Children of Zion realize their oneness with all worlds, and the part they must needs take in the ministries of the Celestial Beings belonging to the Household of the great family of Terrestrial, Celestial and Divine Hierarchies.

Thus it may be readily recognized that the Land of Israel or the Divine Inheritance of the Children of Zion, is rich in promise, rich in Divine potentialities, and rich in service. Within that Land, the Soul can grow, expand and evolute in an ever-increasing fulness of realization, until it becomes Nirvanic and knows its oneness with the Eternal and becomes conscious of being gathered up into the life of HIM Who is the Universal Mystery, even the LORD GOD of Sabaoth. Such an estate is one wherein the Soul knows no more a separate life, though it still has to function through a separate vehicle. The transcendency of such a realization so endows it, that it is no longer a mere earthly individual, or a Soul separate from the Eternal ONE. Though its individuality or individuated consciousness has to be a vehicle for the expression of the Divine potencies within it, yet it is always one in the Eternal, living always in the Nirvanic land as one who is inseparable from HIM.

AH! THAT IS THE REAL LAND OF ISRAEL, THE HOMELAND OF ZION, THE GLORIOUS INHERITANCE OF THE CHILDREN OF THE SUN, THE EXPOSITION OF CELESTIAL CHRISTHOOD!

*   *   *   *   *   *

It was no light thing that the Prophet did in bringing such a Message to Israel amidst the conditions which then prevailed. Nor has it been an easy service for the writer to render for his LORD, to restore that Message for those whom it concerns, and bring it back amidst the tumultuous seas of human thought and action to-day. Nor will it be a slight thing for the reader sympathetically to look upon this Message, respond to it and accept it; for in doing so he will turn his face to the Divine Orient, to the radiance of GOD's Sun, and to the splendour of the ancient Land of Israel. It is no small matter to seek in these days unto the finding of GOD's Ancients, discover the richness of their past glory, and lead them back again into that fulness of realization of Life Eternal wherein they will know HIM Who is the Dweller within the Sanctuary. For to find them again is to re-open the flood-gates of the reservoir of their love; revitalize all their attributes; bring them back into a state of sublime consecration; and lead them to the doors of the Everlasting through which they may pass as GOD's Nobles, to be once more crowned with the diadem of HIS Radiance. Yet it is unto such an end that this Message has been restored for all Israel.

THE DAY OF FULFILMENT

All this is contained in the Revelation given through the Prophet. And this is the day of Isaiah's return through the fulfilment of the prophecy contained in His Message. For the true interpretation of that Message is now given; and its fulfilment will be found in the accomplishment of the Redemption foreshadowed, and the Regeneration so emphatically foretold.

Therefore it may be now proclaimed—

Break forth into joy! Sing together! Sing together, all the places that have been laid waste in this desolated Ierusalem! For the Lord Himself doth comfort His People through their restoration.

58

In the measure in which all can together sing the song of
the Redemption and the anthem of the Regeneration
of the returning ones who have again found the Land
of Israel, shall the desolated places of the Planet's life
be healed; the joy unto the Angel Lucifer, be made an
angelic reality; and the outlook for the future become
glorious for Ya-akob-El, the Planet's Archangel or Divine
Vicegerent.

Behold how the whole Planetary constitution is looking
for the coming of this event and depending upon your
acceptance of this Message! Behold how great a thing it
will be in the life and service of the reader who believes
in this Message, and makes it concrete for embodiment,
revelation and ministry! Behold how the Word of the
LORD doth come again, even as HE was revealed in the
Heavens unto the Prophet, and transcribed by him for
Israel!

THE RESTORATION OF ZION

Consider this also, that the return of Israel to the land
of their ancient inheritance was for the supreme purpose
of the upbuilding of the Holy City of Zion, the City of
the Sun. For they were, and are, the Children of Zion.
And when they are all gathered together, healed, regenerated, and exalted to their ancient estate, they will
form one of the notable communities of the Sun. For the
ancient Holy City of Zion, whose description is presented
with such resplendence, was none other than the sacred
Temple of Solomon, into which such great wealth was
upgathered. The Holy City of Zion as the Temple of
Solomon was, and is, something transcendently greater
and more resplendent than any earthly house built by
human hands and adorned with earthly treasures. Those
who are true Free-Masons will understand that the real
Temple of Solomon was nothing less than one of the great

Temples of the Sun. It was the Temple of cosmic Christ-hood. In the ancient Mysteries it was known as the Temple built upon the Hill of Zion within the Holy City of Ierusalem above. It was, and it is, the Temple of the radiant Life, wherein the fashion of the Soul is of the very radiance of GOD, and in which Life becomes one in and with the Eternal FATHER-MOTHER.

That is the reason why the restoration of Zion is so stressed in the Message; and the appeal unto all Israel to return unto Zion is so constraining. For when Zion is restored, then shall all darkness flee; for the light shall have broken and grown into Divine resplendence. And in that day shall it again be said of Israel, that they are the City of the LORD, and that HIS glory filleth the Sanctuary. Then there shall be given back through the Children of Zion, in a fully restored state, the one-time resplendent Kingdom of Ya-akob-El. And this ancient Celestial Home of Lucifer, shall again become the scene of the Edenic Life; and the twelve-fold House of Judah shall have all her Gates rebuilt, and her Bulwarks restored.

*　　*　　*　　*　　*　　*

Therefore, arise ye! Arise ye! and come to the shining, all ye of the ancient Christhood! For thus alone can it come to pass that the Planetary Household be healed again, and all the woundings imposed upon Judah's children mollified through the Balm of Gilead and the touch of the Divine Physician Who is ever there. Arise ye!

Arise ye! ye who read these Teachings, and anoint yourselves and GOD's Christ within you, with the precious unguent of your own love unto the sharing in the service of your LORD. Give Mind and Heart, Soul and Being, with the measure in which the GOD in you would have you give, and so shall ye be like the LORD of Love, and

60

realize perfect childhood to the FATHER-MOTHER. Should you be tempted by the hurtful influences that surround life, the many misleading voices that may be heard calling to you, and the confused messages uttered by them, to stand apart, to take no action, to be negative towards this call, then remember that the re-building of the ancient City of Zion, the glorious Temple of the Sun, needs your service. There must not be lacking the ministry of one servant of the Most High.

Or, should you be tempted by the glamour couched in the presentation of a segregated people monastically or semi-monastically housed and endowed, as the sure way of building up the Holy City of Zion and the venue of the Christhood manifestation, remember that, whilst such states of communal consecration for service may come bye and bye in order to further the redemptive processes and the manifestation of the Christhood, yet the true manifestation is in and through the individual life; for it is thus that the light-bearers of GOD shed HIS radiance and reveal HIM.

It may be that many looking out upon the conditions of life in the world to-day, and all the difficulties which arise in the path of those who try to bring healing and redemption, will be tempted to say to themselves, that such a state of a world redeemed and an exalted Christhood manifestation, seem afar off, away beyond our time and our strength and, because of this, to tarry in their arising and coming forth into manifestation of the Jesus Christ Life.

It may be that many will account as pure visionaries those who dream dreams that seem beyond realization, who hear this call, respond to the Message, and essay in every desire, motion, and action of their lives to make the vision concrete. For such judgment is frequent.

To all these the Heavens would say—Be not faithless to the vision; nor to the realization of the Life unto which it calls. *Remember the patience of the Lord.*

ARE SUCH THINGS POSSIBLE?

More than four Naronic cycles have arisen and set since the glorious Message was given from the Heavens which filled the Prophet's Soul with a great Divine hope for all Israel and the land of Judah, and constrained him to lay his whole Being on the Altar of Oblation unto the accomplishment of an end so glorious. It does seem a long time as men count days, to think back through four Naronic cycles. And yet each six hundred years is but a planetary day. It is also a great prophetic day. It is likewise an important Celestial day. It is a day of the Stars and the Gods. One day with the LORD is as a thousand years and a thousand years as one day. There is no time-limit where Divine Consciousness obtains. In all GOD's worlds there has to be regulation, and the time upon each one varies according to the estate, order and degree of embodiment and the ministry each world has to render. But in the Universal Consciousness there is no time. Even in ourselves when we are dwelling in the Sanctuary of HIS Presence, there is no consciousness of time. In such hours we can look upon that which took place great ages ago as if the drama were being enacted now. Even in the process of the unveiling of the sublime Revelation contained in Isaiah's Message, it has been given to the writer to look through the four Naronic cycles, or Inter-Planetary-Lunar-Solar days. Within the compass of the vision, time has been no more. Therefore, if when looking forward to the realization of all that has yet to be accomplished, you are moved to say to yourselves— *Indeed, it does seem as if it never could come to pass*—the Heavens might remind you of many things, and especially in relation to the past. They might ask you, where you were and in what state you were, when that glorious Message was given in the Heavens unto the Prophet-Servant of the LORD. Think what the state of Israel as a whole was when the Servant of the LORD was empowered to address them. Think of the Divine Travail of Israel and of her LORD, through the ages that have passed since then. Remember the many times in which you may have thought yourself forgotten, and how the LORD HIMSELF prepared a way by which you were to be found again and brought back into the consciousness of HIS Presence. Think how HE has travailed in HIS Servant, bearing the Burden of the Oblation throughout the three Naronic Cycles which have risen and set since the days of the Manifestation, unto the end that this Message might be given once more, unto the finding, healing and regeneration of Israel.

How wonderful is the way of the LORD! It is always lit up with the glory of HIS Wisdom. Behold how HE calls HIS children, as in the ancient times, through HIS Servant and the Message! HE does not send some appointed one with greatness emblazoned on his vesture such as might attract and hold the multitude. HE has guarded those would-be disciples of the LORD from being enamoured of an individual rather than of the Message. HE has known through the ways of men and women in past ages, how HIS Message has been betrayed and changed, and thus prevented from having its full effect upon those unto whom it was sent. HE has had grievously to witness how HIS own intimate children have missed the meaning of HIS Holy Purpose as unveiled by the Master Himself. For the Divine glory revealed in the unveiling of the Christhood during the days of the

Manifestation, was so changed into earthly and personal glamour, that the millions of the western world who have professed belief in historical Christianity, have never understood the most salient features of that Manifestation, nor the meaning of the Master's Message to the world.

The Church reared in His name, whose torches have been lit in many lands, has never understood the life of exquisite beauty signified by Jesushood, nor the glorious Celestial character of the Soul-estate of a Spiritual Christhood, let alone Celestial and Divine Christhood.

THE FULNESS OF TIME

If any have ever thought in their hearts that the Great Love has forgotten HIS children, such a thought is unworthy of the memories awakened in this hour through the unveiling of HIS Love and Wisdom. HE never forsakes HIS children. HE never forgets even the least. It is of the very nature of perfect Love that its ministry to its object fails not. Though men may oft-times by their conduct reproach the Divine Love, yet HE never changes. HE has nothing in HIMSELF of that false dignity which obtains in the fallen human mind, and which so changes the attitude of men and women towards each other. Even in the perfect human estate, the heart never departs from a state of love; how much less, then, could the Divine Heart cease to love all HIS children.

Therefore, as the result of the operations of the Divine Love in the Travail of the Oblation, you may see before you to-day the mighty triumph of that Love. I see the triumph of it coming. I hear the motion of its wings. I feel its early morning breaths. I am honoured again to hear the long-forgotten Angelic Song, and look upon the long-lost Angelic Faces, and even to witness the effects of the magnetic activity of the Divine World upon yourselves.

It is the day of the triumph. HE Who gave that Message long, long ago, was the Word of the LORD. The ADONAI knew what HE was doing when HE gave it. HE knew that HE would have to wait until "the fulness of time" came for the Manifestation to be made, and then for the Burden of the Oblation (which could only then be projected) to be undertaken and borne.

Then "the fulness of time" came to find the vehicle in the Servant of the LORD. It came for the Messianic Advent upon the Earth-planes to become a reality through that Servant. It was "the fulness of time" for the accomplishment of the Divine Purpose in the Manifestation, when the Master came in triple estate to reveal unto Israel the glorious embodiment of Jesus Christ the LORD; and then to crown the Divine Purpose on behalf of HIS children by bearing the burden of Love's Passion, passing through the midst of the Hells as Redeemer unto the extinguishing of their fires which burned within the Planetary Heavens, and the purification of all the evil elemental states which were regnant there. In all these things the Divine Love has triumphed.

THE CALL OF THE DIVINE

And on the outer planes also it is the day of the triumph of the Divine Love. But the measure of that triumph is also the measure of your response. Herein lies the grave responsibility for each Son of Israel. The redemptive and restorative triumph of this Message of the Divine Love and Wisdom, can be commensurate only with the measure of your Being's response in consecrated life and service. Can any of HIS children who once knew HIM, fail to respond to HIS constraining Love and the call of the Beloved ADONAI? Verily, HE is the chief among ten thousand and the altogether lovely; and those who know HIM in realization yearn more and more to be like HIM in their embodiment and their consecrated giving. Such Souls are always willing to respond unto the uttermost, knowing well that in such motion of their Being alone they can enter into the full realization of their Divine Inheritance. Such are GOD's Christs. It is the way of their going. And if ye would be of that glorious company, such life and service must also be yours.

It was a wonderful vision which Isaiah gave. It was a glorious Life unto which his Message called. It contained a revelation of marvellous hope for Israel and the world. Now that Message is brought back to you; in this day it is unveiled, revealed and interpreted through the motion of the Eternal Spirit. It is a voice calling unto you from out the Eternities. Ye may hear that voice reverberating through all the Heavens of your Being. The voice that calls to Zion, the most ancient City of GOD, is HIS voice. In HIS calling, HE reveals the Wisdom of the FATHER-MOTHER. HE calls you to that Life which is the exposition and revelation of HIS Love. If ye can hear HIS Voice, then come up into the high mountain that once was your dwelling-place, and be once more citizens of the radiant City set upon GOD's Hill!

Children of Zion and of the Sun, arise ye! Arise ye! It is the voice of HIS Beloved One Who calls unto you, that ye may no longer continue to sit in the dust of humiliated conditions imposed upon you by the world states; that ye may ascend into the Holy City to be clothed once more in the beautiful garments of the Sons of GOD; that ye may mediate of Angelic and Celestial things, and make for your LORD once more a company of HIS Christs.

Arise ye! And come forth from the world's night. Lay your full offering upon HIS Altar, even that of your Being.

Give absolutely unto HIM. HE appreciates your giving. HE sets upon it its true value. Should HE seem at any time to chide you, it is only HIS loving urging of you to give yet more and more, until you reach that estate of realization wherein you can give even your very Being without accounting it too great a gift. Such action lies at the heart of the secret of the Gods, and it is something you must again attain unto. It is a most sublime realization to give without knowing it, without having the consciousness that you have done a great thing for your LORD and for this world. The FATHER-MOTHER is ever doing great things for HIS children; and the greater the ministries unto them, the more greatly does HIS Love flow. To be like HIM we must also just love as if it were done unconsciously, and were the natural spontaneous outflow of our Being. The only time when we should permit ourselves to become conscious of our giving is when and where we have allowed our love to be intercepted in its flow of blessing and its giving in ministry; and through such consciousness the disturbed harmonious conditions should be changed and rectified.

Arise ye! Arise ye! And come to the shining, O my people of Israel! Come to the land of your ancient Christhood Inheritance! Come back into the possession of your ancient Divine Estate, even to the consciousness of the full riches of Grace bestowed upon you through HIS Immanence with you!

PRAYER AND ADORATION

O most Glorious One, the ever Blessed and Adorable Father-Mother! We bow before Thee. With Cherubim and Seraphim, with Archangel and Angel, and with all the Heavenly Hosts, including all Thy Saints, we would adore Thee in this day of Divine Triumph.

Our sacrifice in the sublimest giving of our Being, is surely but the giving of what is Thine own for the service of Thee.

Though the shadows of the Earth have fallen upon our raiment, and the waters of bitterness have had to be drunk of deeply by us, Thou chasest the shadows away through the radiance begotten of Thine approach; Thou changest all that has been as Marah in our Being when Thou givest unto us Thy cup of Blessing that we may drink of it. The Living Waters from the fountain of Thy Being Thou givest unto us, full of the sweetness of Thine own perfect Love and Wisdom.

We come to Thee just as we are, to make our offering at Thine Own Altar. The gift is that which Thou gavest unto us in the day of our fashioning by Thee, and of the riches wherewith, throughout the ages, Thou hast enriched our Being. We would by means of these serve Thee unto all fulness.

* * * * * *

Ever blessed be Thy Glorious Name, O my Father-Mother! May Thy Name ever be glorious in all Thy children. And at all times may the revelation of Thee unto Thy children through me, be such as Thou canst bless, and, through them again, unto all the children of this world.

Amen and Amen!

THE BOOK OF ISAIAH

PART FOUR

A DIVINE DRAMA

*Wherein is set forth the dramatic situation which
was the primary cause of the declension and
fall of this world and the consequent disasters
which overtook the Human Races, the
Sons of God upon the Earth, the Solar
World; together with the Way of
the Divine Love and Wisdom
by means of the Oblation
for the recovery
of the Wanderer
and all the
System.*

CONTENTS

PROLOGUE

A DIVINE DRAMA

*"O Lucifer, ancient Son of the morning, and the
Daystar of the heavens of the Earth!*

*How is it that thou art as one who has fallen from his
high estate?*

*Why art thou still captive, lying in the dust of the
humiliation unto which thou wast brought down by him
who came unto thee in the name of the Lord of Hosts?"*

Prologue

THERE is a drama set forth under the form of Parable
in the New Testament which is related to the Celestial
Heavens. It is that of the Prodigal Son. It is so essentially
a human story as it is told in the Gospel of Luke, that none
behold the deeper significance of it. The human element
is so arresting that it holds the reader's imagination from
beginning to end. There are elements in the story which
were not in the Parable as spoken by the Master elements
which were added to it by those who betrayed the
Teachings given by the Master.[1]

For purposes hidden by the Divine World, the Drama
had to be presented as belonging wholly to the Human
Kingdom and human experience. Also, it is much easier
to understand a prodigal of a human order than to
apprehend and understand such an event taking place

---

[1] *vide* "The Logia, or Sayings of the Master."

73

upon Celestial Realms, and having within it a history of Divine Tragedy. It will be an easy element of belief, as stated in the Record, to accept the fact that a human Soul has gone out from the Divine Presence into a far country to spend his days and powers in prodigality; but the same cannot be said for the acceptance of an interpretation of the Parable which touches upon Celestial Realms, and unveils the story as related to one who stood in high estate in the Heavens.

The Master said to His intimate ones that unto them it was given to know the Mysteries of the Kingdom. All the Parables and Allegories were associated with the Mysteries of the Kingdom of the Heavens. These Mysteries embraced the individual Soul, the Planet, the Celestial Systems, and even the Divine World. The Parables and Allegories, therefore, contained profound teaching. The Story of the Prodigal Son is amongst the most profound. It bears within its signature the tragic history of a Celestial Being, the Fall of the Earth, and the conflicts of many of the Gods. The Human Races were deeply affected. The polarity of the Planet was changed and its outer Kingdoms were broken. The Moon became unspeakably stricken. The Solar Angelic Heavens were destroyed through the necessity which arose to change the Photosphere and Chromosphere. The Sons of God who had been long-time visitors to this world as the spiritual Teachers and Interpreters, were sorely afflicted even unto the loss of their Celestial Estate and Angelic powers.

* * * * * *

There is deeper meaning than is wont to be recognized in these words of the Prophet—

"*All we like sheep have gone astray; we have turned every one to his own way; but the Lord hath laid on him the iniquity of us all.*"

Or in the more correct rendering which will be found in the Text as presented in this volume—

"*The children of men have all gone astray; like wandering sheep have they gone along a path other than that appointed of the Lord.*

Upon His Servant hath the Lord laid the burden of their return."

That which was implied in "the going astray" and the "burden of the return," touched the whole of this system; and it involved the Servant in such a process of burden-bearing as has never been even dreamt of by translators and interpreters. That travail will be found unveiled in another portion of this volume.

*　　*　　*　　*　　*

Here the reader is asked to follow the unveiling of the Divine Drama with most reverent steps and sympathetic attitude of mind, even where it may seem difficult to follow; and to hold in remembrance the ever blessed truth that the Love of the Eternal and ever Blessed ONE never fails, nor does HIS Wisdom lack in its revelation and purpose. And also it were well to hold in consciousness the unshakable truth that HIS Love is eternal Righteousness, never varying from rectitude; and HIS Wisdom the resplendence of HIS own Glory. Righteousness and Equity are supreme qualities of GOD the Creator FATHER-MOTHER. They are in perfect balance. They hold in balance the whole Universe of Worlds and Souls.

But just because the Divine Love and Wisdom are perfect, and find perfect expression in embodiment, Stars and Souls are not mere machines driven by irresistible force wherein there could be no room for any volition which was the result of choice and willinghood; rather are they conscious co-operators in the universal activity, and

share in the grand Celestial Drama. They are all sufficiently free-agents to have the right of choice in all the
ministries they may be asked to share in. Within a
certain area of activity, every member in the Divine,
Celestial, Angelic and Human realms has the right of
choice. *Freewill is a reality. It is a most sublime gift of the
Creator to all His Children.*

The Laws of GOD are perfect. Their operations produce
that which is perfect. To violate them would be to
intercept their perfect motion and have, as a resultant,
an imperfect manifestation. Divine Love and Wisdom do
not make mistakes; but the interception of them, or
opposition to them, would lead to mistakes. It was in such
a way there happened that which brought about "the
Fall" of this Planet, an event resulting in all the Earth's
tragedies. Of that history the Story of the Prodigal Son
not only contains the substance of the human elements,
but also the shadow of the Celestial and Divine Tragedies.

The Drama enacted may be divided into five great
acts:—

I   Upon the Divine Kingdom
II   Within the Celestial Spheres
III Within the Earth's Hierarchies
IV   Upon and Within the Soul
V   On the Threshold of the Divine World.

I

UPON THE DIVINE KINGDOM

In the story of the Wanderer leaving his Home for his
pilgrimage to a far country, we have presented a Celestial
Drama. There is revealed in cryptic terms the action of
one who was in high estate, one who had been greatly
honoured by the Divine World, and who had been
exalted to the realm of the Sons of the Gods. No one

could dwell upon the threshold of the Divine Kingdom who had not been gloriously enriched with the Wisdom and Righteousness, Equity and Omnipotency of the FATHER-MOTHER, and thus be great in inward stature. For the inward stature of the Sons of the Gods is immense. They are giants in potency and attribute. But just in proportion to their attainments so are their responsibilities. Their ministries are commensurate with their gifts. Should temptation come their way it will be such as only those who are so exalted could have presented to them. Dwelling near the Source of all their power, and in the consciousness of the Divine Presence as an indwelling and immanent force, no temptation could assail them. But it might, if they dwelt upon their powers rather than the Source of them, and their exalted state instead of upon HIM who exalted them. Then temptation would not only be possible, but it might become effective and bring them down. For upon the Celestial Heavens as well as in more lowly estates of consciousness, potency and regnancy, within a given area of action for the manifestation of potency, there is the freedom that perfect Love and Wisdom give. The Gods, the Sons of the Gods, and the Angels, are no more mere machines, irresponsible factors in the administration and government of the Universe, than are the sons of men upon the Earth. There is, therefore, freedom to expand in growth and deepen in consciousness, and then to ascend in state and become exalted.

It is this freedom of choice that makes it possible for those in exalted positions to fall from their high estate. Being overcome by pride of place or love of power they may oppose themselves to the Divine Will. And though such conduct is rare within the Celestial Realms, it has been witnessed by the Heavens and experienced by some Sons of the Gods.

The Story of the Wanderer concerned itself with one of these. A change took place within him. His attitude revealed that self-desire was dominating him, and as a result, came the creation of inharmonious conditions. He asked for all that he might claim and went out from the Divine Presence. By this latter is meant that he left the Kingdom where he had found a field of service for the Divine, and gradually had to lose the high consciousness of the Divine Immanence which was his inheritance.

Vividly and potently there is revealed his first mistake. He left his first estate when he desired to have given to him the potencies which would enable him to create even as the ETERNAL ONE, as well as rule and administer like one of the Gods.

The Divine Purpose is always most beautiful; yet he purposed to oppose and over-ride it. The Divine Will is in itself the Law of Love, making for perfection in all its operations; but he sought to set that Will at naught by direct disobedience to the inherent Law of the Celestial Universe, for he wished to create conditions amidst the Divine Elements which would fix the poles of the various Elements and destroy their beautiful volatility and responsiveness. To desire other than the fulfilment of the Divine Purpose and to oppose the operation of the Divine Will, by a natural sequence of events led him to go out from the Divine Presence. Herein was tragedy for him; and his Celestial tragedy led to that of the Earth and all her children.

It may not be easy for a human Soul to apprehend the significance of the experience contained in the expression "going out from the Presence of the Lord." In a human Soul's own travail it may feel as if it had sustained some great spiritual loss through deviating from the path of rectitude. And this experience may become intensified to

the degree that the individual may feel as if the Heavens
had closed their windows to any request he may make for
light, so that the wanderer from the path of righteousness
may be, in state, as one whom the Heavens have cast off.
It may be that the reader has had some such spiritual
history. If in an hour of self-seeking and self-will he has
said in his heart, *If this be the Divine Way, I will have none
of it!* So, the reader will know that in such an hour the
windows of the mind and heart-sanctuary became veiled,
and the gates closed to the Heavens.

This is just what happens when the human will opposes
its desire to the Divine Will and accounts its own conceptions of love, service and sacrifice preferable to the Divine;
for in such case the inner light grows dim, and the way
of ingress by the Heavens to the Soul, is closed.

Consider then what it would mean for one who had
attained to Celestial experiences and whose attributes had
been endowed with power to reign within a Kingdom of a
Star, when such a change had overcome him as to lead
him to refuse to serve in harmony with the Divine Law
inherent in the System. If such a loss as described above
becomes the experience of a Soul in human estate, or in
spiritual Christhood, what must the loss amount to in a
Soul in such Celestial estate that it is crowned a Son
of the Gods? How great must be the inward loss to one
who had looked upon the Divine Vision, who had heard
within his audient chamber the Voice of the ETERNAL,
and who had been appointed to serve before the FATHER-
MOTHER with many of the Sons of the Gods, and rule
over one of the Kingdoms within a Celestial System, in
the day when, by his own choice, he goes out from his
Kingdom and from the Divine Presence!

That which he was robbed of or had wasted, was but part
of his possessions. He could not take real estate with him.

This latter he had to leave behind. It was of the Home-land. He had possessed the Holy ONE in the degree in which the Eternal Mystery is realized within the various realms of the Sons of GOD. In that possession he had Celestial Vision and Audience of the Divine; and he shared in the creative ministries unto which the Sons of the Gods are appointed. These Divine Attributes he had to leave behind him. The farther out he went the more impoverished he became.

There is a reflection of planetary history here, that will be unveiled presently. That which overtook a Son of the Gods found a concrete exposition within the Planet's Hierarchy and Kingdoms. The writer is not unaware of the difficulty encountered by many in approaching the question of a fallen world occasioned through the mistake of some Celestial Being in authority. There are those who seem unable to accept the doctrine of a fallen world, and find it easier to believe that all that is, must be the resultant of the outworking of the purpose of the Divine Love and Wisdom. The materialistic doctrine of evolution seems the only feasible explanation of the prevailing conditions, notwithstanding the most obvious truth that so much of what obtains in relation to individual Soul experience is absolutely out of harmony with the mani-festation of the Eternal Love and Wisdom. For notwith-standing the supposed operation of perfect Law, the world is yet full of lawlessness, unrighteousness, injustice, the spirit of oppression, self-aggrandizement and even cruelty. All those states are at variance with the idea of the triumph of Divine Law and the administration of Divine Love.

*　　*　　*　　*　　*　　*

The Scriptures are like great pulses expressing sorrow. They speak of deep Soul-travail. Often they are full of a

motion which reveals the breathings of anguish. The
Prophetic Writings unveil in most remarkable language a
state of grief in the Divine World. Not only is the fate of
humanity implied and the necessity for Redemption
indicated; but there is also set forth in terms and scenes
of dramatic character, the descent from high estate of the
whole planetary household. In unmistakable ways it is
made known that Beings who had held high Celestial
Office, had gone out from the Divine Presence and come
to this system to work havoc by changing the Divine
Order of ministry, and establishing ways of life within the
Kingdoms of the Earth which were a contradiction of the
Divine Purpose and a violation of the way of the Divine
Love. The change effected in this Earth, from a one-time
radiant world full of the blessedness of Edenic Life, to one
overwhelmed by spiritual darkness and evil, is greatly
emphasized; and the satanic influences that brought about
such a change are related to powers and principalities
above this Earth, and to the Planet's own Hierarchy. For
the betrayal of the latter is implied. The revelation of the
cause of the disorganization of the whole system, could
come from the Divine World alone; for only there could
such things be known.

*   *   *   *   *   *

It is from that Source alone that the things which are
herein recorded have come. The Divine Secret has been
held sacred for ages, though the tragedy has been often
referred to. The nature of the mistake that brought
about the great Descent, has been well guarded, both for
the sake of the one who was the cause of the disaster,
and the nature of the work that had to be accomplished
through the Solar World. For the Divine World always
seeks to cover up from the merely curious, those who may
become unfortunate through wrong judgment or false

direction and activity; and of very necessity the secrets associated with the creative energies of the Solar Body and other Celestial Systems, must needs be veiled and guarded. That these secrets may now be partially unveiled is because "the fulness of time" has come when fuller revelation concerning them may be safely given. The Mysteries of the Planet-Soul, of the Planet's Hierarchies, of Lucifer and Ya-akob-El, and the one who went out from the Divine Presence and sought to found a materialized system; together with the Holy Mystery of ADONAI as HE is expressed in and through the Solar World, both in its constitution and ministry, are now to be revealed to the Sons of GOD who are dwellers within this system.

It is not easy to write of the tragedy of a Son of the Gods. There are not wanting those who imagine that temptation to such would be impossible because of their exalted state. But self-exaltation or pride of mind is always possible where there is perfect freedom, and where powers and principalities are entrusted to a Soul. There is the same need for humility and lowliness upon the Heavens as upon the Earth. The hour of trial to all the initiated within the various Heavens, is greater even than that same hour to the Initiate upon the Earth. The supreme sacrifice there is the same as it is here, though naturally more intense: it is the laying down of all powers in perfect obedience to the Divine Will. The more fully the Soul obeys the Will, the less it desires to have power to rule Principalities, govern Kingdoms, and direct Worlds.

II

WITHIN THE CELESTIAL SPHERES

To go out from the Presence of the LORD meant a cessation of Divine motion within that one unto the fulfilment of the ETERNAL's Will. This state ultimately led to antagonism to the way of the Divine World. And this latter state sowed the seed that sprang up as deep-rooted desire to smite some part of the Celestial System, and change it from a purely spiritual manifestation, to one that would be fixed in its substances. For, in this tragedy, *that* happened which we have seen take place in human experience when men and women have revolted against righteousness and equity, and they have proceeded to the extreme swing of the pendulum of life and done many things which, in their more balanced moments, they would have abhorred.

It must also be borne in mind that Celestial events cover ages. The hurt imposed by such a tragedy as the above, may take ages to fully manifest itself. It was ages after the betrayal of the Planetary Hierarchy ere the full consequences of the mistake of Lucifer became revealed. To effect the necessary changes in the substances and elements as would make them cease to be perfectly spiritual, pliable and volatile, meant the changing of the polarity of the Planet; the deflecting of its magnetic poles; the serious alteration of the constitution and motion of its seven planes, especially the lower and outer three; and the changing of its mineral and vegetable Kingdoms. But to accomplish so much, it was necessary for the Planet to be moved away from its place in the Divine Ecliptic, and out of the Celestial Stream of Solar Force which flows through the Divine Ecliptic. This took some ages to accomplish.

But though the process of change was gradual, the effect was great and tragic. Many of the members of the various Hierarchies appointed to minister upon and through the seven planes and within the various Kingdoms, became involved. The one who was hurt most of all, was the Angel of the seventh Sphere. He ultimately became enamoured of the vision of a world with fixed

planes and phenomena which had been presented to him
by the one who had left the Divine Presence full of dis-
appointment which grew to anger and resentment. For
Lucifer was not the original betrayer. He was himself
betrayed. So great was the hurt to him that he fell from
a state of high enrichment to know unspeakable impoverishment; and from being a most radiant star
amongst the members of the Hierarchy, he descended into
the night wherein he had to be deprived of his interior
Divine Light and Wisdom. Indeed, upon the very
Kingdom of his regnancy he became broken in his
spirit, and filled with pain and sorrow. Of late ages,
though hope has now been brought to him through the
accomplishment of the Oblation, from time to time he has
known something of the anguishing of the Divine World.

III

WITHIN THE EARTH'S HIERARCHIES

The reader will understand that it is not without
sharing something of the hidden sorrow in him and others,
some of whom were even in higher estate and entrusted
with greater responsibility, that their travail can be
unveiled. The history of the tragedy that overtook them
is cryptically indicated in some of the Greek and Roman
Myths, and Myths of other lands. And it is very especially
set forth in part of the Abrahamic story found in the Old
Testament. That part of the narrative dealing with Lot
and his Family, contains an awful episode of the tragedy.

* * * * * *

Lucifer was a resplendent Son of the Heavens long
ages ago; and he is still wonderful, notwithstanding the
unspeakable history written within his Kingdom. Since
the Oblation has been fully accomplished, he has regained
much of his long-lost power, and is working in harmony

with the Divine World of this System—which is also the
Solar Body. He is the plenipotentiary for the Planet-Soul
upon the outer planes, and is the seventh Vicegerent in
the Celestial realm of this System, for the Holy ONE Who
is LORD of all.

The Celestial significance of this will become obvious
to the reader; for such an Office could not be betrayed
and changed in the nature of its ministry, without the
whole of the Planet's constitution suffering. The changes
effected in the Planet's Kingdoms were of a most tragic
nature, and the results were soon manifest in all the
Planet's children. Indeed the whole System was so much
involved, that Luna had to make unimagined sacrifices.
Even the Sun, the Divine Centre of the System, had to
close its lower Heavens, indraw many of its elements,
and change radically its atmospheres through which it
ministered.

Should there be a reader of this message of revelation
and interpretation who has doubted the ever-confronting
problem of "the Fall," he is here asked to reflect upon all
that even limited profane history has had to portray
of the awful conditions which have obtained throughout
great ages amongst peoples, nations and races. For we
cannot get rid of a problem of evil by simply denying it,
or relating it to the Divine World as part of the scheme
of human and planetary evolution. Nor can religion be
confined to the unillumined interpretation that would
account it merely the effort on the part of humanity to
find an expression for the emotional nature in superstitious
beliefs and the worship of imaginary powers and Gods.
For the religious motion is inherent in humanity, and it is
of Divine inheritance. Consequently, the Prophets of all
ages and of every land have told of a Golden Age in the
far past; and of that Edenic time the true Poets have sung.

The illumined Poets, Prophets and Seers, have glimpsed the past glory of this world, and sensed the tragedy that overtook it. And almost invariably their whole Being has been affected by, and has moved in deep sympathy with, the sore and most sorrowful travail of the race.

* * * * * *

Of these things much of the parabolic and allegorical teachings in the New Testament, speaks. The whole of the Master's Message was concerned with the history of this world, past and present. Whilst the parables He spake seemed to have an intimate individual Soul reference and application, yet most of them were historical in a planetary and celestial sense. Their deepest meanings were related to the Planet-Soul and her children; and in a very special degree, to the real Children of Israel. And in the case of the Oblation, of which He often spake to His intimate ones in allegory and in cryptic terms, the references were not merely personal, but Planetary and Divine.

* * * * * *

Here it may be mentioned that the supposed lamentation by Him over Jerusalem as He sat upon the Mount of Olives, was an event of far greater moment than anything merely personal in His experience. It was an echo through Him of the Lament of the Divine World over the Spiritual Household of this Planet, which in the Heavens had been named Jerusalem. What the Divine sorrow was He well knew. He often spake of it to those who had come nearest to Him. That that sorrow was most real, and that it was unspeakable, he who writes of these things, knows; for he has often heard the reverberated intonations of it and felt the holy awe and sacred passion begotten of them.

The Divine Love never fails. There is no end to its infinite patience and rich provision. It is always

Righteous. It is full of glorious Equity. Its resplendence is Eternal. Though the lower Heavens had to be shut for ages during the awful struggle with the dark forces which encompassed this Earth, yet, when it was possible, the windows of the Heavens were opened. And though the Solar Heavens themselves had to be guarded, yet there was given from them, as it became possible, an accommodated ministry by means of a marvellous rearrangement of the Photosphere. In this latter great cavities appeared, now spoken of as Sun-spots, which were and still are as windows and doorways through which tremendous electric forces are poured forth for the preservation, healing, energizing, and equilibrating of the Kingdoms, Planes, and Elements of the Planet.

IV

Upon and Within the Soul

In all this ministry the Divine World has sought out the Wanderer to bring him back again to the Estate he left. It has laboured to find and restore all those who became smitten through his betrayal of them. The travail of Divine Love on behalf of the Planet-Soul Judah and all her children, has been beyond recording; and it has been more profound on behalf of, and more poignant in and through, all the Christ-Souls who were involved in the betrayal and its tragedy. For stupendous has been its ministry to effect their liberation and restoration, and the re-exaltation of them all to their ancient Inheritance. Sublime sacrifices have been made to restore Judah and Lucifer; and to bring real comfort to the Planet's Archangel, Ya-akob-El.

Can the reader wonder that there is sorrow in this World? That Divine grief prevails in the Heavens? So great is the sorrow of the Heavens and the grief of the

Divine World, that, if it could be written of fully, no living Soul upon these planes could endure to feel its motion in the lapping of its waves upon the shores of his spiritual life.

It is not like human sorrow. It is not of the same order. It is the grief begotten of travail through others and for them. It resteth not; for it is of the Eternal Sea whose motion is unto the healing of all things. The Joy of the Heavens is found in service. There is no night there, and rest is ever found in new service. The ministry may entail grief, for it may have to be rendered amid most painful conditions; but the unceasing sacrificial Spirit labours on unto the accomplishment of the Divine Will. It is thus the whole Heavens of this System, aided by the Divine ministries of other Systems, work the Works of God for the full restoration of Ya-akob-El; Lucifer; Judah; the planetary constitution; all the Planet's children; Luna and all her children; the House of Israel with Ephraim and Manasseh. In the Redemption, Regeneration, and Exaltation to primal Regnancy of all these, shall all the Gods who have shared the burden and ministry, rejoice with all the Heavens.

* * * * * *

The Divine Wisdom is perfect in the out-working of the Eternal Purpose. The Divine World never fails, however great the burden to be borne. Its provision is always equal to the need. Therefore, though it may take great ages to accomplish the Divine Purpose in relation to the Redemption and Regeneration, yet the fulfilment is assured. Even as it took ages for the Planet to fully descend in its spiritual state till its inherent Divine vitality became so low that its Gods all slept and became as dead; so has it been in the recovery a seemingly long time. To reach the realm, the place, and the state where the Ladder of the Heavens could once more be revealed to the Planet's

Angel Ya-akob-El, and the Hosts of GOD meet him on the way to Penuel, has taken some ages.

Even as it takes a Human Soul who has become opposed to the Divine Will, longer to return than to go out, so is it true of a Household like that of this World. Though it was betrayed and has suffered grievously, yet its return can be accomplished only in the degree in which it is able to respond.

This is true of all the Planet's children; of the Planet-Soul; of Lucifer; of all the members of the Hierarchies; and of him who went out from the Presence of his LORD. In the return of the latter it is difficult to express all that has happened, and all that is still proceeding. The Wanderer went out in anger from the Presence, but was soon full of the joy of having his own way; for it is evident he thought he was on the road to the accomplishment of some great deed for and by himself. He never dreamt of the loss that would overtake him. Because of the seriousness of the loss he had to experience, the return has been made more difficult.

V

ON THE THRESHOLD OF THE DIVINE WORLD

But the Divine Love in His Wisdom has never ceased to care for the Wanderer, nor for any of those whom he betrayed. The Divine·World has laboured through the ages to restore all to the unfallen days when Love and Wisdom were regnant upon the Earth, and through GOD's Sons the Heavens were continually telling of the FATHER-MOTHER, and showing forth HIS Glory. And now, as the result of that glorious ministry, the whole Earth with all her children emerges from the long night of tragedy, into the day wherein there is the light of a living hope. The Day of the LORD breaketh. The Delectable Mountains are clothed with the radiance of GOD, and the hills of

Zion are reflecting the glory. The Angelic Hosts are choiring their song of joy, and the songs of triumph are being sung by the Sons of GOD. The desert conditions are giving place to the becoming of the Garden of the LORD through which the streams of the Water of Life will once more flow. The world's wilderness will be cleansed, purified and changed, until within its borders shall blossom again the Rose of Sharon and the Lily of the Valley.

* * * * * *

Herein is hope. Notwithstanding the apparently hopeless conditions of the world, and the dread that haunts the mind and heart of many, the wandering world is returning. The Redemption is at hand. It is nigh every one; it is even at the door. The LORD is near. HE has returned to HIS Temple. The Ark of the Covenant and Testimony has been recovered, and is restored to HIS Temple. HIS Shekinah overshadows the Altar of Oblation. Once more HIS Cherubim minister before HIM, and HIS Seraphim from HIM. From between the Cherubim where the Cloud of HIS Radiance is, HE doth speak unto HIS Servant of these things.

And there HE would minister unto all HIS sons and daughters who once knew HIM within the Sanctuary. HE would reveal HIMSELF as in the ancient times when Zion was the Holy City of the LORD, and Ierusalem a reflection of the glory of the Heavens. In this way HE would find again the whole House of Israel, and bear back every Tribe to its ancient estate. For the Tribes of the LORD must have a most real part in the return pilgrimage of the Planet's Household. They must contribute by their service to this return, and have Divine Joy again in witnessing the trekking homeward to the redeemed life of the Ierusalem which is from above, of all the Earth's children. Having found once more the Presence within the Sanctuary, they must rejoice to share the Divine Travail of the Return. They must acquire the power to move, with sublime surrender, in harmony with the motion of the Heavens, and be again the channels of its Breaths unto the healing of all Life and the restoration of the Planet's Kingdoms. Through the Divine Balance of all their powers and perfect equilibration of all their own Kingdoms and Planes, they must contribute to the restoration of the Celestial status of the Earth till, in all its polarity, it moves in obedience to the Divine Law as in the unfallen days.

Thus must they aid the Divine World in its Travail, sharing the burden and rejoicing in the honour of such a service. For in so doing they will be fellow-workers with the Heavens in the Restitution of the ancient House of Ya-akob-El, the Redemption of the Kingdom of Lucifer, and the Equilibration of the Poles and Planes of Judah.

*　*　*　*　*　*

The Divine Drama may now be understood in relation to the five aspects which have been outlined. These have been presented in their order:—

Upon the Divine Kingdom:
The Assembly of the Gods.

Within the Celestial Spheres:
The Choice of a Son of the Gods.

Within the Earth's Hierarchies:
The Challenge by Betrayal.

Upon and Within the Soul:
The Tragic Effect upon the Race.

On the Threshold of the Divine World:
The Return of all through Divine Ministries, Redemptive and Regenerative.

And in relation to the last great work it must be perceived and understood that the Divine World is looking for vehicles, living Souls through whom it may transmit the power of its Blessing unto the world's Redemption and the full Regeneration of the Sons of GOD. Unto this end is the Solar World—the Divine Centre of this System—most active, rendering an intensified ministry. Every man and every woman who can truly say, *I will arise and go to my Father-Mother to live before Him, to be obedient to His Holy Will and make manifest the righteousness of His Love in all the service of my Life*, and who accomplishes such a noble purpose, becomes GOD's vehicle for the new Christhood Manifestation.

The Divine World is looking for such vehicles. In and through the recovered Message of the Christhood; the Divine Mysteries; the Celestial story of the Sun; the history of the Planet; the adventure for ministry of the Sons of GOD known as ancient Israel, with all their tragic travail; and the Sin-offering Oblation on behalf of the System unto the accomplishment of the Redemption and the Regeneration—the Divine World is calling for such vehicles. It needs for its great ministry those children of the Gods who are willing to seek only unto the fulfilment of the Divine Will; in whose Mind there is no false hope of being first in the Kingdom; in whom that lovely attribute of GOD known as Humility, reigns, so that the last desire of the Heart would be to seek the chief place.

THE WORK needs such Souls. The Kingdom cannot come upon the Earth without them. They are those who are to reign with Christ. In them Love is to be triumphant. Its regnancy is to be manifest to all. Through the Sons of GOD, Divine Love is to be revealed in its majesty as the potency of the Gods, and in its tenderness and beauty as the bloom of sweet lowliness. For only through such a revelation of the lowliness of Love and Wisdom can the Earth be brought through its travail, out of the slough of despond, through the valley of the shadow of death, and delivered from the fires of Gehenna which burn within its children, and the deep darkness of Gehinnom which has made Life for them one long night of fear, sorrow and pain. Only by such a manifestation of the Sons of GOD can the Earth and all her children know again the sacredness, beauty and joyfulness of Life.

* * * * * *

If the reader of these things be gifted with the faculty to hear the groaning of the burdened Earth; the travail-cry of all her oppressed children; the intonations produced by the motion of the Heavens and the language in which they speak; to recognize the Divine Call to share in the world's Redemption, and find himself able and willing to respond; then surely he has known sonship to the Gods, and must needs yield up all for the work of the Divine Love and Wisdom.

To know GOD, is to give as GOD gives according to the measure of our stature in HIM, and in our love and service to be as HE ever is towards all HIS children.

* * * * * *

O wondrous Love! Thy Glory is too transcendent to reveal in human terms, and Thy motion is too profound to interpret.

But we may Manifest Thee in Blessing;

We may Adore Thee in Embodiment;

We may Worship Thee in Serving Thy children;

We may Praise Thee in the harmonious Motion of our Being as we seek to fulfil Thy Commandments and accomplish Thy holy Purpose.

This honour Thou bestowest upon us that we may wear upon our Fashion, the Insignia of Thee.

93

THE BOOK OF ISAIAH

PART FIVE

THE MYSTERY OF THE SIN-OFFERING

Wherein is revealed the reason for its need, the
tragic events that called forth such a
Purpose on the part of the Divine
World, the Nature of it, the
Process of its Burden, the
Path that had to be
followed, and what
has been accom-
plished
by it.

CONTENTS

O Most Blessed One, our Father-Mother! The Mystery of Thy Love deepens to Thy Children as they contemplate the Majesty of Thy Love's Sacrifice on behalf of this world, and sense in some degree the depths of its Motion.

Amid the Great Deep, the Way of Thy going is beyond fathoming; the Mystery hidden in the Oblation of Thy Love is above the comprehension of any man till in his Being he comes to know Thee.

From out Thy Glory Thou hast looked upon the fallen estate of this Earth, the one-time glorious member of Thy Celestial Household, and though its conditions filled all Thy Heavens with grief unutterable, yet didst Thou not account it too great a thing to do for the healing of all its Children and the restoration of all its kingdoms, to make sacrifices most sublime, even unto the carrying away of the Burden of its fallen Heavens and the generation of new Planetary Heavens.

The full Mystery of the Oblation is understood only in Thy Heavens; for there alone amid the High Sons of God, could the Passion of the Lord of Being be fully apprehended.

How Thy Children will adore Thee when they understand this Holy Mystery of Thine! How they will marvel at the vastness of the Work which Thou didst accomplish in the Divine Travail! How absolute will be their own sacrifice unto Thee, when they behold all that Thou didst accomplish for this stricken World and the whole House of Israel!

They will sing of Thy Glorious Deeds, and proclaim Thy Wondrous Works.

O Holy Father-Mother! Thy Servant would adore Thee evermore.

Amen and Amen.

THE MYSTERY OF THE SIN-OFFERING

THE Mystery of the Sin-Offering is most fascinating. To the Saints as well as Theologians it has ever been attractive yet elusive, commanding belief in its reality but refusing to be unveiled to the Understanding. The ages have witnessed it held fast in the toils of tradition, and strangely averse to yielding up its secret in the laboratory of the theological schools. The Church has held its tradition, believed in its necessity, commanded acceptance of the fact, but found itself unable to interpret satisfactorily the Mystery. Howsoever frequently ecclesiastical authorities have put the Mystery into the crucible of their judgment, the Mystery has come forth almost as it went in. The various alloys have still clung to the pure gold of the Divine Truth; the fires of their criticisms have only issued interpretations of contradictory nature, and have not enabled those who sit in the seats of religious authority to discern the secret. Consequently different Schools have given different interpretations, most of which have been far afield from the Truth; and some of them have been most dishonouring to the LORD of All, misrepresenting the manifestation of HIS Righteousness and Equity in the administration of this world.

* * * * * *

All the theories built up around the Mystery of the Sin-Offering are associated in the most direct and intimate way with the Master Jesus. Whether it be the doctrine of Commutation by a Son of GOD through atonement, or Identification with fallen Humanity; a spectacular display

99

of Righteous Indignation against Sin in order to impress Humanity, or the Self-martyrdom of the Master in human service in order to reveal His love and compassion unto the healing of the race, there is utter failure to solve the Mystery. All are equally in the dark regarding the real inner meaning of the Sin-Offering, its nature, its path, its duration, and what it accomplished.

* * * * * *

In approaching the Mystery it is absolutely necessary for the right understanding of it, that the seeker divests himself of all the associations which traditional beliefs and interpretations have woven as a garment and with which they have clothed the Mystery. The only premises permissible are those which embody Love, Righteousness and Equity: for God is Love, and His Love is ever righteous and just. But Righteousness and Equity are the expressions of the Eternal Law of His Love and Wisdom. Of perfect Love it may be postulated that it doeth all things well. Of the sentient conscious objects of that Love it may be said that they would be responsible actors within the circumference of the operations of the Eternal Law, and not mere machines. And this would be true of a Celestial or Planetary Soul-system, as well as of the individual Human Soul. The Eternal Law of God is the same throughout the Universe, and is unchangeable. It varies only in the degree of its accommodation to System, individual Celestial member, and solitary Soul. It is in this sense alone that it may be truly affirmed that the ETERNAL ONE is unchangeable, and at the same time said most truly, that HE is ever accommodating HIMSELF unto the needs of all members of HIS Universe—Solar, Planetary and Human.

THE NEED FOR THE SIN-OFFERING

The reason why the Sin-Offering became necessary

arose as the outcome of changes effected in the Planetary administration and constitution. It was not occasioned by the Fall of Humanity, as that tragic event has been interpreted. Nor was the primary act of the Fall associated with the Planetary administration. The scene of it was within the Celestial Heavens. That which brought about the Fall was witnessed within the threshold of the Divine Kingdom of this System. The Divine Kingdom of this System is the Solar Body. Concerning the Nature, Constitution and Ministry of that Body of the LORD, some more definite teaching will be found in another volume of Divine Revelation.[1]

In one of the Assemblies of the Gods belonging to this System as Servants of the Most High, there arose one who had been greatly honoured of the Divine LORD, and who had been appointed one of the Plenipotentiaries and Chief Administrators in the Celestial Kingdom of the Sun. He was a glorious Being who had risen to great heights of power for service. He had attained the status of being accounted "a Son of the Gods." According to their status, the Sons of the Gods have to administer the Laws operative amongst the Elements out of which Planetary Systems are fashioned and Human Souls generated. Their position is one which demands of them absolute self-surrender to the Divine Will; and their ministry amongst the Divine Elements is one of most grave responsibility.

The original status of this System was more sublimely glorious than it now is. Every member of the System was perfect in fashion, motion and ministry. There were no dissensions in the Assemblies of the Gods, for the ministry of all was perfect. The Solar World, which was the Body of the LORD for this System, was then

---

[1] "*The Mystery of the Light Within Us.*" By Author

in far greater estate than it is now; for all its Kingdoms were open and its glory was undimmed. Its manifested planes extended far beyond its present dimensions; its Photosphere was the Cloud of Radiance through which it accomplished its ministries; and its Chromosphere was the scene of Angelic manifestations, and the magnetic circuli wherein the spectra of the ELOHIM were revealed.

*　　*　　*　　*　　*　　*

The gifted one who had risen into the status wherein he had the right to enter into the Assembly of the Gods, became obsessed with the ambition to rule over this System, and to create conditions amid the Elemental Kingdoms other than those which obtained. He desired that within certain areas there should be introduced fixity of all the Elements as these were made use of in the outer realms of manifestation, and thus have permanent phenomena.

Such an adventure would have meant the effecting of great changes in the constitution and combination of the Elements, the loss of their inherent volatility by means of which they were always able to respond to the Laws of the Divine Kingdom in their centrifugal and centripetal motion. It would also have necessitated a change in the Elements and motion of the Solar Body. Indeed, such a change could not have been accomplished within a Planetary Household, such as this world, without such an alteration of its polarity as would necessitate a change in its motion and status. And if such a decision were made and the change in Celestial status brought about, the Planet would be compelled to move out of the Divine Life-stream which flowed from the Solar Body and formed the Divine Ecliptic of the whole System.

It was this very change of motion and status some ages

later that brought about in the most dramatic way, the tragedy of this Planet's fall, the desolation of all its Kingdoms, and the breaking of its outer Planes. The Fall was not that of a human pair in the childhood of their Earth-life, but nothing less than that of a minor God.

THE DECISION OF THE GODS

The Assembly of the Gods refused to countenance any such change in the order of the Universe, or the least deviation from the Divine Law. They regarded the suggestion as one at variance with the purpose of the FATHER-MOTHER, and counselled the brilliant member to put from him any thought or desire of doing anything contrary to the Divine Will. Even from the innermost realm counsel was sent forth to him that such request on his part be withdrawn, as it was contrary to the way of Love in any member of the Assembly to seek through fellow members to change the Laws of the Divine Wisdom manifest throughout the glorious Celestial Heavens. And it was a season of anxious awaiting his reply to the tender Divine greeting and counsel by the acknowledgment of his mistake, and his beautiful obedience once more to the Divine Love.

But he gradually closed his audient chamber to the Voice of the Divine World, and allowed his ambition to prevail; so in pride of heart he went away from the Assembly, and passed out from the Presence of his LORD. Though the various members, acting upon the counsel of the Divine Love, sought to find him and bring him back, he eluded them. He chose his own path and became a wanderer. But his ambition still remained the dominating influence within him. He therefore sought out a field for the realization of his ambition. And he found that field upon one of the Planetary Homes of this System.

It was from this field of activity, where his counsel was listened to by those who agreed with his wishes, that he set out to bring down the glorious Home of the Planet-Soul Judah, by influencing her Hierarchy to adopt his counsel and have a system with permanent phenomena. He became the friend of Lucifer the Angel of the outer Kingdom, and prevailed upon him to change the Elemental Kingdoms. To accomplish this, the whole Planetary Household was compelled to move out from the Stream of the Divine Ecliptic. The effect of this betrayal of the Divine Law of motion and status was to bring about the materialization of the whole of the sphere of Lucifer, cause the fixity of the poles and, consequently, of the polarity of Substances and Elements.

*   *   *   *   *   *

Even the Heavens of the Planet became changed. Every generating station, such as this world, has its Angelic Heavens. These are contained within the upper Atmospheria, and are media and venues through which Angelic and Celestial ministries are rendered to the Planet-Soul, her System, and all her children. These circles are also in direct communication with the Vortexya or Celestial Magnetic Atmosphere through which the Solar Body renders ministry to the entire Household.

The Planetary Heavens had also a high spiritual service to the Human Races; for as Souls came into the outer manifestation life for purposes of education and, having fulfilled the number of the days of their service, passed away, they came out from and passed back into those Heavens. The Heavens formed the higher training ground. It was within them that the individual Soul gathered up the fruits of its experiences upon the more objective realm, and had these confirmed or crystallized as enrichment of potencies and attributes, with corresponding expansion and deepening of consciousness.

THE EFFECTS OF THE BETRAYAL

The tragedy that overtook the Planet when the counsels of the betrayer were listened to and acted upon, involved these Heavens to such an extent that Angelic ministry through them became more and more difficult. Indeed, there came a time when they were so infested by evil things that the Angelic Hosts had to be withdrawn, to the sad loss of all the children of the Planet-Soul Judah. And the loss was even greater to that race of Celestial Beings spoken of in the Old Testament as the Sons of GOD, and also known later by the terms, the Ancients, the Magians, the House of Israel, and the Children of Zion. For these Souls had come to this Planet in various offices of ministry unto the Human Races, from another system. They were friends of the Angels, and throughout long ages before the great betrayal, were companioned by them.

*   *   *   *   *   *

The Heavens of the Planet in their fallen state, became the home of those who had brought about the disastrous conditions. It was against the principalities set up by the dominating evil powers that the Human Soul, individual and communal, had to wrestle. These powers in their regnancy in those Heavens, made pandemonium conditions for all the Souls who were resident. They contained the elements of death, Hades, and Gehenna. Some of the circles became even Tartarean.

*   *   *   *   *   *

Amid such Planetary conditions it was impossible for the Soul to grow truly and evolve towards the realization of the radiant morn of full Soul-illumination and the perfect Life. Tragedy succeeded tragedy upon the outer

planes and in those Heavens, till at one time it did seem
as if the entire Planetary manifestation would have to be
abandoned. Solar ministries of a specially accommodated
order even, failed to effect the purgation of the Planetary
Heavens and the rescue of the Planet's children. To
have made the intensive disintegrating and transmutory ministries sufficiently great to destroy the evil
principalities and the sodomic degrading images which
filled the Planet's Heavens, and restore these latter to a
state of purity and equilibrium, would have involved the
utter destruction by annihilation of the younger Human
Races; for they could not have endured the Solar Rays
that would have had to be projected. So another way
had to be found.[1]

That other way was by means of The Sin-Offering.
In order to save the Human Races and make it possible
for the complete return to their Celestial Home of the
Sons of GOD, the real Children of Israel, it was proposed
to send one who had attained to Divine Sonship in estate,
to deal with the situation in an individual capacity.
That one was to be the Servant of the LORD. He was to
be the vehicle through whom the Divine World could act.
Constituted in his estate a Son of GOD in the inner Kingdom, he was to be as a son of man upon the Earth. And
in and through his Divine Humanity he was to be the
medium for the expression of the Passion of the LORD.
The world's burden was to become his burden as the
Divine Love took it upon HIMSELF unto the taking of
it away.

*   *   *   *   *   *

How pregnant with the Divine Mystery of the Sin-
Offering are all the references in the Prophet's Message

---

[1] For fuller explanation see *The Mystery of the Light Within
Us*. By Author.

concerning the bearing of world iniquity by the Servant of the LORD, and the redeeming back of Israel!—

"All men, like sheep wandering, have gone astray; every one has gone in a way other than that unto which he was appointed; upon HIS Servant hath the LORD laid the burden of their return.

"He shall make his graves amid the wicked and lie down with the fallen.

"There shall be an hiding of faces; for none shall know him in his generations.

"He shall be wounded and tormented in bearing iniquity and the sin of many; yet by his stripes shall many be healed.

"Behold saith the LORD of SABAOTH, I will thus create anew the Heavens of the Earth, and righteousness shall dwell in them and upon the Earth."

THE PLACE CALLED CALVARY

The place of Golgotha had a significance greater than the physiographic location with which it is associated. The Sign of the Cross and the suffering one upon it, are related invariably to the Roman Crucifixion of the Master; therefore it will not be easy for those who turn their thoughts and sympathies thitherward, to accept the statement that the real Calvary was not there, and that the "green hill without a city wall" was not in Palestine. The outer story as told in the Gospel Records is confounded with events which were Soulic and Divine. That the Master suffered crucifixion at the hands of the Romans through the instigation of the rulers of Judaism, is quite true. But such an outer tragedy was related to the Blessed Manifestation of the Christhood, and had naught to do (except in a symbolic sense), with the Sin-Offering. For the Roman Crucifixion took place some years before the closing days of the Manifestation, as has been revealed in earlier writings;[1] and the Crucifixion related to the Sin-Offering only began after the Master had laid down His Christhood (which was the laying down of His Life), and had taken up the burden of the Cross unto Redemption, wherein He became a bond-servant. His Crucifixion was on Calvary. But the Cross He bore there was that of the Divine World; for He was representative of HIM Who is the Sign of the Cross in the Divine World. And the Calvary where He suffered crucifixion was outside the City Walls of the Christhood Estate, outside the holy Citadel of the abiding Presence. For Him it was the place of spiritual death, the realm of false powers and principalities, the home of beasts of prey represented in evil desires, the Hinnom of the outer darkness and the Gehenna of the fires of consuming ambition. It was within the circuli of the Planet's Heavens whose atmospheres had all been changed and whose magnetic potencies had been misdirected and misused.

*　*　*　*　*　*

Verily it was the place of the skull which has come to be the symbol of death, though it originally had relation to the various circles within the Vortexya or magnetic atmospheres by which the outer planes were encompassed. The Divine Cross had to be borne there unto the full crucifixion of the LORD of Glory in and through the full crucifixion of the Christhood of the Master. For, to enter those circles and function in them in such a ministry as

---

[1] See *The Master*, *The Logia*, and *The Divine Renaissance.*—By Author.

was required, meant the sacrifice of the consciousness of
the Holy and Blessed Presence of the FATHER-MOTHER,
and the direction and use of all His attributes amid
conditions other than such as are associated with the
Christhood. For He had to lay down His Life unto the
uttermost in the work of the purification of the Planetary
Heavens. It was there the three crosses were to be seen—
the cross of the Man of GOD crucified between the spirits
of negation on the one hand and superstition on the other;
and it was there that the great burden of the Oblation
was borne on the three Crosses of the three realms of the
Being—the Mind, the Heart and the Soul—the realms
of Vision, of Audience, and of Divine Realization. For
the crucifixion or veiling of the Vision had to be lovingly
endured; the closing of the doors of the chamber wherein
the Voice spake to Him, had to be submitted to; and, until
the close of the Oblation, all the glorious realizations had
to be lovingly yielded up.

Thus it will be seen that it was no hill clad with the
verdure of the Heavens of the Divine LORD, since Love
had been banished from those realms, and Wisdom
supplanted by confusion and disorder. To bring back
the Love that had been so cruelly betrayed, and restore
order and harmony expressive of the Divine Wisdom,
the Cross was projected into the midst of the Vortexya
and Elemental Kingdoms. That which belonged to the
Divine World ministry of pure and exalted Adoration,
Worship, Praise, Blessing, Thanksgiving, Mediation and
Sacrifice, was lowered into the hells generated in the
midst of the loveless states and disordered conditions that
made of the one-time paradisical Heavens, a place of the
skull or spiritual death. It was there the one who had been
in such high estate as to be designated a Son of GOD, and
become known to all those to whom He had ministered

as Mediator and Messenger from the FATHER-MOTHER as the Beloved One, carried His Cross and suffered upon it the pains of Soul-death. It was within those realms that He fulfilled the Stations of the Cross, as these had to be repeated in the Divine Passion, and where He fell three times beneath the burden as He accomplished the redemption of the Astral Sea, which had to give up its dead. For His Mind had given to it the cruel crown of thorns which pierced His Soul's brow; His Heart was wounded by the sword of the bitter irony of His position; and all the attributes which His Hands and His Feet represented of creative, manifestive, and mediatorial potency for the Divine World ministry before the High Altar, became bruised beyond telling as He carried the burden of the Planet-Soul and that of all her children; and even that of the Travail of the House of Israel.

HOW THE EARTH'S HEAVENS WERE PURIFIED

The process of transmutation by which the Planet's Heavens were emptied of the evil magnetic images which infested them, is one that must needs remain hidden in great part. Only in general terms has the writer been permitted to state its Mystery. Herein may be seen the way of the Divine Wisdom. Those who are merely curious could not look with true reverence upon such a sacred mystery. They might repeat the vulgarity presented in the Gospel Records where it is reported that during the Roman Crucifixion, many who passed by the suffering crucified one, wagged their heads and said, "He saved others; Himself He cannot save." "If thou be a Son of GOD, come down from the Cross." For they could not understand His burden, being as yet ignorant of the majesty of Divine Sonship and all that it implies of absolute trust in the Divine Love and perfect obedience to the Divine Will, even unto the enduring of such a cruci-fixion as implied the sacrifice of all that the Mind, Heart, Soul and Being held most dear, and the doing of many things in the redemptive service that filled Mind, Heart and Spirit with ignominy, pain, sorrow and anguish.

Therefore it is asked of all who read what follows that they do so with lowliness and reverence. The measure of the Divine Awe that fills the reader will also be the measure of true apprehension of the way of the Divine Love and Wisdom revealed in the majestic Divine stooping for the Redemption of the whole Planetary Household.

Behold the Love of the FATHER-MOTHER in the pro-vision which HE made, and HIS Wisdom in all the Path of the Oblation!

Behold HIS Love in its sublimest giving, and HIS Wisdom in its transcendent revealing!

That which might not be accomplished by means of the direct intensified Solar Ray without grave danger and loss to so many of the Planet's children, it was purposed should be done by means of the mediatorial ministry of one who was in the estate of a Son of GOD. Through Him the Solar World was to effect the destruction of the fluidic magnetic images begotten of evil desire and action which had been written upon the atmospheric walls of the Planetary Heavens, the overthrow of all who had set up the evil kingdom and reigned there over all the Souls who had to enter those Heavens in their transit from the outer planes, and who also made their regnancy felt throughout the Planet.

Unto this end the Servant of the LORD had to be very specially constituted in His vehicles; for the Solar Ray was to pass into Him and through Him in a way most marvellous in the Divine Wisdom of it. The Servant having the Divine status of a Son of God, was one with the inner Life of the Divine World; and this enabled that World to act for the Lord of Love towards the Servant and hold Him magnetically by means of His magnetic poles, as well as affecting those poles to give Him direction in the oblatory work, at the command of the Divine Will. In His Being He was placed in the position, through His various estates, between the Heavens of the Divine World and the Earth. Through His magnetic body He functioned upon the outer Kingdom of the Earth: in His Mind He was cast into the den of wild beasts within the lower atmospheres: in His Heart He had always to function in the Kingdom of Divine Love: and He had to seek unto the realization of that Love amid all the conditions which prevailed within the magnetic Vortexya and Atmospheria of the Planet's Heavens.

Thus it came to pass that in all His mysterious travail begotten of His endeavour to express His love and devotion, He was ever seeking the Divine Presence even when He had to go into the far country in ministry.

Placed as He was through His Divine Estate within, and His fallen Human Estate to correspond to the needs of the without or lower Kingdom of Soul-manifestation, in the Innermost He received the Divine Urge through the Solar Electro-Magnetic action, to act upon the lower or outermost in a way that led to the attraction of the evil magnetic conditions. When these came to Him they were held as by a great magnet; then they became magnetically drawn into His body and absorbed, and there the power of the direct action of the Divine Ray transmuted them; and then the influx of the Divine Magnetic Stream separated these changed elements, destroyed their power for evil, and afterwards caused them to be eliminated.

It was in this way the Sin-Offering was made. It was in this way that the Servant became as one deeply involved in the world's Sin. This is how He came to be the bearer of the effects of human iniquity. Though the prince of this world came to Him yet found nothing in Him to respond to the evil conditions which had to be changed, nevertheless He became affected in His vehicle by those conditions, and felt Himself to be part of the burden of Sin as He held the evil images, absorbed their magnetic elements into His body, endured the process of the extinction of their fires, suffered the awful darkness they left behind them, and then anguished till all the elements were eliminated.

The way of the prodigal had to be His. The depths of fallen Humanity He had redemptively to explore. The distress of the Planet-Soul He had to share. The fallen estate of all His Brethren He had to know, even unto the state of the least. He had to languish with Lucifer amid his fallen Kingdom. He had to know the dread that beset Ya-akob-El and all the Hierarchy. And He had to be even as the one who went out from the Presence of His LORD, and become as a Celestial Wanderer.

Thus from the least to the greatest, and from the lowest to the highest of all who had become involved, He trod the winepress alone, covering the ground of all their needs as the Holy One, whose Servant He was, led Him. For He was led of the Holy Spirit.

THE DURATION OF THE SIN-OFFERING

The story of the Roman Crucifixion, including the trials before the Sanhedrin, Herod and Pilate, and the events associated with the Resurrection, barely covers a week. Historically and ecclesiastically, the Sin-Offering did not exceed three days. The official and supreme Act of Sublime Sacrifice progressed through three hours only. The momentous Seven Words, supposed to have been uttered on the Roman Cross, though actually spoken during the Gethsemane[1] which came long after the Roman tragedy, are related to the suffering endured and expressed in the cry of despair as the darkness closed about His vision and He felt Himself GOD-forsaken. Thus the events which were Cosmic, and all the individual experiences before and during the Crucifixion which were Celestial, are compressed into a few Earth-days.

The Sin-Offering was something far greater than anything that has been conceived of and set forth in Christian Beliefs. In its events it covered a period which has to be expressed in Celestial terms. It was commenced when the Master had completed the Christhood Manifestation; and it continued for three Naronic Cycles or prophetic days which were related to Celestial positions of Sun, Earth and Moon, covering over 1,800 years. The references by the Prophet to the Servant's *Generations* are related to the duration of the Oblation. The Generations were His Forty Incarnations, which it was affirmed no one would know; for "the hiding of faces" would prevent anyone from recognizing who He was. And during each of those Incarnations He was cut off out of the land of the living or state of Soul-consciousness of the Presence, because He was smitten by the transgressions of the people. The burden of sin weighed Him down to spiritual death. The death was Soulic. Not only were there dead and dying things around Him everywhere, but within Himself He had to know the state of Soul-death in the loss of all remembrance of the Divine

---

[1] For fuller explanation see *The Master, The Logia,* and *The Divine Renaissance.* By Author.

Countenance. His Incarnations during the Sin-Offering were actually forty; but none knew the fashion of any of them. They were "the forty days" or rounds with the wild beasts in the wilderness, during the period of which ministry it is said He was tempted of the Devil; and the Devil is the spirit of negation.[1]

The Sin-Offering as a Divine Office had its super-structure. There was a most definite arrangement of Office in its processional. It had its Divine Plan to be followed from beginning to end. Indeed, right through the ages, from the hour of the Assembly of the Gods when the Sin-Offering was projected, and then that hour amid another Assembly wherein the Servant of the LORD was chosen to be the Divine Vehicle of the Burden, to the Day of the Manifestation, preparations were being made for the revelation of the Christhood, which was to be followed immediately by the Oblation.

And of this latter, every step was arranged by the Divine World so far as the Office could be filled by that World. Great were the provisions made for the Servant in His Work. Each Life had a certain amount of the redemptive burden-bearing apportioned to it. As an Oblation, it began with the passing of the Master from the Life of the Manifestation, and it continued until "the fulness of time" was fulfilled. It lasted from the year 49 (using the common setting of A.D.), and it obtained as an Office until the year 1903. It was then consummated.[2]

* * * * * *

But the return journey by the one who was the LORD's

---

[1] For fuller explanation see *The Master*, pp. 369-401, *The Logia*, pp. 230-1, and *The Divine Renaissance, Vol. I*, pp. 261-301.

[2] *The Divine Renaissance, Vol. I*, pp. 217 to 240. By Author.

Servant had then to be undertaken. For it was necessary that the LORD should celebrate the Passover—the passing away from the Christhood Manifestation and the Return —in the House of that Man. The Message of the Christhood had to be recovered, and the whole of the lives and the path of the Sin-Offering, retraced. The time drew near when, through that recovery, the Mystery of GOD in Christ travailing for the world in and through HIS Servant, must needs be revealed.

But there followed *The Aftermath* which had to be borne during the Return, the poignancy of which lasted until 1914, in which year the third *Naros* closed and the fourth *Naros* opened.

* * * * * *

It is not easy to decide which was the hardest to bear, the tragedy of the Sin-Offering or that of the Awakening and Return. But both were beyond telling. In the Return from Edom with all His garments of the Christhood red-dyed as one who had trodden the wine-press, no one knew Him as the Soul through whom the Manifestation was made. Could they have been told that He was that one, they would have accounted it presumption if not blasphemy, for any one to think so. The traditional concept of the Master would have prevented any one from discerning His Return in the man who had nothing really attractive about Him in either His appearance or estate. His visage was indeed marred more than the sons of men; but no one knew it, for it was only visible to the Heavens in the hours of intense anguish. He did weep and agonize; but it was chiefly in secret, so that the occasions were very rare in which the Soul-travail could have been witnessed by human eyes.

Nor could any of His Brethren have understood such sorrow even if they could then have discerned who He was.

Peter and John[1] who had to find the Guest Chamber and prepare it, had no easy ministry; for during the celebration of the Return from the Passover, what they had to witness from the inner planes often overwhelmed them; and they would fain have fled from the sight of such a Calvary. For the Gethsemane of every life was upgathered into the last life, with most momentous effect upon all the attributes and vehicles.[2]

It was the Travail of more than an individual Soul. It partook of the character of the Burden itself. It was Planetary. It was also Racial. It was likewise Solar. And it was none other than the Pulse of the Divine World throbbing its profound sorrow. It was thus that it became most true of Him—there never was sorrow like unto His sorrow, nor grief like His.

What the Sin-Offering Accomplished

That which was supposed to effect a change in the relation of Mankind to God, did not alter one iota the attitude and purpose of God towards humanity. But it did effect great changes in the Heavens of the Planet; and it made Redemption possible. It cleared away the obstacles to the Planet-Soul regaining her most ancient estate in the perfect balance of her magnetic Poles and the equilibration of all her Planes. It opened up the way for all the Elements to be purified and redeemed back to their original status, and for all the Planet's Kingdoms to be restored. It enabled the Sun to open up more fully his Angelic Kingdom and begin the Avatar movement which would herald the coming of the Lord in

---

[1] Though these two represented the Understanding and the Love-Principle they were also two intimate friends of the Master.

[2] Of these things see *The Logia*, pp. 219-225. By Author.

and through a restored Christhood. Through the healing of the Earth's Heavens, an intensified Angelic Ministry could be given to humanity such as would gradually accomplish the real Redemption for which the Oblation was made and the burden borne; for all would be called to the pure way of living upon every plane of consciousness, and find the true path of Love, Compassion and Pity to walk therein. And though these latter long-looked-for manifestations of nobler ways on the part of humanity seem as yet afar off, they are coming; for though, like the prodigal in the far country, men still satisfy their hunger with the swinish elements associated with carnivorism, they are gradually awakening to their wrong states and turning their faces towards the Homeland of the Soul where the Divine Inheritance awaits them.

The Redemption is on its way. The Hosts of the LORD are hastening its coming. The unsettled state of the World to-day is the sure testimony of the Divine activity. The Solar Heavens are pouring out upon the nations such electric streams as must purify the polluted channels of social and national life, and make of these helpful venues for the enrichment and ennoblement of individual, communal and national character. True religion will ere long be welcomed as the motion of the Being towards the embodiment and manifestation of every good thing. Though there will be the cessation of much that is associated with religious creeds and ceremonials, yet there will be a clearer vision, a truer understanding, and a less self-regarding aim crowned by a much nobler purpose.

*　　*　　*　　*　　*　　*

In this redemptive work the Planet-Soul will have an ever-increasing power to serve; for, as it progresses, that noble Plenipotentiary will have greater freedom in ministry through the healing of the Elements and the

liberation of the Planes. And Lucifer will again be equal
to faithfully filling his Office; for all the outer Planes will
be restored and balanced in their motion, and be able to
express the Divine Will in their ministry. It will then be
possible for the children of the Planet-Soul, Judah, to
function more beautifully upon them. For them to live
will then become a real joy. They will take upon themselves the glory expressed in the Planet-Mother's name,
and be radiant with the light and joy of the Angelic
Heavens. All the Angels of the Seven Planetary Spheres
will once more become exalted; for they will regain
power to serve their LORD as in the unfallen days.
Ya-akob, the Planetary Angel, will behold his one-time
glorious Household restored to the radiant estate of
the Ierusalem Above, and know the blessed regnancy
that once was his as Ya-akob-El, the Vicegerent of GOD,
when the Holy City was still intact, and its terraces and
palaces were the delight of all who beheld them.

THE STORY OF LUNA

And in that day shall the glorious Goddess of the Night
shine with a resplendence she hath not known for great
ages; indeed, not since she gave up her Celestial regnancy
in the gift of her Seas, Atmospheres, magnetic Plane and
all her Celestial Children, in an age of the Earth's
greatest need.

Few know what the ancient Estate of the Moon was.
None of the various names bestowed upon her describe
who she was and is, nor her real ministry. Perhaps the
names that best express her ancient estate are those of
Phœbe, Diana and Cynthia. She was not only daughter
of the Sun in her origin, but she was also as the Sun's
sister in her ministry. In the realm of interior Wisdom,
she not only represented the Higher Mind, but she was
the Guardian of the illumined Understanding. The arc

of light seen in her rising and setting was taken in mystic ages as the Symbol of the Holy Spirit; and also of the Soul floating as the Ark or an Argosy upon the face of the Great Deep. As Diana she was the huntress of the Night— the symbol of the awakened Mind ever seeking amid the world's night for the *raison d'être* in relation to everything.

Many great minds think the Moon is now a dead world. She may appear so when observed by astronomers; for she is without Seas, Atmospheres and magnetic Plane. But now, in a new motion, she is gradually coming nearer to the Earth to receive back those Seas, Atmospheres, magnetic Plane and Children which she lost when she made her supreme sacrifice on behalf of this world. Gradually her Seas will return to her as vapour; and all the Elements of her one-time highly magnetic Atmospheria find their way to her through the Earth's Vortexya;[1] for her Seas are amongst the waters of the great oceans of the Earth which she so greatly influences, and her Vortexya, or Celestial Magnetic Circulus, is entangled in that of the Earth.

The effect of the Sin-Offering upon her has already been great; for by means of it the Earth is now able to receive so much more fully from the Solar Body that, without loss to the potencies necessary for the support of her Kingdoms and all who inhabit her Planes, she can gradually restore to Luna the Elements and Powers which belong to her.

*　*　*　*　*　*

In addition to all these, and yet in a Divine sense a most integral part of them, there is now manifest in many directions the awakening of the Sons of God who have long slept upon the Earth. It is the break of *the Day*

---

[1] This has actually begun to take place.

when all the Gods should arise to manifest and serve.
For in such a return shall all the Ancient People share.
For, the first great arising as the resultant of the Oblation
and Sin-Offering, is to be associated with the Return of
Israel and the manifestation of the Christhood. It was
said of them that they would be redeemed from their
captivity, liberated from all bondage, and come back
to the Holy Land of their ancient inheritance and the
Holy City of their Spiritual commerce. For the real
Children of Israel were the ancient Sons of the Heavens
who manifested as God's Christs, and whose Holy City
bore the sacred name of Zion, the City of God.

*   *   *   *   *   *

All these Souls were related to the Solar World as the
inheritors of Divine Love, Life and Light. And they knew
the Planetary Archangel, Ya-akob-El and shared in the
ministries of the Hierarchy. They loved Luna as Diana,
Phœbe and Cynthia in the unfallen days, and suffered
unspeakably when Luna had to make her supreme
sacrifice to save Judah the Planet-Soul. And they had
great regard for Judah whose children they came to
teach. Therefore, all that concerned Judah and Luna
made demands upon themselves. As no man liveth unto
himself neither doth any world, whether Sun, Planet or
Moon; so that what affects one affects all. And in like
manner a great community of Souls could not live to
themselves, but for all unto whom they were related and
to whom they ministered. So, in their return, these
Sons of God will live and serve for all. They were Cosmic
in their Christhood and ministry when they came to
this world; and in their arising they must again become
Cosmic. For their arising and coming doth the stricken
Earth wait, and also all her groaning children; because
in their coming, the wilderness is to be fully changed

and the desert conditions made to give place to an Edenic Life. Indeed in their coming, their manifestation and their ministry, GOD the Eternal and ever most Blessed ONE is to be revealed as once more walking with the Sons of the Heavens in the Garden of the Soul.

THE BOOK OF ISAIAH

PART SIX

A MOMENTOUS PROMISE

*Being the sequel to the Sin-Offering where-
in the effect of the Travail of the
Oblation becomes manifest in the
assurance of its triumph, the
Return of the Servant,
and the Arising
of the Sons
of God*

CONTENTS

O Lord of my Being, unto Thee turned I in the day of my Travail, for Thou alone couldst succour and comfort me, and restore unto me a Living Hope.

Thou hadst given to me, as an Eternal Inheritance, a portion in Thy Kingdom, and a part to play in the Mystery of Thy Holy Passion.

Thus didst Thou crown me with the glory of Childhood to Thee, and the great honour of sharing in the Burden of Thy Holy Passion; for unto such Thou didst appoint me.

The Ages have borne witness to Thy great Love and Wisdom, though Thy Children knew not of Thy Travail for their recovery and the healing of all the afflictions that befell them.

To those in Thy Heavens who have watched for the Dawn the Night must have seemed long and almost hopeless, so dense has the darkness been, and terrible the conflict with the forces of the enemy.

Throughout the Travail Thy secret has had to be held sacred; for those who smote the glorious Vision of Thyself unveiled by Thy Servant in the Days of the Manifestation amid the Syrian Hills, have sought to defeat even the purpose of the Passion of Thy Love.

But in the Might of Thy Love Thou hast accomplished the Oblation, changed the Heavens of the Earth, opened up a way for the Return of the House of Israel, and made it possible for the distraught Earth to be redeemed and restored.

Thus hast Thou caused the Night of Sorrow to pass away and the Morning of Joy to break forth.

Thou has filled the Sanctuary of Thy Servant with the Glory of Thy Resplendence, and made full the Chalice of His Being with the Wine of Thy Love.

O Adorable and Most Lovely One! How shall Thy servant Praise Thee as Thou shouldst be praised!

For Adoration, Worship, Praise and Blessing his Life is evermore Thine; for he would be Thine in perfect Life and Service.

Amen and Amen.

A MOMENTOUS PROMISE

ERE writing further of the great Mystery of the Oblation,
I would pause to give praise and thanksgiving unto the
FATHER-MOTHER for all the tokens of HIS Love and
Wisdom vouchsafed unto me. For, through HIS encompassing and overshadowing of me, HE hath brought
me back from the world's dense night, and out from the
midst of the awful maelstrom begotten of the meeting of
its many evil streams, to behold once more the glory of
HIS Countenance, and meet again those Angel-faces and
friends lost awhile in the Heavens and on the Earth.

For HIS sustaining, preserving and guiding Presence
throughout the ages, I would praise HIM; and in HIM I
would rejoice for the coming of this day of the Return, and
for all that which it heralds of the triumphant issues of
the Divine Passion.

I am rejoiced to be so honoured of HIM as to be able to
mediate from HIS High Altar, of HIS Holy Mystery
revealed in the Sin-Offering. For, to write of it is to speak
of HIMSELF; of the glory of HIS Love; of the wealth of HIS
giving unto, and on behalf of, this distraught Earth and all
her children.

TEXTUAL CRITICISM FAILURE

Language is too inadequate to express in words all that
stands out in my vision, and which has become realized
by my Being concerning HIM, as I endeavour to unveil
the meaning of the momentous prophecy expressed in the
sublime Revelation of the Divine Travail found in

Isaiah. Towards the close of that chapter of Mystery set forth in the Book we have these words:—

"He shall see of the travail of his Soul, and shall be satisfied."[1]

Except in certain sections of the School of Higher Criticism, these words have usually been applied to the Master. The Servant spoken of by the Prophet has been associated with Him. Some of the greatest scholars have rejected the idea of the fifty-third chapter of Isaiah having any reference whatever to the Sin-Offering and a suffering Messiah.[2] Nor is this to be wondered at; for the interpretation given to the passage concerning the suffering Servant, has often been such as to turn serious-minded students from accepting the possibility of, or even the need for, such a Sin-Offering as the Church has believed in.

But whatever good textual criticism may have done in clearing away many foreign elements, and breaking up traditional and stereotyped beliefs, it has not succeeded in unveiling the real Message hidden in the Text. Indeed it has got little farther in that direction than the usual national and racial prophet of Jewry. There is not even an approach to a Cosmic vision of the Message. The latter is circumscribed by the religious, social and national life of one small country and race. The hopes and fears, the successes and defeats, the conflicts and conquests, the captivity and deliverance of one branch of the Human Race, hold the stage in the drama of GOD and HIS People.

A RECORD OF DIVINE TRAVAIL

Yet above and beyond all that textual criticism has done, and all the mistaken application and interpretation

---

[1] *Vide* Isaiah LIII, v. 11. Also the Text given in this Volume.

[2] *Vide* Encyclopædia Biblica, and the late Dr. Cheyne on Isaiah.

of the passage by the Catholic and Evangelical Schools, there is a profound Cosmic Revelation contained in the whole Message of the real Isaiah, which breaks forth into the revelatory Travail of the Divine LORD. It is of this Divine Passion the Prophet speaks in the fifty-third chapter. It is descriptive of the projected burden-bearing of the LORD of Being through HIS chosen Servant; the great need for such travail arising out of the condition of humanity; the nature of the Burden to be borne; the way by which the Servant would have to go in the carrying of humanity's load; the chief characteristics of the Travail; the multiple lives the Servant would have to live and the deaths he would have to experience; his aloneness and unknown-ness; the torments he would have to endure in bearing the world's Karma as he made his bed with the wicked; the long silence imposed upon him during his generations of burden-bearing; the sacrificial character of his ministry; showing that his afflictions, whilst begotten of humanity's evil states, were nevertheless appointed by the LORD of Being to be borne by him; that it was in response to the Divine Will that his Soul was made an Offering for Sin; and that, when the Offering for Sin was fully accomplished, he should see of the Travail of his Soul and be satisfied.

Thus will it be seen that the glory of the meaning of the whole description has been dimmed, and the revelation hidden. The interpretation given to them even at best, has reduced their cosmic sublimity to an individual and a personal realm. The profound universality of the Oblation in its relation to this world, the Solar body, the System, and all Israel, has remained throughout the ages unperceived. The inner burning flame of the Message has been unseen and unknown throughout the ages, whilst the LORD of Love travailed for all HIS children in the whole System. Whilst the historical Christian Communities have believed that there was some great mystery implied in the Sin-Offering itself, and in the manner in which the Burden of it was borne by the Master, yet they have all been as those who have eyes yet see not, ears that receive not, and hearts or intuitions that perceive and understand not; for the wealth of Divine Love and Wisdom expressed in the Sin-Offering has remained in the deep mine of its Mystery.

*   *   *   *   *   *

It is to the LORD of Being that the momentous prophecy refers. HIS has been the Travail through the ages. The burden in the Servant was borne by the LORD of Love. The Servant was the LORD's vehicle. He had to carry the Cross of Sacrifice. But the measure of the Servant's consciousness of pain, sorrow and anguish, was the measure of his realization of the Divine Indwelling. The Mystery of the LORD's Passion could only thus be borne by him. Consequently, the triumph of the Travail is the LORD's. It is HE Who shall see of the Travail and be well pleased with the glorious result. Love's conquest in and through the Servant, is of the LORD. Its quality and quantity are of HIM. And in the tierce of its quantity and the eternal nature of its quality, lay the measure of the poignancy of Soul-travail.

*   *   *   *   *   *

It is thus with all GOD's Servants. They are all sensitized to the Divine World, and are held by it. They have power to feel divinely. This power is commensurate with the degree realized of the Indwelling Presence. *The capacity of the Servant unto sorrow, is the measure of the stature of God in him.* In the degree in which the deific potencies have been realized by him, so is the capacity reached by him to endure the pain of world-travail, and to share the burden of ministry undertaken by the Celestial and Divine Worlds. The glory of the Divine Mystery in any one, is commensurate in quality and quantity with that one's power to grieve with Divine Grief over a world in which negation reigns where love should triumph; low conditions of life obtain where righteousness should be manifest; and equity has become a meaningless term because dethroned from its Divinity.

The measure of our Divinity realized is commensurate with our capacity to be one with GOD in Divine Grief as well as in Divine Joy. And it thus comes to pass that, as the ETERNAL moves in and through a Servant unto the manifestation of HIMSELF in some great redemptive as well as revelatory ministry, that one senses and carries within himself the burden of a fallen world, and that of all its children; the sorrows of a Planet-Soul; the travail of the Angel of the Planet; the Karma of a planetary Hierarchy; and the grief of the Divine World.

THE BURDEN OF VICEGERENTS

The LORD travails through HIS Vicegerents. Those who are the Excellencies of the Heavens are HIS vehicles. The chief Potentates of the Sun and the Earth are embodiments of HIM. The Angel of the Sun and the Angel of the Planet, are HIS Regal Representatives. Through them HE reigns. They are HIS Manifestors in Divine and Celestial estates. They are centres of HIS Administration. What HE is to them, they also become to the spheres of their regnancy. They execute HIS Law and fulfil HIS Purpose through the various Hierarchies under them. The members of the various Hierarchies preside over spheres, and are responsible for the fulfilment of the Divine Will in their realms. They reign within their own Kingdom, and are the centres of all Soul activity. Thus, in their degree, they become Shepherds of Flocks; Agents of

Angelic ministries; directors of the elements; controllers of the magnetic and electric forces within the Planetary and Solar Kingdoms. They are so intimately related to all within their sphere that, if any member were hurt, they would feel it; if any wrong states and conditions arose as the result of the hurt of any member, such would be a smiting of themselves.

In this way our own System has come to suffer in every part of it, through the hurt given to one member. When the radiant Being named Lucifer was betrayed, and his once glorious Kingdom became smitten, the whole Earth reeled under the blow, and the spheres of the Angel of the Planet were brought low. For all the Earth's Kingdoms became affected, and the members of the triple Hierarchy were put under limitation. All suffered through the change. And the results were felt in the Solar Body, the Divine Centre of the System. For what affected one was felt by all.

From this unveiling of the Mystery of Divine oneness, from the Divine Kingdom to the lower realms of manifestation, it will be possible for all to understand how the ETERNAL ONE we name the FATHER-MOTHER, lives in all HIS children, manifests through them, and suffers with them should they become afflicted. As HIS Life-stream, named the Blood of the Lamb, pours itself into the many great Celestial Centres, and through them as reservoirs into the lesser Centres, and thus through all HIS worlds and into all HIS children, so HE giveth Life unto all. All live from HIM. All are nourished by HIM. All are sensitized in HIM. Thus, all may come, indeed all are meant to come, to feel HIS Presence with them, HIS Cloud overshadowing them, HIS Life-stream flowing into and through them.

But surely the corollary of such a union is found in the

great truth of Divine Travail in and through all His children? If a world goes wrong, HE must know it. HE must feel its burden and grieve over it. And should it need some very special ministry involving the Divine World in great sacrifice, surely the cross-bearing is of HIM.

It was thus the fallen Earth's burden became HIS own. HE took up the Earth's need to meet it; so in the ministry called forth by that need the Travail has been HIS. Nor has it lessened the direct nature of the burden upon the Divine World, in that a Servant who was a Son of the Heavens, was chosen to be the vehicle of the LORD's Passion. For a Soul capable of such a ministry must have been, in his love and will, one with the LORD. The Life-Eternal in him was from the LORD. His power to carry the Burden of Oblation, to endure the humiliation and crucifixion, to travail throughout the ages full of a poignant grief which often resolved itself into dire Soul-anguish during the process of purifying the Planet's Heavens, was the power of GOD in him. And as that power was contained in the Life-stream, or Blood of the Lamb which flowed into him, whatsoever was felt and endured by him, was felt and endured by the Heavens of the Divine LORD.

Therefore it was verily the Travail of HIM Who is the Soul of all Life. HE was the Lamb of GOD in the Servant, bearing away the sin of this world. And whatever may come to the Servant, it is of the LORD the momentous prophecy is spoken, that HE shall see of HIS Travail and be well-pleased.

WHO MAY FATHOM THE MYSTERY?

But who may be able to fathom the depths of meaning contained in the Prophet's outlook and prophecy? What sounding line could touch the bottom of such a sea of

133

Mystery? Who has the vision to compass the length, breadth and height, as well as the depth, of the accomplishment of Divine Purpose implied in the resultant? What would satisfy the LORD of Being as full fruitage for all the Travail of the Oblation? Surely nothing less than the full restoration of all the Kingdoms of this Planet, with all their Administrators; all the children within them; all the Sons of GOD upon the Earth, now known as the real Israel, and their re-enthronement as the regnant manifestors and revealers of GOD. The ages testify to the fact that men have assumed that the Travail and the Redemption effected by it, have their resultant in Ecclesiasticism, Christian Beliefs and Ceremonial. But if the historical Church be the true resultant, then surely it is a poor fruitage for so great a work; for the Church has been a most lamentable failure as an embodiment of the ideals of Jesus Christ, and the interpreter of the sacred Mystery of GOD in Christ and the Soul. It has failed utterly to understand the nature of the Manifestation and the work of the Sin-Offering. It has not yet learnt the language of the Redemption. To its leaders and teachers, the Divine Terms of the Oblation are the signs and symbols of an unknown tongue. The world has not witnessed redeemed communities where the ecclesiastical influence has been greatest. Even in its segregated Monastic Institutions, there has been an amazing absence of illumination and pure spiritual manifestation.

Therefore, the ecclesiastical institutions cannot be regarded as a satisfying and well-pleasing fruitage with which to crown the Travail of the Oblation and the Passion of our LORD. A Church that knows not the true Way of Life, that encourages the destruction of the creatures for food and clothing, and their oppression in laboratories for scientific and medical research, could add no diadem to the LORD of Glory; its crown would be, as of old, one of thorns. The Church in its false claims and most sad failure, continually pierces the Brow of GOD—the Divine Thought, Purpose and Travail. Its sword enters the Divine side. It smites the crucified One.

COSMIC RESULTS OF THE OBLATION

As the Oblation was Cosmic in its nature and range, so must the fruitage be. It must find expression in and through Sun, Moon, Earth and Humanity, and most notably in the coming again of the Sons of GOD. All these are so inter-related, that one cannot be affected without the others sharing in the blessing. The changes in the Solar World have brought joy to the whole of the Celestial and Divine Heavens. One of the great resultants of the Oblation in the form of Solar fruitage, is the more intensive ministry now possible from the Divine Kingdom of the Sun, unto all the Planet's Kingdoms. Already it has been found possible to begin the work of restoration of the outer Heavens of the Solar Body. Those Heavens were once in a most exalted state. The disaster that overtook the Earth, so affected them that they had to be changed in order to meet the new needs. The glorious Angelic Spheres of the outer realms had to be closed, and the elements of which they were built up had to be changed by lowering their status, and then formed into a new order of Heavens through which the ministry necessary to the Earth could be rendered.

The changes taking place in the Solar Body are chiefly in the realms now occupied by the Photosphere. That encompassing sea of elements in a state which physical science describes as fiery incandescency, is at once a veil, a protection, and a combination of media. It curtains the Inner Kingdoms. It protects these latter from being hurt by the conditions that have arisen through discords in the System; and it is so marvellously composed and formed that the Divine World can make use of the accommodated elements within all its circuli, as media through which to project electric forces, disintegrating and transmutory rays, and nourishing and upbuilding potencies.

The activity through the Photosphere is now greater than it has been for ages. So much has the intensiveness increased, that the Earth is being shaken to her foundations. What is visible upon the outer Planes and Kingdoms, is the reflection of all that is happening within the Planet. Potencies long shut up in the Planet's general captivity, are now being liberated through the intensified Solar action. The magnetic elements hidden in the unseen Planes and Kingdoms of the Planet, are being raised from the state of inertia or spiritual torpor which long ago overtook them, and are being re-charged in all their containers; and in the process they are being re-exalted in their state, and thus re-empowered to fulfil their original service in the Planet's spiritual recovery.

*   *   *   *   *   *

The possibility of such increase in the Solar World output of electric force unto the healing and redeeming of the Earth, has brought great joy to the Divine Heavens. It is the first-fruit in the Celestial realms of great issues to follow. For that which made such an intensive ministry possible was the Redemption of the Heavens of the Earth. For all ministry unto the Earth from the Sun, and from all the other Celestial members who share in the fulfilment of the Divine Purpose concerning the Earth, had to be given through the Heavens encompassing the Planet as part of its system. But when those Heavens were brought down in their state, to represent the darkness of Hades and the evil fires of Tartarus, they were unable any longer to receive from the Divine Kingdom of the Sun.

That was the chief reason why the Oblation had to be borne. Through the ETERNAL CHRIST ministry gathered up into and concentrated in one of the Sons of GOD, the Solar rays played upon the Planet's Heavens through that Son of GOD who was the Servant of the Most High and the vehicle of His LORD, and effected such drastic changes as made it possible for the true Solar ministry to be restored for all. And as the LORD, through the Servant-Redeemer, has effected the Redemption of those Heavens, and the Divine World is now able to act upon the Kingdoms of the Earth more effectually, the LORD of Being is witnessing the resultant, and is well-pleased that so much Celestial fruitage has already become manifest. For it is the prophecy of yet greater things, of which the arising of the Sons of GOD is the harbinger.

THE LIBERATION OF ISRAEL

The Liberation of the Sons of GOD or Ancient Israel, was one of the Mysteries hidden in the Divine Purpose expressed in and through the Oblation. For their Redemption from all the elemental powers which had for ages held them in captivity, was absolutely necessary for the larger Redemption of the whole of the Earth. Without their liberation, regeneration and ascension, the Heavens would be bereft of those vehicles capable of receiving from the Divine World, and making manifest the Christhood. Therefore, whilst the Oblation was occasioned through the state of the Earth's Heavens, the primal purpose of its burden was the finding and restoration of all Israel. To liberate them, provide the means for their regeneration and ascension, and then have them all re-endowed and enthroned, was a resultant of no mean value.

In this work of the Return of the Sons of GOD the Heavens have a large share. The Return has begun.

The Vision has been restored, the Divine Purpose unveiled, and many are beholding, hearing, understanding
and following. Very soon there will be a great uprising.
There will be a re-marshalling of the Sons of GOD, and a
refashioning of the Christhood for Manifestation. The
restoration of the ancient Christhood communities and
ministry, is to be the crown of the Divine Passion. It is in
this arising and rehabilitation that the LORD shall see of
the Travail and be well-pleased with the fruitage. Nothing
less than this would satisfy the Servant through whom the
LORD accomplished HIS Passion, for the Sin-Offering was
borne and the Oblation made unto this end. And if the
Servant would not account as worthy fruitage anything
less than the full return of all Israel and the re-manifesta-
tion of the ancient Christhood, could it be imagined that
the Most Blessed ONE would be satisfied with a less return
as fruitage of the Burden of YAHWEH?

* * * * * *

But this return of the House of Israel to the estate of the
ancient Christhood must not be anticipated under any
of the forms of religious or ceremonial revival, or ecclesiastical claims, or new far-reaching movements. There have
been many such revivals of ecclesiasticism, ceremonial
and doctrinal, which have left the world no better for
their arising. Indeed where there is found the greatest
ostentatious display of such revival in Belief and Ceremonial, the Divine Travail in its most poignant reality, is
rejected. When weighed in the balance of the Life unto
which the Master called His intimate ones to be found in
the states of Jesushood and Christhood, such forward
movements have revealed themselves to be strangely
lacking. There is absent from them the true inner vision.
GOD's Divine Man remains unperceived. The states of
Jesus Christ as degrees of Divine Life to be embodied in
and manifested through everyone, remain veiled to those

who are swept away in days of new enthusiasm, by the streams of the new movements. There is an obvious danger of the recrudescence of the Pauline days when historical Christianity was inaugurated, and the Church arose in the name of the Master. That ostentatious revival that swept Asia Minor and the Grecian Isles, and reached unto Rome itself, was a most successful adventure on the part of the enemies of the Christhood. It gave to the Cosmic Message of the Master, a direction which practically defeated the purpose of the Manifestation. The states of Jesushood and Christhood revealed by Him, and the Cosmic nature of the Oblation, were gathered up into and concentrated upon His own personality in the new religious expression, devotion and service.

It was thus the fruitage that should have been gathered in as the result of the Manifestation, was prevented; though it is generally thought that the founding of the Church and the development of historical Christianity, was a glorious achievement. That it was no fruitage such as the Master and the Heavens hoped for, is evidenced by the fact that the world does not yet know Jesus Christ, and that the Redemption has not yet swept away its evils and brought healing to humanity.

*   *   *   *   *   *

Such betrayal of the Manifestation also made any immediate fruitage from the early lives of the Oblation impossible. The Brotherhoods had been broken up, the Master's Teachings stolen and changed. It was not until the course of the Oblation was half run by the Servant, that any real signs of true fruitage appeared. And these were but fleeting; for the inimical forces were hard at work; and they lost no opportunity of crushing any spiritual arising. The Heavens had to wait till the opposing principalities in the Planet's Heavens were overthrown.

139

That part of the work has just been accomplished in these last days of the Travail. That is the reason why the full resultant of the Oblation can only now come. It is the hour in which *the Patience of the Lord* is to find fulfilment. And in that fulfilment the Earth is to find Redemption. All her Elements are to be healed and her Kingdoms restored. Her Planes are to be equilibrated and her magnetic Centres readjusted. Her Heavens have been purified, and now all her children are to be so conditioned that true spiritual growth and ascension of Being will become possible for them. They are to derive benefit from the resurrection of the Sons of GOD. For, when the manifestation of the Sons of GOD is fully accomplished, great will be the healing of the groaning creation.

For that arising have the travailing Hierarchies of the Earth had to wait. These administrators have had to witness and share in the pain and suffering of the whole planetary household. The Angels of the Seven Spheres of the Planet have had to carry out their administration under states imposing great limitations in their ministries. They have had to wait and watch for the coming change in the Atmospheria of the Heavens of the Planet, and thus learn that the time of the Redemption was at hand. And the head of all the members of the Hierarchies of the Planet, the Divine Vicegerent Ya-akob-El, concerning whom much unveiling has been given in other sections of our Message, has also had to work, watch, and wait, for the coming of this hour when the Heavens could be safely opened again, and the Mystery of the Divine Travail revealed.

THE FRUITAGE OF THE OBLATION

The full restoration of these glorious ones to the

fulness of their ancient estate and ministry, is to form a part of the fruitage of the Oblation. It is difficult for those who are steeped in the elements of historical religions and occult philosophies, even to imagine that any of the administrators of the Kingdoms and Spheres of the Planet, could have had anything to do with a planetary fall, or that the whole of the Planet's Hierarchical members, including the Angel of the Planet—the Vicegerent of ADONAI—could have been so heavily involved that they were all dependent upon the accomplishment of the Divine Passion in the Oblation for their restoration to full Celestial regnancy, and the Redemption and equilibration of their Kingdoms. The effect of the subtle work of the betrayal is most evident in such an attitude of mind. In historical religion the Fall is related only to Humanity; and in occult philosophy it is either denied or accepted as part of the evolutionary processes in the development of the Human Races. In neither system is there any place for a Redemption such as the bearing of the Sin-Offering implies.

But surely the day hasteneth in which even all such attitudes of mind and heart will become changed and recognition be given to the great Work accomplished by the Divine LORD through HIS Servant. Assuredly the arising of the Sons of GOD and the manifestation through them of a Cosmic Christhood ministry, will affect the philosophical outlook and change historical religious interpretation. For the Sons of GOD will be the revealers of Truth. Once more they will become the true Prophets, Seers, and Priests of the Most High. In their lives they will be Divine Embodiments; and in their ministries, Divine Interpreters.

In these great changes, which have already begun, the LORD shall see of the Travail effected by HIM through the Soul of HIS Servant, and be well-pleased.

Here it might be well to note what such anticipation implies for those who once belonged to the ancient communities of the Christhood. Their vision must be of the Heavens of their LORD. Their concepts of Life must be other than those which hold and enslave the world devotees. They will know that the world's Redemption cannot be accomplished through any form of politics as understood and regnant to-day. All their policy must be Theocratic. The world's concept of purity must be exalted. As expressed in and through them, purity must affect the tastes, desires, feelings and ambitions. It must be shown to be full-rounded; touching Life at every segment of its circle; chastening and exalting every attribute; removing from mind, heart and will, pride and falsity, unrighteousness and inequitableness. Through them the standard of Righteousness must be raised, and the balance of Equity restored.

There is no other way by which the world can come to know the joyful sound of the Redeemed Life, which is the Salvation of God to Man.

* * * * * *

As I write these words my vision travels across the world as it is to-day; and I see it shaken to its foundations. All nations are caught by its contrary rushing streams, sped into the conflicting motions of its maelstrom, and tossed to and fro like ships upon tempestuous seas. That such are some of the signs of the Divine Appearing, is well known to me. That my LORD is behind the intensive Solar activity, the transmutory and transforming ministries unto the Healing of the Earth and the Redemption of all her children, has been revealed and made manifest to me; and I am assured it is coming. Yet amid the Travail of the Return of all the Souls who comprised the Brotherhoods of the Sons of GOD, and the results as

Aftermath of the Oblation, my whole Being cries out to the Heavens of His dwelling:—

How long, O Lord! How long, until Thy Righteousness once more shines upon the Earth with noonday splendour, and Thine Equity tempers unto perfect balance, the judgments and actions of all men and women!

Only in the coming into Realization of those blessed states, shall HE truly see of the perfect fruitage upon the Earth of HIS age-long Travail.

THE BOOK OF ISAIAH

PART SEVEN

THE TRIUMPH OF ADONAI

*A further sequel to the Mystery of the Sin-Offering,
showing forth yet more fully that the Oblation
was the Work of the Divine World
through the one sent, that the accomplishment was by Adonai,
and that the full
fruitage will be
Planetary and
Solar.*

CONTENTS

147

O Most Holy and Blessed Adonai, Lord of the Treasury of our Father-Mother, Thy Servant would adore Thee.

Thou art the altogther Lovely One, for Thou art the express Image of the Eternal.

Of His wealth of Love and Wisdom Thou dost administer, bestowing the Riches of His Grace upon all Souls as they are able to receive from Thee.

The Flight of Ages changes not Thy Ministry, for Thou art always the exposition of His Holy Mystery unto all who come into Thy Presence.

Thou art ever Blessed; and blessed are they who approach unto Thee and dwell in the Light of Thy Radiance.

How marvellously Thou didst make the Holy Mystery of Thy Cross to triumph over all things and powers opposed to the Father-Mother's Will, and cause Thy Servant, who was the vehicle for the motion of Thy Holy Passion amidst the Fires of Gehenna and in the Deeps of the Valley of Hinnom, to return from Edom with all its sorrow, unto the Homeland of Bozrah whence he went out on Thy Service clad in glorious apparel!

Assuredly hast Thou made open the Way for the return of all Israel to the estate of their ancient Inheritance with which Thou didst enrich them.

In the day of their Return they shall know Thee again and dwell in the consciousness of Thy Presence.

Thy Triumph shall find echo in theirs as they return to the Holy City of Zion with the Eternal Joy within them and serve Thee again as in the Ancient Days.

Most ever Blessed One! Ineffably Glorious! Adorable in Thy Loveliness! In lowly reverence Thy Servant bows, feeling overwhelmed by the Majesty of Thy Love and Wisdom.

Amen and Amen.

THE TRIUMPH OF ADONAI

TO speak of HIM, in itself would seem to ensure triumph. HE is the All-conquering ONE; the supreme and sublime Manifestor in creation Who comes forth into manifold manifestations in and through the Children of the FATHER-MOTHER. For all Souls have been begotten in HIM. From HIM they derived the Principle of their Being. Through HIM they are all fashioned and nourished, enriched and developed, evoluted and expanded, and translated in their Being from height to height, until every one comes to know HIM in blessed realization as the Indwelling Presence and the Enfolding Cloud of Radiance. HE is the magnetic centre by Whom all are held in Spiritual, Celestial and Divine relationship, whilst they move within the circumference of their several Kingdoms of experience. In and through HIM all Souls attain to Nirvana; for all are to become one with HIM. The consciousness of the individual is to become so full of the glory of HIS vision that everything beneath it, whilst still remaining in its own Kingdom, will be swallowed up as the Being realizes perfect oneness in HIM.

HE is the All-conquering ONE. HE is all-conquering within the individuated Soul, evolving from the Arche or first Principle, all its potencies and deific forces, until HE HIMSELF becomes the glorious fashion within its Sanctuary. In so far as HE can take fashion for manifestation within and through a Human Soul, a Human-Angelic Soul, a Human-Celestial Soul, in its glorious path and transcendent realizations, HE is the All-conquering ONE within and upon all realms.

THE REGNANCY OF ADONAI

Thus from first to last HE is meant to reign, was meant to reign, must ultimately reign. HE reigns now in the Divine World. HE reigns within and through all the Celestial Spheres where there has been no shadow cast—and the systems within which the shadows have fallen are few compared with the innumerable hosts. For a fallen system is most rare. There is scarcely a single Star of the glorious systems upon which HIS regnancy is not supreme. HE reigns throughout the whole Celestial Universe. HE reigns as LORD of all within the Angelic Kingdom. HE once reigned in all HIS Children of the Kingdom of the Sun who were sent forth to this world. HE reigned through their realization; reigned within their consciousness, even unto the revealing of the fashion of HIMSELF. And HE accomplished this, not only within their Sanctuary, but in the fashion of their manifestation. In and through them he reigned in the degree in which the Planetary Household could receive of HIM, even within the estate of the little child, as well as in the maturer child; and in greater degree in those who had reached early manhood and womanhood in the Human evolutary processional. HE was then the Regnant ONE; KING of all the Kings who were then representing HIM. For HE was the Administrator and High Mediator through them, of HIS rich and glorious blessings unto all Judah's Children.

That HE has not so reigned in this world for vast ages, has been a great grief to the Heavens. The Divine Heavens have been sore vexed—pained and grieved at the conditions which have obtained and prevailed upon the Earth. But in the apocalyptic, prophetic vision, we are

informed that HE shall reign again, not only in the
Heavens above us, and around us, and beneath us—the
all-encompassing Celestial Hosts; in the Innermost
realms of each system; and in the Innermost realm of all;
but that HE shall again reign within the realms of this
Earth, upon all her planes and within all her spheres;
and that HIS government shall prevail and obtain
eternally. HE shall once more be the Regnant ONE in
every sphere, as in the olden times, through HIS holy
representatives, the Sons of GOD.

Alleluiah! Halleluiah! The LORD GOD Omnipotent is
become again; and HE shall reign for ever and ever!

ISAIAH FORETELLS DIVINE TRAVAIL

But the recovery of that regnancy is a resultant. And
my thoughts take the flight of the Spirit back through
the ages, and very specially to the Work purporting to have
been the Book of the prophet Isaiah. That Book reveals
the Travail of the ADONAI. It reveals the reason for that
Travail. It portrays what it meant for the ADONAI to
go out, by means of mediation, after that one who went
forth in anger from the Assembly of the Gods, and from
the Divine Presence, to found another kind of Celestial
Kingdom—a kingdom of a different order from that
purposed by the FATHER-MOTHER in HIS Love and
Wisdom. That Travail implied a very special mediation
unto such an one, and all those whom he influenced to
turn their faces away from the Eternal Light Whose
radiance lit up with glorious resplendence, the Divine
Purpose. For he caused them to fail to fulfil the Divine
Will.

You will understand this mystery more fully as your
conceptions become more and more cosmic. As the
result of your enlarged vision, the Oblation will become

less personal and more Divine; less earthly, and more Solar and Planetary; less individual in relation to the Servant, and more and more cosmic in relation to HIM Whose Passion it was, and Whose Energy wrought out all that the Oblation was projected and undertaken to accomplish.

The ADONAI is revealed in the prophet's vision as one in sore Travail, even whilst HE is also portrayed as the All-conquering ONE. And although the language would seem to relate to the Servant of the LORD, of whom Isaiah had much to say, yet everything had to be, and has to be, and must ever be, related to the Divine Love and Wisdom of our FATHER-MOTHER expressed in and through the holy Passion of the ADONAI. For the Travail was HIS in that Passion which seized upon and filled unto all fulness the Being of the Servant who became HIS vehicle, and in whom HE chose to go forth as Son of GOD to war against the awful inimical conditions, Planetary and Solar, which had been generated by the false system which arose as a result of the betrayal, with the intent to defeat the holy purpose of the FATHER-MOTHER.

Try, therefore, to realize what the fulfilment of the prophecy would mean that "*He shall reign for ever and ever,*" and how fully it is related to the Travail.

There are four prophecies, all wrapped up in two or three sentences. I will just name them in a form in which you may remember them, and unveil something in relation to them.

"*He shall see of the travail of his soul, and shall be satisfied*";

"*He shall see his seed*";

"*He shall prolong his days*";

"*The good pleasure of the Lord shall prosper in his hands.*"

Thus the Will of the FATHER-MOTHER shall be realized

through that which the ADONAI shall accomplish in the Travail.

What a world of hope opens up here!

"*He shall see of the travail of His Soul and shall be satisfied.*" The LORD ADONAI shall see a glorious resultant for all the Divine Passion expended and borne; for all the exceptional ministries* of a Cosmic order which have had to be rendered through the Solar World; and also through some other members of the system, by means of limitations that had to be imposed upon them.

WHAT WORLD RECOVERY IMPLIES

He shall see of the travail of His Soul. What, think you, does that resultant imply?

It is lovely to think HE shall reign for ever and ever. We can sing the Halleluiah Chorus rejoicingly to think HE shall reign upon the Earth once more. We can exult to know that all the kingdoms of this distraught world shall become the centres of the regnancy of ADONAI and the Christhood, through the Sons of GOD—HIS Christs in manifestation. Yet, when we sing of such things—and they fill the heart with hope and the vision with a clearer outlook, and raise the Being to pinnacles of the Divine Temple of realization for the hour—do we reflect upon all that such experience signifies?

It implies the recovery of the one who went out from the Presence. There could be no complete fruition as resultant to the Oblation, without the recovery of that one. He has had to be met in the way many times during the ages of the Travail. That one has had to be very

*Concerning these ministries, Cosmic, Solar and Planetary, fuller unveiling will be found in the Teachings which contain Celestial History—The Author.

specially mediated unto, drawn magnetically by the Divine Love towards the Altar of the Most High, in the degree in which he has so far been able to retrace the path of his going out. Throughout the ages there has prevailed a living hope that the Divine urge reawakened, shall conquer, and enable him to process back again, even till he comes into the courts of his LORD. Thus will he return back from the outer darkness into the first glimmering dawn of recovered consciousness of that which he lost; back to degrees of the resplendence of the auric glory in which he once dwelt; back from the bondage and the effects of the tragedy he wrought upon the Earth, until he finds that which he of necessity gave up when he went out; back again from "the far country" of rebelliousness of will, into the homeland where all hurt is healed, and the Will of the FATHER-MOTHER is always done by HIS Sons.

* * * * * *

It may seem hard sometimes to save a Human Soul from himself or herself. It may seem difficult at times to those who undertake healing ministries that touch the circumference of life and the centre of the Soul, and deal with a suffering body, mind and heart, love-principle and the will, to effect perfect healing. Intensify such an experience a thousandfold, aye, even more, then it may be possible to glimpse the significance of bringing back from the outer darkness, one who had been a minor God; one who, in the strength of his deific forces, has to learn again how to become as a little child, humble and lowly, gentle even in the majesty of strength, sweet and beautiful in obedience to the Will of the FATHER-MOTHER, whilst holding Divine Knowledge and exercising Celestial power. The return and restoration of such an one is to be part of the fruitage. *It is in process of accomplishment.*

THE BURDEN OF LUCIFER

I have indicated that Lucifer unto whom the betrayer came with emissaries, belonged to the Celestial Hierarchy of this Planet; and that he was ensnared by the satanic presentation of the illusion of fixed phenomena, and led to disobey the Divine Command. He has been involved in that Travail of ADONAI. He has been the cause and object of much of that Travail. He has known, in the earlier ages of it, rebellion produced in him by the conditions arising out of his misjudgment that led to the betrayal of the Planet. The Travail of ADONAI embraces the return of Lucifer. That Angel is a glorious Being; the one-time radiant Star of the Morning of this world in its Celestial estate; a great administrator of the elements which were used for the upbuilding of Souls in their spiritual fashioning, during their evolution upon the planes of this world. It is blessed to know that Lucifer is able to rejoice in this day, though he cannot yet get rid of the long shadows of the ages thrown upon his threshold, nor arise out of the unspeakable sorrow which broke within him in his awakening and, naturally, has continued through the great ages of the Divine Travail. But it filled him with the joy of a great hope to learn that his sphere was to be redeemed, re-balanced, re-equilibrated; that he himself was to be restored to his former glory and power of administration; and though the realization is in large part still only prophetic, the prophecy is of such an order, and so much has been accomplished, that he is able to rejoice in the outlook, full of assurance. Thus in a measure he shares our own joy.

THE BURDEN OF YA-AKOB-EL

And what shall I say concerning Ya-akob-El, whose spirit was broken in the great betrayal when the descent of this system had been fully accomplished, and his servants—those who were mediators from him within the Planetary Heavens—had hearkened unto the betrayers, and not unto the Divine Voice which spake through him? He came to feel as if the Fall had been his own; as if the cause of the descent had been his fault; as if the mis-direction and lack of strength in administration in those who should have been faithful to him as the Divine Vicegerent, had been the outcome of a lack in himself. Flashes of illumination on this great mystery are to be seen in many of the wonderful passages found in the Old Scripture, prophetic and psalter, concerning the remark-able history of Jacob—the Planet's Angel, Ya-akob-El, the Divine Vicegerent at the head of the Earth's triple administration.

* * * * * *

This has been a wonderful School of joy,* and I want it to close on the note of joy. But it is necessary that you now understand all that was involved in the Divine Travail, and the resultant hoped for. It will strengthen the urge within you to manifest your Divine Childhood in the estates of Jesus Christ; to realize for, and manifest on behalf of, the accomplishment of the Divine Travail, so that your manifestation may hasten it. For the Great Love is dependent upon His Children who were the ancient Sons of God in this world, for the accomplishment of the Travail. The sons of Ya-akob-El—the Planet's Inner Hierarchy—can sing for joy in this hour. They share our gladness, though they are not free from travail in their upper realms, whilst they mediate to the lower. Ya-akob-El can share with us the joy of the Heavens. Yet how great that joy will be when all that circumscribes it, and all that causes the inrush of the dark shadows thrown

---

*Summer School held at High Leigh, Hoddesdon, 1933, at which this unveiling was given.

at times across its threshold owing to the unredeemed conditions on Earth, have passed away, and the regnancy of Ya-akob-El is fully restored. Then the whole world will sing for very joy. The joy of child-life will be restored. The joy of virile manhood will come back, and the joy of the consciousness that GOD is ever present in HIS world and revealeth HIMSELF in all its beauty, power and motion, even though the individual may not have evoluted far enough to realize HIS Mystery to the extent that the Sons of GOD realize it. To know that GOD's Spirit breathes upon and through the world; that HE encompasses the world; that HE overshadows all things; and that HE sheds benignly HIS blessing continually upon the whole Earth, is joy indeed.

Thus shall it come to pass that HE shall see of the Travail when the one who went out from the Celestial Assembly; and Lucifer and his co-workers within the Hierarchy; and Ya-akob-El, with his Divine Hierarchy; are all able to be re-enthroned and restored to such a regnancy as once they enjoyed, and reign over a world which has become a new Earth, encompassed by Heavens which have been re-created as the result of the Travail of ADONAI.

THE BURDEN OF ISRAEL

In that resultant ye yourselves are included. The first joy of the Return is in the issue of the Oblation; that Divine Sacrifice, having accomplished the purification of the Planetary Heavens, is immediately to be followed by the Saints rising out of the graves of non-spiritual and material conditions wherein they have long lain buried, and going to appear in the Holy City. For therein they will be coming back to the Christhood, and making that holy estate manifest unto many. Even now you may hear the Halleluiah Chorus sung as it can never be sung on the

Earth-planes, with a meaning transcending anything that the children of men have ever dreamed of, even when expressed through the best musicians.

"*He shall reign for ever and ever.*" "*The kingdoms of this Earth shall become the kingdoms of our Lord and His Christ.*" How glorious when it can be truly said "*For the kingdoms of this world have become the kingdoms of our Lord and His Christ!*" What hope for the Earth when all its kingdoms are redeemed and have again become the field of the ministry of the ADONAI through HIS Christs! But the regnancy of HIS regnant ones is not to be thought of as power in the earthly sense. HIS Christs are not ambitious in that way. If they were they would utterly fail. A Soul divinely rising toward GOD and reaching unto power, is unconscious of it. We attain divinity unconsciously. If we reach out for power, we shall miss it. We shall get hold of something that is not of ADONAI in us, nor the revelation of the FATHER-MOTHER through us. The regnancy of the Christhood is to be the regnancy of the ADONAI Who is the sublime and glorious embodiment of the FATHER-MOTHER in the Eternal World, with an individuation of HIMSELF in every staral embodiment, and in every member of all the systems. There are individuations of HIMSELF in the Divine and Celestial realms, just as in each one of us there is the individuation of HIMSELF. We are part of HIS glorious Body. But we know *that* in consciousness only when HE becomes realized in us, and we are one in HIM. Our very Being then becomes a part of the Body of the LORD, for manifestation. Our Temple is HIS Tabernacle where HE reigns in the beauty of holiness. Our attributes are HIS powers through which HE doth make HIMSELF manifest. Our substances are HIS own substances dynamically raised to the field of HIS direct operation, so that they can receive the electric streams from the Innermost World and become divinely magnetic.

It is thus we are to become regnant. There is no other way of reigning. Of what value would it be if we proclaimed ourselves to-day to be the risen Christs of GOD? Who would believe it? The world would laugh. The cynics would scorn. The unholy would blaspheme. Our mistake, our unwisdom, would even hinder the grand processional of the Christhood, and the descent from the Inner Worlds of the glory of our LORD into and through HIS Christs.

To be regnant for HIM is to have open the flood-gates of our Being that the King of Glory may come in resplendently; that HE may enrich our potencies; that HIS own consciousness—which is HIS Omniscience—may fill us to the full capacity of our Being, so that we may know all things in HIM, and function in the realm where we may know all things HE permits us to know; that HIS Omnipotency may fill us until everything that proceeds from us is nothing less than a power from HIMSELF; that our government and our governmental acts, our administrative acts and the whole deportment of our Being, are not those of one who desires power to sit and govern upon an earthly throne and have multitudes bowing the knee, but of those who bow to HIM, who adore HIM, who worship HIM, who love HIM, and who become the revelation of HIMSELF through manifested regnant potency and interior Divine Wisdom that flashes its glory upon all things; who chase away the shadows in which men and women dwell, though they do not see and cannot understand; who throw the light of heavenly Wisdom as HIS Light, and always refer it to HIM, claiming it only as from HIM, reigning only as those who would rule, govern and direct for HIM and from HIM alone.

That is the regnancy we have to declare. "He shall reign for ever and ever," in and through HIS Christs. The kingdoms of this world shall then become HIS Kingdoms.

Then shall HE see of the Travail of HIS Soul in the Return of all the Children of the Kingdom. HE shall see them going back to the Sun, in their consciousness and life; rising up in Soul-estate-stature so as to be held by the Sun, and nourished directly from the Solar rays whilst ministering here. For the glorious, Divine electric forces will re-charge all HIS Christs from the Inner Kingdom. (Here I am not speaking of the light and the heat generated by the Solar Rays after being projected electrically through the photosphere, and transmitted into the vortexya and atmospheria of the Earth. I am speaking of Rays no physical science can tap, that come directly to the Being. They are not of the realm of manifestation and, therefore, could not be discovered through the outer manifest-world methods.) To receive those Rays into the Being and be containers of their force, is to become individual transmitters as from generating stations. The Divine World having filled us, we become dynamos; we are full of creative, electric force from HIM. And we are sent forth with HIS energy. We reveal HIS Light. We live for HIM. We manifest from HIM. We interpret HIM. We are HIS absolutely.

That is the Divine-Solar-Soul regnancy which HE is to see as the fruitage of the Travail of HIS Soul.

THE NEW EARTH-HEAVENS

The new Heavens have been generated; the new Earth is now to come. Let us hasten it. We cannot change the Divine Purpose. We cannot move the Heavens to do more quickly that which they have set out to do. Yet we can further what they are accomplishing. The Heavens inform us, and we know it to be true from experience, observation and interior knowledge,—aye, we know it from direct communication with HIM Who is our LORD— that the Children of the Kingdom, the Sons of GOD, can

hasten the ministries of the Divine World. The Divine
World is awaiting the arising of all Israel; for every
member of that ancient House of the Heavens is to be a
vehicle for the accomplishment of the healing of the
Earth. Israel as a community of Christs, is to complete the
work of its redemption, re-habilitation, re-organization
and re-constitution; to aid the Heavens in the dynamic
exaltation of all the Earth's elements; to re-establish its
upper seas and its lower seas; its substances and its
kingdoms; and restore again the perfect equilibration
of all its planes.

In such a resultant of the Travail of HIS Soul the
ADONAI shall be well pleased.

* * * * * *

In the process HE is to see HIS seed. Even the Servant
is to see his seed. What is it that is implied in the Old
Scripture sayings? They speak of the seed of Abraham;
of the seed of Isaac; and of the seed of Jacob. And we all
know that such statements are interpreted in the sense of
human personal posterity. Yet they are divinely significant.

For the ADONAI to see HIS seed, is to see all HIS children
in the manifestation of Christhood; see them all grown up
again and fully returned to their Sonship.

The Servant through whom ADONAI revealed and
spake, and then travailed, was to see of his seed also. He
was to come unto his own; and even though many might
not receive him, because the hour in their Return had not
yet come, those who did receive the Message would
become his own again. (There is nothing personal here;
banish it from your thought. We have to function through
vehicles. But the vehicle is not the Being: it is a servant
also.) To such as received the Message, to them did that
Message give back the Power of GOD. But to receive

the Message is not simply to receive something written or spoken in the sense of hearing it and believing it to be true. It is to receive it back into the understanding until it becomes part of the Being, something concrete and in the fashion of GOD, and of the very substance and life-stream of the Being.

Unto those who receive that Message, to them will the ADONAI give power to become the Sons of GOD, to recover their lost divinity and deity. Such Souls are re-born, but not of bloods, nor of the flesh, nor of the will of man. In such a heritage there is nothing personal, nor physical, nor tribal, nor national, nor that which is racially proclaimed after the manner of men. Such Souls are born of GOD. They are those in whom the vision of GOD is ever first and last, the Alpha and the Omega.

Thus shall HE see HIS seed. Such Souls will be HIS posterity.

DIVINE RELATIONSHIPS RESTORED

Behold, what this signifies in the Return in these days, and our relation to one another as a spiritual family that once was a great family in the Heavens! Behold the relationship of all Israel to the ADONAI as HE is represented in HIS high Vicegerent in the Solar Body! For verily that glorious Being is as a God in ministry for the LORD GOD of Sabaoth. Think what it means for the ADONAI to see the return of the seed of Abraham! For such is the seed of Brahma, as HE was embodied in the Sons of GOD and manifested through them as A-Brahm. See what it means for the Divine Travail to have accomplished so much that even in these days the Heavens may look out upon and watch for the hastening return of those who are inheritors of this Divine Seed, beholding the partially maimed, halt and blind ones, and sending to them special Angelic ministries, since the outer world cannot minister to them to aid them in their return; nor the ordinary religious venues suffice for their needs. For the Divine Heavens are sending special Angelic ministries unto all Israel to intensify the Divine Urge within them, and cause their aura to be filled with the breaths of the Angelic World and take on their ancient beauty, and once more fully reflect the Divine Resplendence that is thrown upon them from the Inner World.

The Heavens would thus heal all your spiritual lameness, haltness, blindness and every impoverished attribute. They would enrich and re-empower all your powers and vehicles that you may come back again to know something of the Omnipotency of GOD and HIS glorious Omnisciency, and HIS Wisdom that lights up everything, that all these may be realized by you and expressed through you.

It is thus that through HIS seed HE shall prolong HIS days—the days of the manifestation. HE shall prolong HIS days. HE will recover the great ages of manifestation that once were. HE shall prolong the revelation of the Divine Love and Wisdom through HIS seed, and the Will of the FATHER-MOTHER shall be accomplished.

How beautiful it is! How full of radiant hope, a hope illumined with Divine certainty! What a call is here as the result of the vision presented to you! What a memory to hold in the Being, even that of the Travail of the ADONAI! The fruitage in and through you is to be HIS fruitage.

We are all servants of the Most High. Even the one who is Servant in a special sense because of the nature of the ministry, is brother of all. He is Servant of all unto whom he is sent. All that is revealed through him of omnipotent and omniscient Love and Wisdom, is the ministry of the LORD ADONAI.

Ah, lovely ones! You have travelled far since we first met on the way in these latter days. You have come up out of the night of the world's darkness, to glimpse the roseate hues of the early dawn of this new age. And those who have risen with the Sun—mystically understood those who have risen higher as the Divine World has drawn them—are able to see the highest peaks tinged with the glory of the breaking dawn, and they are able also to behold the foothills take on the reflection of that Radiance. Standing above the world in their state, looking out upon its tumultuous conditions and reading through the deep waters of all its commotion, they can see that the Divine Radiance is stealing down the foothills to the plains, and across the plains into the valleys. And though the world knows it not, they know that it is the dawn of God's Day. It is the breaking of God's own Sabbath for the Children of the Kingdom who are dwellers upon the outer planes of the world. For them it is the dawn of perfect balance in Him. And through them, the spirit of Divine peace and exquisite equipoise in Him, will come for all the Children of Judah—especially the elder children of this Earth. And in such wise shall come to pass the cessation of the world's rush, the world's conflict, the world's misconceptions, the world's misactivities; and in place of these, a meeting of the world's real needs.

Those who rise with the Dawn, who ascend to see the Glory, who stand above the Earth in vision, can look down and behold the accomplishment of the Divine Travail and realization in part of the Divine Purpose, in the rich fruitage of the Travail of the Soul, and thus the fulfilment of the promise "*He shall see of the Travail of His Soul, and shall be satisfied.*"

The sublime meaning of these Scriptures will now be apparent. And in that day we shall all sit down with

Abraham, Isaac and Jacob, in the Kingdom of GOD. We shall meet them again. Sometimes in consciousness one has to do that even now. We shall meet them again in larger fellowships. We shall rejoice with them. We shall know the fellowship which obtained within their kingdom in the perfect day. For the glory of a world perfectly redeemed shall be restored to Ya-akob-El; the glory of a recovered Christhood laid on the Altar of Oblation shall be once more the Isaac part of the Solar ministry through the Christhood for this world. And we shall sit down in the Divine Kingdom with Abraham as the friends of GOD, as those who have realized HIS encompassing, HIS overshadowing, and HIS indwelling Presence again. It will be a wonderful festival—Spiritual, Angelic, Celestial, Divine, when we can look into the faces of those who have had to be recovered, and who are being recovered to-day, and laugh with them, rejoice with them, in the consciousness that we have done our part. In no self-conscious self-glorying way shall we rejoice, but in the consciousness of having been a sharer in the accomplishment of so great and glorious a work for the ADONAI and our FATHER-MOTHER.

*　　*　　*　　*　　*　　*

I would take you all into my heart, into the bosom of my own love, into the Sanctuary of my very Being, and there name you before the High Altar, as one family in HIM, to be HIS Christs again in manifestation and service upon the planes of this world, unto the re-making of the Earth; bringing back joy to it; redeeming it; healing its woundings; and uplifting all its life to the realm of the ETERNAL, till it can endure the encompassing of HIM as Avatar, and the overshadowing once more of the Cloud of HIS Radiance.

Ever blessed be HIS Name within and through us all, unto Whom be all the honour and the glory!

THE BOOK OF ISAIAH
PART EIGHT

THE DRAMA OF ISRAEL

*Being the history of one of the Households
of the Sons of God whose members were
sent to this Earth to minister as Manifestors, Revealers and Interpreters
of the Divine Love and Wisdom,
the sufferings they endured in
this world amid its fallen
states, and the Mess-
age of Messianic
import unto
them.*

CONTENTS

O Shepherd of Israel! Praise be unto Thee at all times! Assuredly Thy Way is in the Great Deep, and Thy Paths beyond finding out.

The Children of Thy Love whom Thou didst fashion, and upon whom Thou didst write the sacred signature of Israel, would adore Thee.

Thou didst send Thy Children into this world to make Thee manifest and interpret Thy Holy Will; and it was their delight to serve before Thee and fulfil Thy Commands.

But those who became enemy unto Thee and smote the Earth unto the loss of most of her Inheritance, also smote us, and in our affliction carried us away into a land most strange to us.

Our great loss was to find our vision of Thee intercepted by a veil we could not penetrate.

Our cry was unto Thee for succour; but the more we sought Heavenly aid, the more the enemy afflicted us.

Then didst Thou seem lost to us, and the Heavens of our ancient dwelling-place closed against us.

It was thus Thou didst again find us; for we were in bondage to the ruling powers of the strange land.

How wonderful are Thy ways! Thou didst find us when succour seemed hopeless, and Thou hast upborne us through the ages and ministered unto us of Thy Love and Wisdom through Thy Holy Messengers.

And now Thou hast recalled us to enter into our ancient Inheritance, and be once more Thine Israel in fashion as well as name, that we may make Thee manifest, and reign with Thee, though remaining for a Season upon the Earth.

May we all be Thine Israel indeed, clothed in the Robes of Thy White Light, showing forth Thy Glory, and serving Thee in the Praise-motion of all our Being.

Evermore would we thus Adore Thee.

Amen and Amen.

THE DRAMA OF ISRAEL

IT is a most fascinating story that is hidden in the name Israel. The history written by the Children of Israel within that of the drama of this world, is a very different record from that which we meet with in the Old Testament. In the Bible Records they are usually confounded with the Jews; yet these latter were only a secondary sub-race who became attached to Israel at a later period. That the Jews came into possession of the Mysteries known and taught by the Elders of Israel, is evidenced in many of their Books; but the heritage became theirs through attending the Masonic Schools of the Prophets. For in this way they learnt much of the mystical Teachings given by the Elders, Seers and Prophets of Israel. But not understanding the inner significance of the Teachings, they applied them to outward events and histories, and identified themselves with these, until Israel and Jewry became synonymous. It was in this way that the real *diaspora* took place; for Israel gradually ceased to be a distinct race from Jewry, though the two outer Kingdoms arose named after Israel and Judah. These are said to have had separate Kings, and even to have gone to war with one another.

THE STORY OF THE HOUSE OF ISRAEL

But the true history of Israel and Judah was spiritual; and the great dramatic and tragic events associated with them, separately and in combination, were Planetary and Solar. Much of the Teaching given under the Mosaic economy, whilst it was ostensibly biographical, tribal, and national, had relation to this world in its spiritual and celestial status, and to the ancient House of the Christ-hood—the community of the Sons of GOD.

Great ages ago, long antecedent to the change which overtook this cosmos or planetary manifestation, and brought about such a descent from spiritual conditions as resulted in the evil states of life with which the Earth and all her children have been smitten for ages, a certain community of the Sons of GOD came to this Planet to aid its elder children in their spiritual evolution. These Souls belonged to another System. They had accomplished their lower degrees of initiation upon another world, and had reached the status of Sons of GOD, as that exalted term may be used when indicating Solar attainment. They had, therefore, passed through many orders of generation as they grew in estate, deepened and expanded in con-sciousness, and ascended into ever-increasing degrees of realization of spiritual and celestial things. They knew many of the Angels. They often took part in the ministries of the Heavens of the System to which they belonged. In some measure they had all come into the consciousness of the overshadowing Presence; and some of them were able to receive from the realm of the Archangels.

They were sent to this Planet to be the super-teachers and interpreters of the Divine Mysteries contained in and expressed through its various Kingdoms, including the Human. At one of the Assemblies of the Gods, they were chosen for such a ministry and asked by the Heavens to come to this Earth. That is why they afterwards came to be known as *the Chosen People, an Elected Nation,* a People specially endowed for mediatorial ministry, and desig-nated, *a Kingdom of Priests.*

Though as a nation of a higher order of Soul, they were absorbed by and then lost amid other nations—and especially so during the best days of Jewry, by that race; yet they have always remained a distinct Order of Soul in this world. This will become obvious as their history is unveiled.

* * * * * *

When the Sons of God were sent to this world, the latter was then unfallen. The elemental Kingdoms were in perfect state and equipoise. The elements were pure. They were all responsive to the ministries rendered to them and demanded from them by the Law of the Divine Love and Wisdom, as that Law operated within their realm of manifestation. The difference between the elemental Kingdoms as they were, and what they became and are now, is immeasurable. No student of physical science could imagine what the phenomenal World was prior to the tragedy that befell the Earth and all her children, unless the Truth had come to him in inner vision and Soul realization. When the Sons of God came, the vehicles or bodies through which they functioned for service unto the children of men, were built up out of elements in primal state. These corresponded to the elements out of which the Planet's Heavens were constituted. The Sons of God were therefore able to descend into the Atmospheria of the Heavens of the Planet, and dwell there. From those spheres they ministered for ages, descending as required to the lower Bethlehem of the Heavens to meet with and minister to the elder races of humanity. They had the Office of Shepherdhood. As Souls rose in spiritual culture, vision and understanding, they were formed into Folds. They were led into the Angelic pastures where they were nourished upon the Divine Love and Wisdom. It was thus the Sons of God became the Shepherds upon *the Planes of the Bethlehem.*

During that time of the Earth's *golden age*, the Sons of GOD, though dwelling upon the Bethlehem and ministering from there, were able to retain in their consciousness, the memory of the land of their nativity and the blessed ones whom they had left behind. They were also able to remain in such an exalted spiritual state that they continued to dwell in the consciousness of the over-shadowing Presence. They were therefore able to speak to those unto whom they were sent, of those things which they understood, and of the Angels whom they knew.

*   *   *   *   *   *

But there came a time when they lost such a consciousness. The changed conditions of the Planetary Heavens resulting from *the Fall*, affected them in no small degree. As the density of the Earth grew greater, they found themselves unable to function within the Bethlehem of the Planet in and through the refined vehicles which were used by them as the media of their manifestation. Either they must leave the Earth-spheres altogether or assume vehicles such as were generated upon the human Kingdoms. As their presence was greatly needed, and as they loved the children of the Earth unto whom they ministered, the Heavens decided that they should be asked to remain within the Earth-spheres and continue their ministry. This they were rejoiced to do.

The increased densification of the Planet's Heavens, however, so affected them in their power to see into and hear from the Homeland, that gradually the memories of all that they had been, all they had left behind, grew dim. The countenances of the Angelic Friends, Patriarchs and Messengers, faded in their consciousness; and with this tragic loss came that of the Overshadowing ONE.

Amidst this tragedy they never lost their love to give in ministry. Even in the worst times, selfless service was a

passion with them. It was of the nature of the Divine
Passion. To save from great disaster many of the children
of Judah, [the Planet-Soul] who had descended into the
Saurian Hells, they followed; and in doing so suffered
untold agony. The Saurians had been generated and
fashioned out of the awful conditions in the outer and
intermediary planes, and had become the prison-houses
of many of those unhappy children who had been drawn
down by him who went out from the Presence of the LORD.
And these continued their betraying influences upon the
children of Judah.

THE FINDING OF THE LOST PEOPLE

The night of that tragedy is now past, and the deep
shadows of it which persisted through great ages, are
gradually being blotted out; for the Oblation accomplished great things for all the Christ Souls. Our reference
to these tremendous events in the Planet's history, has
relation to the Sons of GOD. For it was owing to these
events that their cosmic Christhood manifestation was
betrayed and their communities were broken up, till every
Tribe became scattered, and as a Celestial People they
were lost amongst the tribes of the Planet's children.
Nor from that time have they in any age been regathered;
though when the Messengers appeared, small groups of
them were formed for the transmission of the Message
sent through the Messengers from the Divine World.
Throughout their most sad travail in this fallen Earth,
they have sought to recover some long-lost knowledge,
vision and realization. They have yearned for the
Christhood, the Divine Man, the realization of the
Presence. They have always been those Souls who have
felt an irresistible urge to seek unto the finding of the
Divine Superscription within them, and to bring it forth
into manifestation.

The seeking unto the finding of Israel in the midst of the world's débâcle, has been a momentous work. It has covered great ages of ministry from the Divine World. As they were the interpreters of the Divine Love and Wisdom unto the children of men, when they were borne down by the avalanche of evil that overwhelmed the Kingdoms of the Planet, they were not only lost on the Earth as the revealers and manifestors of the Divine Purpose in all Soul and world creation, but they were likewise lost to the Heavens as its vehicles of transmission of the Divine Wisdom unto the elder children of the Planet. Therefore, in the sublime efforts of the Divine World to recover the Planet and bear her back to an unfallen state, the first ministry had to be the finding and recovery of the Sons of God.

* * * * * *

It is this ministry of the Heavens that lies behind all Revelation given through the Messengers, Priests in high mediation, Seers and Prophets. What are known as the seven great Religions, were aspects of that Revelation unto the finding of Israel. For the House of Israel was composed of communities of the Sons of God. The communities were named Tribes; and these represented various degrees of attainment and ministry. The Bible contains, though mostly in cryptic form, many of the elements of that Revelation in both the Old and the New Testaments. Though in the Old Testament the name Israel does not occur until the story of Jacob is reached in which the vision of the Presence is given him; yet all that the name signified is contained in the Revelation given through Adam, the first Messenger; and in succeeding revealers, such as Enoch, Noah and Abraham. The Old Testament contains many of the greater Mysteries within the compass of its opening proem of Creation and the appearing of Moses. They are cryptically stated under the forms of biography, history, and great physical events such as the Deluge and the Fall of the Magnetic Plane upon the land of Sodom and Gomorrah.

* * * * * *

The going down of Israel into Egypt, with their subsequent tragic experiences, is set forth as an emigration of the whole House of Jacob owing to famine in the land of Israel. But that is a cryptically told story of the travail of the Planet-Angel, Ya-akob-El, and how the House of Israel came to be involved. For the aid of the House of Jacob, and for ministry unto the House of Israel, Joseph was raised up. Some of these Mysteries have already been unveiled, and others will follow bye and bye.

The story of Israel in Egypt is a mystical outlining of the path which they followed in their own Processional. In Egypt they were oppressed by the false Pharoahs. The powers opposed to all that they stood for, smote them. With the Planet-Soul, the unfallen members of the Celestial Hierarchy, and the Angel of the Planet, they suffered pain, sorrow, and anguish. The glorious day had given place to a night of dread; the darkness overwhelmed them in the degree that they had once known the Celestial radiance.

But amidst the awful night a Star of great luminosity shone. That Star was the Messenger Moses. He came as the Divine World's answer to the cry of the Sons of GOD. He came to find them amid the darkness. He was sent to deliver them from the thraldom of the false Pharoahs. But they had to be found by means of Revelation; for they could be delivered only through illumination and re-initiation. To find them was the awakening of the sleeping divinity within them, the arising of all their attributes and powers from the graves of material conditions. The world whence they had come, thus spoke to them. The ministries were Divine; but they were rendered through the Solar Body. For Moses was a Messenger of the Sun.

MOSES, AARON AND ISRAEL

It may thus be seen how the Old Testament contains many of the gems of Revelation given unto Israel; but the gems are lost amidst the erroneous biographical and historical settings. Flashes of their beauty may be beheld as the Light from on high falls upon them. But the secrets at the heart of them are hidden. Even unto this day, whensoever Moses is read, few discern the Mysteries couched in the Revelation given through him.

In the work of finding Israel, Aaron played a part in the drama. He was the brother of Moses, according to the story. He was another Celestial Star. Like that of Moses, his Office was Solar. Whilst Moses revealed, Aaron mediated. He was the High Priest of the Realm to which Moses belonged. To Israel when found, Moses revealed anew the Law of the LORD as it appertained to the Mystery of the Soul, the Planet, and the Sun; Aaron revealed through his ministry, the nature of the Priesthood which Israel once knew, and the order of sacrifice by which alone the ancient heritage of the Christhood could be recovered.

Such was the ministry unto Israel. The Revelation contained in it was related to the Sons of GOD; and as such it could appeal to and be understood only by Souls who had been in that high estate. For who could understand the Law of the LORD as that Mystery was expressed in the superstructure of the Soul, the fashion of a Planet-Soul, or the Divine embodiment in the Sun? Only those who had accomplished high degrees of spiritual and celestial evolution.

All Revelation concerning such Mysteries was given to find the lost House of Israel. As members of that ancient community of the Sons of GOD were arrested and drawn by the Divine Magnetic power of the things revealed, out from the bondage of Egypt, these formed themselves into small communities such as might be associated with a true Masonry. For many ages there were Lodges and Fellowships of this order, in the Himalayas; in Mesopotamia; in the Sinaiatic Peninsula; and later, amidst the Syrian Hills. To these Souls the Messengers came. But though the prophetic faculty in them was re-awakened, the veil lifted that had obscured their once illumined vision belonging to their Seership, the elemental conditions were so greatly against them, that they could not rise up into the Angelic Realms in their inner state, and recover the power to embody and make manifest the ancient Christhood. The Apocalypse of Moses helped them greatly; but they were in great need of a Manifestation.

To give them a Manifestation and prepare them for the full recovery (as a result of the Oblation) of all that they lost in the Earth's débâcle, the Master was sent unto them. His great work in the days of the Manifestation was to seek unto the finding of the lost sheep of the Fold of Israel. He sought not merely personal following: no Messenger could ask for that. He sought out those who could hear His Message with the inner ear, and who were willing to follow whithersoever it led them. He knew well that some who might desire to listen would, nevertheless, not follow; and that there would be those who, though arrested by the Message, would go back. For He understood those whom He met in the way. What He sought for in those who would follow, was loyalty to truth, compassion and pity, and the Being's consecration to the Way of Life as set forth in the Manifestation. Discipleship to the Message meant true initiation; and every initiate became enriched as he rose into the consciousness of his LORD.

DIVINE WORLD ADVENTURES

The Manifestation was the climax of many adventures on the part of the Divine World to find Israel. It was the fulfilment of the Divine Love's Purpose in the fulness of time. Though gross darkness still covered the Earth, and its pall lay over the land of Jewry; and though in a general way the Flame of the Lamp of GOD in Israel, burned but dimly, and in many had become little more than as the smoking flax, yet the time of His appearance had arrived when the Christhood estate should once more be unveiled to the communities amongst the Syrian Hills, afterward touching Samaria, and then reaching as far East and South as Peraea and Idumæa, in the hope of finding some of the lost Sons of GOD.

Having found some of His ancient intimate Brethren, and uncovered many Divine Mysteries for them con-concerning themselves, the Planet, and the Solar Body, He left them as a heritage the vision of Christhood to follow, whilst He went into the nether-world—*the planetary atmospheria*—to accomplish the Divine Purpose in the Redemption of the Planet's Heavens by means of the Oblation.

And now in this day that sublime Purpose is to be fully accomplished. All Israel is to be found and saved. The vision of the Christhood is unveiled; the Apocalypse of the Master has been restored; and in these the call to all Israel has been renewed, to arise out of the dust of all earthly humiliation and bondage, and come into the Christ-realms of Light and Service—the realm of their ancient Inheritance and the Order of Divine Sacrifice.

The finding of Israel proceeds. Many are coming from the East and West, the North and the South, mystically and geographically. There is now joy in the Presence of the FATHER-MOTHER. The Angelic Kingdom resounds with songs of triumph. Jesus lives again; Christ radiates the glory of the FATHER-MOTHER; and the LORD once more reigns.

The beginning of the return of the Theocracy is with us.

THE RE-SEALING OF ISRAEL

In the Apocalypse there is a passage relating to the resealing of the whole Household of Israel. It is connected with the Divine Assembly wherein the great multitudes are participators, the world Redemption, and the Regeneration of the Sons of GOD. Every Israelite was to be sealed on the forehead.

Many attach great importance to outward ceremonies. Sometimes these are nothing more than the dead signs of a forgotten language, or the meaningless shibboleths of symbols and rites that once were vital with the Breath of Divine Reality. But Soul recovery and re-initiation belong to the realm of living things. They are Spiritual, Celestial and Divine, according to their order and degree. They are such as no man can confer; for they are the gift of the Divine Love and Wisdom. Though there may be outward rites and initiations of a masonic order, these do not necessarily imply spiritual illumination and realization of the Mysteries signified. But the re-sealing did imply such Divine enlightenment and becoming. It was no mere outward action in the transmission of Blessing. It was an inward motion that was signified. It was nothing less than the re-awakening of their consciousness to many memories of the past, and the bringing back to them of the high realization of the Presence of their LORD.

In and through this profound experience there is the renewal of the Divine Vision; the re-opening of their audient chamber so that they can hear again the Divine

Voice; the bringing forth again into blessed manifestation the Image or Fashion of their LORD, which is the superscription upon the Seal. It is the KING's Seal. It bears HIS impress. HIS countenance is upon it; HIS glory radiates from it. To receive that Seal, is henceforth to be in the Image of HIM.

The re-sealing of the House of Israel is for manifestation. The revelation in the manifestation is concerned with the estates of Jesus, Christ, and the LORD. These estates are set forth in the numerical and geometrical values. Of each Tribe there were twelve thousands; and the whole Household numbered one hundred and forty-four thousands. The number values relate to attainment, realization, and service. They do not give the numerical composition of the Sons of GOD. The Tribal powers are attributive. The twelve relate to the twelve attributes. Each attribute must needs be re-sealed. It must have superimposed upon it the Divine Image. If the eye's vision has grown dim, its sight must be restored. If the doors of the audient chamber have been closed, the power to hear the Presence of the King must be re-gifted to the Soul. Every impoverished power must be renourished until it can once more reflect the glory of Christhood. The infinite resource of the Divine Love and Wisdom must be gathered up into and revealed through all the attributes. And the fulness of the value will then become expressed in the perfect Jesushood, the radiant Christhood, and the Divine regnancy. For the attributes of a Son of GOD are twelve; and their sum of dynamic force is three—or the realization of the Holy Trinity: the FATHER, the MOTHER, and the SON. And the one hundred and forty-four thousands which represent the sum of the value of the twelve attributes squared, is the sum of the dynamic power of cosmic Israel for manifestation. Every attribute or Tribe can become squared. In each right angle of each square, the Divine Love and Wisdom, Righteousness and Equity, are revealed. And these speak of powers, vision, balance and sacrifice. All right angles proceed from the Cross; and all other angle-values are partial, and are accommodations for Celestial ministries.

As ancient Israel represented upon the Earth the high Estate, spiritually and celestially, of the Sons of GOD, it will be evident how important it is for the coming Divine Manifestation, that all Israel be found, re-squared, and re-sealed.

THE TRANSLATION OF ISRAEL

When the LORD of Love returns to the Earth, all HIS Saints are to arise and meet HIM in the air. They are to be translated from the Earth. All who have passed into the great unseen Spiritual World are to accompany HIM, and all upon the Earth are to join them. The dead in Christ are the first to arise, and then all who fell asleep in Jesus. All these are to be ever with the LORD; and through the former the Christ is to make manifest, and in the latter, Jesus reign.

The Translation of Israel is co-ordinate with the return of the LORD to HIS Temple. Neither event is physical. Enoch walked with GOD, and the LORD took him. But the ascension of Enoch was not in any sense spatial. The translation of the Being is a dynamic process of the exaltation of the potencies, attributes and vehicles. It is what might appropriately be termed, Divine Levitation, or a state of Soul-consciousness such as enables the inheritor to move at the Divine Will's command, from plane to plane, and from Kingdom to Kingdom.

When one language is translated into another, the ideas and meanings in the one become expressed by means of the new signs and terms of the other.

This process of translation lies at the heart of the

Regeneration. What may be named the travail of the Regeneration, is the outcome of the motion of dynamic forces accomplishing the miracle of transmutation. For Translation is the crown of Regeneration. Without the latter the former could not take place. It is thus the translation of the language of the Soul which it has acquired upon its world of manifestation, into the signs and terms of the language understood and spoken within the realm to which the Soul is exalted. The Divine Ideas in the Soul are elevated to a higher Kingdom, and partake of the power and glory of that sphere.

When all Israel are translated by the LORD, they will not only be fully regenerate, but they will be able to dwell continuously in the rarified Atmospheria of the Cloud of His Radiance. They will again have become Celestials in their Soul state, and in consciousness be able to function within the Angelic and Celestial realms. And they will be able to do this whilst dwelling and serving upon these planes. For they are not to leave the Earth-spheres till their ministry to the Earth's children be fully accomplished. But being regenerated and translated in state, they will have the power to dwell in their consciousness, in the presence and operation of the Celestial Spheres, and be ever with their LORD as HE is there embodied and made manifest.

Such a Translation of all Israel would be a rehabilitation of that ancient community to the status once enjoyed by the Sons of GOD who were commissioned to this Earth. It would be their return to the land of their ancient Inheritance—the light, power and glory of Christhood.

The purpose of the Message now being restored to them is unto the end that they may all arise into the consciousness of the Presence within them, and regain the power to dwell in the Cloud of HIS Radiance. To attain to so much, is to recover their Vocation. The "high calling" or Vocation of Israel, is to be revealers of the ADONAI as HIS Manifestors and Interpreters. Through the corporate body of the Christhood in manifestation, ADONAI will unveil HIS Glory, and shed it upon the world. Commensurate with the recovered power of the Sons of GOD through the exaltation of state which will crown their Translation, will be the restoration of the Theocracy.

THE RE-ENTHRONEMENT OF ISRAEL

The corollary of the Translation of Israel is found in the re-enthronement of them. For the Sons of GOD it is a glorious resultant; and for the distraught Earth a blessed living hope. In it lies Humanity's Redemption. The issue of the Planet from the confusion and hurt of the present débâcle, is dependent upon the recovered regnancy of Israel.

In the day of the Return, the twelve sealed Tribes of Israel were to reign from twelve thrones. In their degree they were to sit upon the twelve thrones that encircled the Throne of the ETERNAL. In the day of the coming again of the Son of Man, HIS reign in them and through them was to be glorious. They were to reign with HIM. They were to share HIS Glory. They were also to reign upon the Earth for HIM.

For all Israel to reign upon the Earth for HIM, means an individual and communal realization of the Christhood. To realize such a state of regnancy, is to become the Body of the LORD for Manifestation. To share HIS Glory is to radiate the Light of Christhood and shed HIS auric electric streams. And for HIM to reign in every Son of Israel, is for all Israel to be executants of HIS Will in the accomplishment of HIS Holy purpose.

In all this attainment and enthronement, there is no

room for mere personal ambition to possess powers and reign amid principalities. For all who would truly ascend and reign, the lowly path lies with open gates. The way to the realms of powers and regnancies, is one of lowly mind and humble heart. Those who would be greatest must know how to be even as the least. Those who would become one with the LORD, must, like their LORD, have the power to be the servant of all, without any conscious loss of dignity, potency or majesty.

* * * * * *

Live thus, all ye who would be of HIS ISRAEL!

Live, all ye who read this drama, as those who are HIS Children and the vehicles of HIS manifestation upon the Earth!

Live ye, as those who dwell in HIS Presence and whom HE hath enthroned!

For through such lives shall the world's tragedy be healed; the streams of its bitter sorrow dried up; and all its errors be corrected and its wrong states changed, until Righteousness is once more the standard of GOD in its midst, and Divine Equity gives balance to all its ambition and motion. Then shall the long night of travail pass away before the dawn of GOD's everlasting day.

It shall be, if all Israel respond.

It must be that the Sons of GOD meet the world's great need, and bring to it redemptive healing.

It shall soon come to pass that the stricken Earth is made glad, and all the Sons of GOD shout for joy.

THE BOOK OF ISAIAH
PART NINE

THE SIGN OF THE CROSS

*The Book of Isaiah scintillates with the
magnetic action of the Cross, the Mystery
Passion permeates its Message, showing the unity of the Revelation with
that given through the Messenger Moses and fulfilled in
Teachings given by the
Master concerning the
House of Israel
and the Divine
Passion.*

CONTENTS

189

Most Radiant One, we know Thee to be the Centre of the Glorious Universe, and the Life of all Beings and Systems within it!

In Thy Most Radiant Cross we witness the exposition of Thy Mystery.

Thou art the Standard of the Universe, and holdest in Divine Balance all its Spiral embodiments of Thyself.

In all things Thou hast expressed Thy Mystery, and in each of Thy Children the Sign of Thy Cross appears.

Most Glorious Father-Mother, we would be Thy Children in very deed, and show forth Thy Glory in bearing and revealing the Fashion of Thee.

We would know continually, through Thine Indwelling Sign, the perfect Motion of Thee.

Upon our Countenance and Attributes we would reveal the Sign of the Cross, even as Thou hast engraven it upon Thine Image within us.

May we be true Children of the Cross in all the Service of our Lives, sharing in the Blessed Ministries of Thy Love and Wisdom, even as Thou dost minister unto us through Thy Holy One.

Amen and Amen.

THE BOOK OF ISAIAH
in relation to
THE SIGN OF THE CROSS

THE impress of the Cross is visible in the whole of the revelation given in the Message which the Prophet Isaiah was empowered to give.

The Message is concerned with HIM Who is the Sign of the Cross in the Eternal Heavens, Who is ever the sublime and exalted ONE, Whose Dual Mystery is at the heart of the Universe and in the seat of every manifestation of HIS regnancy; for HIS impress is found in all embodiments of HIMSELF, even in the lowly degrees in which a Human Soul might be accounted an expression of the fashion of HIS Mystery. Not only is the impress of the Cross upon all the Message, and its subject-matter concerned with HIM Who is always the Sign of the Cross in the highest realm of glorious embodiment and manifestation, and in the lowly degrees with which man may be said to be chiefly associated—the realm of a Human Soul's evolution, growth, expansion, deepening, and ascension to meet the necessities of the coming age-flight when HE shall reveal HIMSELF in HIS resplendence, and in the majesty of HIS overshadowing—but, in addition, the Message is primarily unto those who were most intimately associated with the life and ministry for which the Cross stands as sign and symbol, and who not only bore within themselves, as all Souls do, the impress of HIS

Holy Mystery as Sign of the Cross, but who were the Cross-bearers, and, in their degree, the expositions of the motion of that Cross in its sublime ministries unto the children of the FATHER-MOTHER.

That the Cross has found expression in realms beneath the Human Kingdom, is added testimony to the great reality that in the heart of the Universe is hidden the Mystery of the Sign of the Cross, which is also the Mystery of the ETERNAL. It is that secret which gives potency to the Cross, enspheres the Life of the Cross in mystic splendour, leaves its impress even upon minerals and solidified elements, reveals itself also through vegetation, and finds in the Human the sum of all that is beneath, and from there begins its ascending motion as it bears each Human Soul onward and upward through the ages, pausing at every Station for the Soul to take the Degrees which mark the path of its progress unto the vision of HIM Who is the Holy Mystery within it, even the FATHER-MOTHER.

THE MEDIUM OF THE MESSAGE

The revelation is that of the ETERNAL ONE. It is given to a Prophet-Soul. But the Prophet-Soul, as the Medium in his innermost Being, must have been in accord with such revelation. Had it not been so, such a revealing of Divine Majesty would have overwhelmed him. The radiations would have consumed him. The electric force would have so greatly affected him, that he could not have endured to receive.

The term "medium" is used oft-times in a very loose way. Every Soul has the capacity of mediumship, otherwise it could not receive Spiritual things. It could never become illumined, move forward and ascend, expand and deepen. It is because it is a medium for the

Divine Influx that it can grow and evolute, and continue to grow and evolute from degree to degree.

Much that is associated with what is termed "mediumship" is only reflected light within the Astral Circulus, or within the higher magnetic plane. For, those who are truly Spiritual mediums live purely. Their lives are beautiful; otherwise they could not endure to receive that which they must realize. When a Soul has a real vision, it realizes the vision; and it does so because it inherently knows. That which is the corresponding quality of the vision, is within the Being. The Heavens have called forth that quality; the Soul has responded; and in its response it has received.

For anyone to receive a vision of so Cosmic an order, comprising Angelic, Celestial, and Divine motion, implies that the receiver was *en rapport* in state and willinghood; and through the Soul's deep yearning, it had been lifted in its vision to become one with that which the Divine World unfolded to it.

For, when a Soul receives Divine revelation, it is not simply reflected light that comes to it. It is not ordinary illumination broken upon the retina of the mind that is flashed into its Sanctuary. It is a revelation of profound import because relating to the ETERNAL ONE, which becomes realization within the Sanctuary of Being so that the Seer beholds, sees, and realizes. He becomes an actor who has a part in the Divine Drama, and who is inseparable from it. He understands the revelation as it is presented to him.

Historically there is put forth a theory that the Prophet Isaiah prophesied under several Jewish Kings; that he began to prophesy under Uzziah, and finished his prophecy some half-century later under Manasseh. It is recorded that he poured forth warnings against the ways of Manasseh, and as a result he suffered martyrdom.

THE PROPHET'S DIVINE VISION

The Isaiah who is presented in the real Message is an unknown quantity, and of Divine quality. To the outer history he is an unknown Prophet. The name is not that of a man; it is the name of the Message. He received the revelation within the Sanctuary of his Being. When the Presence is beheld, it is within the inner Sanctuary of the Being. The day can come to the Soul in which it can be so lifted up in state, that it can look from the altar of its own Sanctuary, into the Sanctuary of the Inner World and behold the glorious Presence unveiled there. The Light of the Glory of His Presence passes into the inner Sanctuary of the Soul. The spectacular of the Divine World comes to the Being's inner vision.

*　*　*　*　*　*

"I saw the LORD"! With this statement the Book opens. He could not have seen HIM if the vision had not been reflected within him; nay, he could not have seen the LORD Presence except in high realization. He could not have looked upon the vision if his own Being had not, in every part of it, responded to the electric forces that poured themselves forth from that vision, to fill his own Being. Had he not been *en rapport*, he would not only have been overwhelmed in his consciousness through the contrast between his own state and that of the glory of that ONE, but he would also have been overwhelmed altogether in his attributes, vision, potency, had he not been in union with the Divine Will.

It was the vision of the Sign of the Cross, The Eternal Mystery. The Message was concerned with the Sign of the Cross and the Holy Mystery of the Passion. The Message given to him to unveil and to proclaim, centred in the Sons of GOD, and found its exposition in the Holy Mystery of the Oblation which was to be made manifest bye and bye. The Mystery of the Cross is thus found throughout the revelation the Heavens gave. It was the vibrant testimony of their Love and Wisdom. By its motion were the Sons of GOD and Children of Zion to be found again, redeemed and regenerated.

There is ordinary revelation given to the Soul as it grows and evolutes, until the time when it attains the consciousness in which it seeks to find something of the atmosphere of the Presence, and feel its childhood to that Holy Mystery in some degree through its desires and its attributes, and to rejoice that some day through its growth and ascension it will attain even to know HIM, as it has been promised. Such revelation comes to every Soul growing and evolving, gathering in and becoming enriched; then taking a new degree and another arc of ascension, as the result of the ingathering; descending in the sense of deepening, as the outcome of that which has been ingathered; realizing more and more the meaning of that which has been received and appropriated; and then as the grand resultant, an ascending arc for further degrees in which greater revelation comes, greater empowerment is bestowed. Here all the active attributes are enriched; and those that have not been called forth into great activity, may be awakened and energized to bear the others company in some ministry. But in addition to such revelation, distinctive revelation comes when the Heavens have to reveal in a very special manner. In this sense most distinctive was the revelation given through Moses.

THE UNITY BETWEEN ISAIAH AND MOSES

Now, there is no difference in the subject-matter, except in one aspect, of the revelation given from the Divine World which is found in the teachings of Moses and the revelation given through Isaiah.

You will find in the Message of Isaiah many "sayings"

concerning the Sacred Mystery of the Tetragrammaton. The Sacred Name occurs many times. There is much revelation of HIM Who is the "I AM THAT I AM." The great revelation associated with the Messenger Moses, was the unveiling of the Holy Mystery of the FATHER-MOTHER unto the ancient House of Israel. Nay more, at the very beginning of the revelation, though presented as outer history and under parable, that Holy Mystery appeared unto Moses as the Tree of Fire—the Sign of the Cross. That Mystery is reflected in many sayings and many acts attributed to Moses, especially in connection with Aaron's Rod by which the Magicians of Egypt were confounded, the Red Sea divided, the people healed, and waters given from Horeb. For the Mystery of that Rod is that of the Sacred Name whose very utterance wrought wonders. It brought forth the potency hidden within a rock in the form of waters, and gave great refreshing unto the thirsty people. The Rod could bloom like a flowering plant, and confound the uninitiated. It could assume the form of the Spirit's Sign. It is this most Holy Sign that is confounded with that of the most fallen of the Creatures—the Serpent. For this latter signifies the absolute perversion of Wisdom.

Aaron's Rod was the Sign of the Cross. Here you may glimpse shadows of vestiges of a great truth concerning the White Magic of the Sign of the Cross which obtain unto this day in the Church's belief in the power of the Sign of the Cross when made before the Altar, or over the person in devotion and prayer. It is said that Moses raised a brazen serpent in the wilderness for the children of Israel to look upon in their affliction, and find healing. That Sign was none other than Aaron's Rod. It was the Sign of the Cross made manifest unto the people amid wilderness conditions, to lift their thoughts to the realms whence they had come, and help them to recover the consciousness of that Sign.

There is something magnetic and electric in it. It is not mere superstitious belief, as some affirm. *There is the Divine Duality in it.* Any superstitious associations which may have grown around it are the shadows of the great reality which was known in ancient times. The consciousness of that reality had departed from Israel amidst their travail. Through great ages they have sought for the Divine exposition of that Sign and Symbol to come back to their consciousness. It was part of the mission of Moses to restore it. Isaiah comes with the impress of it upon all his Message.

*   *   *   *   *   *

Who can doubt that we are in the fashion of HIM Who is that Cross? That even the symbol of our fashion, when understood and rightly used, can communicate something of the great truth that lies behind it, or that the Presence of HIM Who is the Sign of the Cross, can dispel, exorcise, transmute, change, elevate, redeem, transform, and, when realized, transfigure all the attributes, until the Being becomes as the Sign of the Cross, and is the exposition of HIM Who is the ever blessed FATHER-MOTHER?

THE RELATIONSHIP OF THE PROPHECY TO THE MASTER

There is no difference in the revelation of HIM Who is ever the "I AM THAT I AM"; between that which Moses had given him to reveal, and that which Isaiah had to transmit. Throughout there is remarkable unity, though there is an extension of the Mystery prophetically stated in Isaiah. Moses, who was a Divine Messenger, as previously stated, presented HIM Who is the Sign of the Cross as the Mysterious Presence whose radiations are tremendous, and whose glory is overwhelming: Isaiah revealed the purpose of the Sign of the Cross to find the House of Israel and restore the ancient Christhood. He had to tell the

story of the Holy Passion of the Christ Manifestation
through the travailing and suffering of the children of the
FATHER-MOTHER who were once known as the Sons of
GOD and the Children of Zion, and to reveal unto them
what that Holy ONE purposed. *His is the Book of the Passion.*
It throbs with it from the beginning to the close. When
once you understand it you see the Cross at the heart of it,
touching every part of the revelation, and its motion
reverberating through every call sent forth unto those for
whom the Message was given, and unto whom it was to be
declared.

* * * * * *

Then when we turn to the revelation given through the
Master whom men call Jesus Christ, and know the Teachings which were given by Him, we find them in unity with
the revelations given through Moses and Isaiah. There is a
Divine sameness in the three revelations. And the inner
relationship of Isaiah to the Manifestation and the Oblation is guardedly unveiled. Moses revealed the Eternal
Christ in the majesty of the Rod of GOD in its potent
ministries of revelation and accomplishment unto and on
behalf of the Children of Israel. Moses in the revelation
expressed the hope that Israel would be able to return to
their ancient inheritance. But after many ages of the
religious Mosaic economy and the revelation which was
given through Moses, it was discovered that more would
have to be revealed and accomplished. Then was projected
the Office of the Oblation, and the Message concerning it revealed unto him who was to be its vehicle. Later
there was transmitted unto the Sons of GOD through the
Prophet, the nature of the Office.

The revelation through him is considered to be the sum
of all prophecy. Unfortunately it is thought of in relation
to the Kings of Israel and Judah and their peoples, unto

whom he is said to have prophesied. Yet his prophecy was not of national or racial character at all, except in the sense that it did affect the race known as the Sons of GOD, and then the races who belonged to this world. The Subject-matter of his vision which he entered into the realization of, was Cosmic. There was no littleness in it; nothing merely personal, national or racial. His was not an ordinary Jewish Document, but a Divine Revelation concerning the Sons of GOD and the Divine Purpose to deliver them from their bondage in this world, and restore them to the ancient estate of Christhood.

*   *   *   *   *   *

A Prophet such as Isaiah is of no one race, though he would come into manifestation and for ministry through a race on the Human Kingdom. Yet in himself he is of Universal Vision and Life. He belongs to the Realm of Universal Government; and in his desires, visions and realizations, to the Theocracy and Regnancy of GOD. Therefore, he prophesies, not for this King or that people, this city or that land. He reveals that which is given to him for whatsoever specific purpose; but his Message belongs to the Cosmic whole, and is not for the benefit of one people at the expense of another, nor to glorify one nation and make it conqueror over all the other nations. He is not the vehicle of GOD, as the ETERNAL is conceived of and worshipped by any nation, as one who would work through the nation to overthrow other peoples. GOD as conceived of and prayed unto by the nations, would make Redemption and racial Unity impossible.

It was by such confusion that the Messages of ancient Prophecies were changed. It made those Messages to be merely of national and racial value. All the sublime Cosmic, Soulic, Angelic, Celestial and Divine import was swallowed up by national thought and desire, racial greed and aggrandizement. Religious narrowness and bigotry prevailed. All the Higher Mysteries which had descended from the Sons of GOD, were materialized beyond recognition. The Master came to restore these during the Manifestation.

Moses revealed the Cross. The Sign of the Cross was Aaron's Rod of Omnipotent Love. Isaiah portrayed the motion of it in his description of the Passion. The Master had to speak of it as that which was then to take the world's burden of sin and bear it away. The Ram of God was to accomplish the Planet's Redemption.

There is unity; there is oneness in the triple Mystery of the Message. The first reveals the sublime Actor; the second, the path of HIS Action; the third, the Mystery of Soul-recovery and Planetary Redemption.

THE MESSAGE WAS UNTO THE SAME PEOPLE

The Message in the three different ages was unto the same people. Moses, Isaiah, and the Master, addressed the Message to the Sons of GOD. Even under Moses they had the capacity to become as Gods. "Said I not unto you, ye shall be as Gods?" Between Moses and Isaiah ages seem, historically, to have risen and set. Between Isaiah and the Master, the ages were considerable. How then could it come to pass that the people were the same unto whom Moses, Isaiah, and the Master ministered?

People are accustomed to live in days of twenty-four hours, in years of three hundred and sixty-five days, and in a life-time extending, at the most, to seventy years, eighty years, or a century. Souls are here to grow, or to serve in special capacity. All come either to grow or to serve. Even in growing we serve; for all learn through service. Everyone must serve. The tiny bush serves as truly as the majestic tree. Though the degree of its service is less, yet its service is equal in purpose.

The vehicles are temporary, whether Souls come for service or to acquire and grow. Souls come into them at birth. They take possession of them. All Souls are held from the inner realms. They are spiritual units of the Cosmic whole. They have had a long history in their growth and evolution. They come and go, taking on new vehicles at each birth. In more intense degrees is this true of Souls who come for service. Then the vehicles are accommodated to the service which they have come to render.

All are children of the great ages. Where do you think the Light that is in you, and that is able to respond to yet greater Light flashed into your mind, came from? How is it that you have the power to apprehend things Divine, and to comprehend such in great degree in these days? Have you imagined it is simply through your fortunate birth, through noble parents, within a good home, and within the radius of a given age? *Then, why are not all Souls in the same home and age and country, alike? Why are not all endowed like yourselves? Why are there so many inequalities found in children of the same parentage? Why do so many suffer from inequalities that ought never to exist, and would not if all things were equitable and righteous?*

Even if the world were redeemed back again to its ancient equipoise in all its activities; if Eden as a state were restored, and all Souls realized it, there would still be degrees of consciousness, apprehension, and comprehension. Lives would be as varied as the leaves and flowers. Souls are the fruitage of the growth of great ages. Consciousness is a gift from the Absolute and the ETERNAL ONE. It is of the Eternal in its quality. In us its intensity and radius are ever-increasing quantities. Its potency is such that it can deepen, expand, and ascend. Souls grow through the great ages by means of their expansion, deepening, and ascension in consciousness. That which makes up the consciousness of a Soul in a thousand ages, in ten thousand ages, is in *the Principle of its Being*. But during ages of growth it has gathered in of the Divine Ætheria which is pregnant with consciousness. For the Divine Ætheria is of the primal substance out of which all things have been fashioned. *It is in the midst of polarized Divine Ætheria that consciousness becomes manifest and finds individuated self-expression.* The Soul gathers in of that glorious living Divine atmospheria. The Divine Ætheria enriches the Being. By this means the consciousness grows from the single to the multiple; from the unit to the power of the few; then to the power of the many; to the power of the multitude; to the power of the race; until the Soul, having attained to Planetary Cosmic Consciousness, has the power to be in touch with the whole Planetary racial consciousness. And the Soul who grows yet further, who may not be of this Planetary evolution, but who may have come here for special service, and who has still to expand and grow even as the children of this world do, but within higher realms where consciousness is of the higher order, may attain to Cosmic Consciousness of a Solar order. Here consciousness is the same in nature. It is the same in principle. It is only in the degree that a Soul can not only look out through the realm of a Planetary consciousness, but can look into a realm which has a circumference expanding to the radius of Solar Cosmic Consciousness.

THE ILLIMITABLENESS OF CONSCIOUSNESS

It is thus we grow, even until, with the wings given to us, through the lowly adoration of HIM and the ennobled, consecrated, purified, and divinely energized though veiled feet of service for HIM, the Spirit takes flight even to the Absolute. But the individuated Being is always relative. For though the Soul can attain to function within the Solar realm and know Solar Cosmic Consciousness, yet it does not become the Solar body. It has just attained the power to be one with its Citizenship.

This will aid you to understand the illimitableness of consciousness, and how it grows until the Being can realize HIM Who is Universal Being—the Eternal and glorious FATHER-MOTHER. It is with the realization of consciousness the Soul has power to apprehend and to comprehend; it has power to sense or sound the great Deeps. It has the power of expansion in the degrees of the Circle: it has length, breadth, depth and height. It gains power to ascend, to seek unto the ETERNAL; and, in the degree in which the Being can receive HIM, to possess Divine Vision. Such power is the outcome of great æonial growth.

How can a mind think that way? The mind has sometimes to use language in making statements concerning great things, which in itself it does not really properly comprehend until it has fully reached the Divine. For instance, take this scientific proposition on the material or physical Kingdom. The Sun is said to be fully ninety-two millions of miles from us. It is difficult to think of millions of miles. A journey round the Earth seems a great journey, but it is only twenty-four thousand miles if you just make a circle of it. How difficult it is to comprehend the meaning of ninety-two million miles, the apparent apartness of the Sun from us, spatially! How much more difficult it would be to put into terms which Science tries to do, the distance of the next nearest star! The star that is supposed to be the nearest to our Sun, is computed to be not less than a million times the distance of the Sun from us. The mind cannot take it in, outside the realm of realization. When a Soul soars to the Sun in consciousness, it does not require these measurements.

Time and space are not. And when it attains to Cosmic consciousness, it may look through a thousand ages. And it will remember many things which were objects of vision, experience and realization. Indeed, in Cosmic Consciousness one thousand years are as a day, and less. Even the visions of the Soul known and realized ten thousand years ago, may appear as if they were present-day empirical experiences.

This does not mean that there is no time-regulation within the Celestial realms. There is time on every Celestial embodiment. On every world, time is the result of triple motion. And such motion differs on every Planet and Star. Even consciousness is the resultant of motion. Life and Light are begotten through motion. There is motion everywhere: there is no rest anywhere. There is rest in the sense of recreation. There is pause in special activities. Yet even in those times, everything in the Universe is in motion. But the consciousness transcends these planes. It takes Soulic flight into the great Beyond where there is no consciousness at all of time's limitations. Then the Soul can look upon that which took place a Naros ago (600 years), even thousands of years past, without having any consciousness of earthly time.

Should it be given you to look into the face of one whom you have known upon these planes many years ago, but who passed from your threshold, and who may now be ministering in the Angelic World, in that moment you will feel as if all the intervening years had fled, and it is with you as if the passing had not been. Should you come to the vision of HIM Whom you have not seen in glorious estate for great ages, and you behold HIM, as Isaiah beheld HIM, as Moses beheld HIM, and as the Master beheld HIM, you will not be conscious of tremendous cycles of years having intervened since the time when the veil fell over your vision. For, the very moment in which you look on HIM, you will simply know that you have always known HIM; and, once you realize it, it will seem as if you had never been away from HIM; except in the sense in which it is expressed in Isaiah's vision when he felt the poverty of his own attributes, the limitation of the motion of his own Being, and became overwhelmed with the grandeur of the Cosmic Vision and the consciousness of his own limitation, in contrast with the sublimity of the Presence, the Seraphic motion, and the Arch-Angelic and Angelic anthems.

This should help you to understand how revelation comes to all Souls, and very specially to those Prophets and Seers who have been sent with Messages of high import. For the Prophet can receive with the Understanding, only that which he has known of old time. The Seer could not understand the visions given him, unless he had realized in his very Being the truths revealed to him. In high degree it was thus with the Messengers, Moses, Isaiah, and the Master.

THE CHILDREN OF THE CROSS

The Message of Moses was unto Israel. GOD's Israel were the children of the Cross who had been sent to be interpreters and revealers here, but who had lost their way amid the gross spiritual darkness upon the Earth. It was a darkness that overtook all the planes of the Earth. GOD's Israel, who once dwelt in the Light of the Eternal, came to know this exquisitely beautiful world to be turned into a veritable wilderness of wild growth and, in parts, a desert land.

All the Messengers brought revelation to Israel. The revelation was to restore to them the things they once knew great ages before they came to this Planet. How were they to be recalled? How were they to be found again? Surely by revealing to them those things which once were their Angelic and Celestial heritage. The revelation was gradual and in aspects. It was thus they were able to endure the Divine unveilings, and welcome the approach of the Heavens through the Message.

So the Message of the Messengers was always unto Israel. And later, when it was found that Israel could not return into the full consciousness of the Laws of the LORD and their operation within them unto high realization, and through them into sublime manifestation of the Ancient Christhood in which state they once manifested as the Sons of GOD when they came to this world to be Manifestors, Interpreters and Revealers, then it was projected to change the Solar ministry, and to accomplish the return of Israel by a miraculous event of another nature. For then the Great Work known as the Divine Passion, in the Oblation and Sin-offering, was purposed and projected. The Ezekiel and Isaiah revelations were concerned with this Divine event.

*　　*　　*　　*　　*　　*

The vision of Isaiah that seems to open the real Prophecy, was given more than six hundred years before the coming of the Manifestation. He who was the vehicle of such a vision, had also dwelt in HIS Presence Who is the LORD. But the time came when the vision had to be made known, therefore it was transcribed from the screens of the Divine World into a language that Israel could understand. And then it came to pass that not only the vision of the Sign of the Cross was given, but the motion of the Passion of the Cross in its redemptive ministry was also unveiled.

Isaiah is considered to be one of the most beautiful books of the Bible because of the exquisite English into which it has been put; for it was an age of wonderful

English when the Bible, as we have it, was translated. Yet the renderings are oft-times far removed from the real Message; and the interpretations are often far afield. Later editors affected the MSS. when these passed into their hands. *The real Message has not been understood.*

But the Message was given to Israel, not to the Jewish nation. It was especially revelatory to the Sons of GOD; but it could not have been understood by a religious system such as Jewry. The Message came to the illumined ones who were at the head of the Prophetic Schools where the Mysteries were understood and taught in some degree. It was revealed to the few who could receive the Message.

*   *   *   *   *   *

Later, the Message suffered change in many parts. This was not to be wondered at. The times through which the Message passed were difficult and dark, and the power of Jewry was great. Because of this, the essentially spiritual Schools of the Mysteries passed under a dark cloud, and the true vision became obscured. When the Master came, a considerable number of these lovers of Truth had migrated to the Syrian Hills; for when Divine Events are to take place, there is always direction given from the Inner Heavens to meet the need of those events, to those who are to be the recipients and vehicles. And so, many of ancient Israel had gathered in the valleys and on the slopes of the Galilean and Syrian hills. It was there the real Manifestation was made. The Divine revelation of the meaning of Jesus, Christ, and the LORD, was given on the hill-slopes of Galilee, and by the waters of the Lake of Gennesaret. Sometimes to intimate ones, or those who drew very near through the Message, the Divine Mystery was unfolded within a home circle. For the Master who came to find Israel and reveal the Laws of the LORD, unveiled the sacred Passion when meeting His beloved ones in the quiet of the home-circle. It was more often in such gatherings than in more public places that He found His friends and drew aside the veil.

It was in such hours that He intimately interpreted Moses and the Prophets. He interpreted Moses and the Prophets in a way that showed that those who held the Books literally and according to tradition, did not understand. How many of the Western world understand the Mysteries of the Old Scriptures; or the Mystery of the Passion revealed in the New? If the Western world understood, what a different world it would become! There could be no war. There would be no injustice. There would be no element of hatred. There would be a cessation of conflict. Barbarisms would cease. There could be no more conflict amongst mankind in any degree whatever; nor would there be any grievous burdens imposed upon the creatures. If the Western world knew the Scriptures which they profess to hold sacred, what a power for righteousness there would be! Alas! through not understanding, the peoples have oft-times entered into conflict. If the Scriptures were understood, the Western world would become idyllic; and all nations and races would bask in the radiance of the Divine Love and Wisdom.

The Master brought the glory of the Divine Mysteries revealed through Moses, right from the threshold of the Heart of GOD, back to the heart of Israel; and He interpreted Isaiah as the Prophet of Zion, and told them of the glorious revelation of the Divine Passion which was then prophetically projected, and which was now to be actively undertaken and carried through until fully accomplished.

THE RESTORATION OF THE MESSAGE

Now you will understand how it comes to pass that this Message is restored for Israel. It is not given to the world, except incidentally and in a secondary way; but all the world will benefit. No one can live beautifully without helping the world. The Message is primarily for the Ancient People; those unto whom Moses spake from the heights of Sinai and Horeb; to whom Isaiah prophesied of the coming Manifestation and Travail; and those whom the Master came to seek unto the finding of, and who were privileged to hear again the Message concerning the Life known as Jesus, Christ, and the LORD. The ancient Mysteries are again being unveiled to some of them, and for all the Christhood. Moses and the Prophets are being re-interpreted. The Message of Isaiah has become alive. It is vibrant with the potency of Divine Love, and is luminous. Unveiled, it is seen to pulse with Divine emotion, from its opening prelude to its closing cadences of Divine Hope. That for which the Master was sent by the FATHER-MOTHER; the Life for which He stood; the interpretation of the Life which He had to give for His LORD; have been in these days restated, re-interpreted, and revealed.

*　　*　　*　　*　　*　　*

Now, as Moses was one with Isaiah in the subject-matter of the Message given unto Israel; and as both were one with the Master in the Message He was given to declare as He regathered Israel; and as He was one with the Sign of the Cross in His Life and holy consecration for the ministry that the Sign of the Cross had undertaken through Him in bearing the burden of the Divine Passion: so are you all one—one with Moses and the Prophets; one with that Israel unto whom the Message of Moses was given; one with those who felt the throb of the Divine Passion in the language of Isaiah; one with those who heard from the lips of the Master in the days of the Manifestation concerning the Passion of the Sign of the Cross, the redemptive burden of the Divine Love, the ministry to be undertaken within the circles where Gehenna and Gehinnom reigned—Herodian and Tartarean realms of darkness, degraded passion, and inverted desire; those realms where satanic powers and principalities became dominant, which were so much out of harmony with the Kingdom of our LORD and HIS Christ, that the Passion had to be borne to overthrow them and change the direction and use of their powers, and so redeem them that they should ultimately contribute to the coming of the Kingdom of Divine Love and Wisdom all over the world.

You are inheritors of the Mysteries to-day; of the redemptive ministry to which all the revelation of the estates of Jesus, Christ and the LORD calls. You are the inheritors of the glorious Message that you may also be the manifestors, revealers and interpreters of it. For you are to be inheritors of such great gifts unto the embodying of them. Knowledge of the Mysteries unveiled to you is food, but it can only nourish when it is absorbed, appropriated, assimilated, transmuted, and raised dynamically into the vehicles, clothing them with the power of its life.

* * * * * *

Bear with me should I seem impassioned. The Passion of my LORD moves me, and calls to you to awaken, arise and understand the meaning of this Sign. HE calls you unto the realization of HIS approach; HIS becoming within you; HIS revelation unto you; HIS return to the Sanctuary of your Being; HIS encompassing of you; HIS overshadowing through the Cloud of HIS Radiance.

Children of a thousand ages, whom HE has borne in the bosom of HIS Love with exquisite patience and tenderness beyond telling, awaken to the fact that HE calls you to be the receivers of HIS Radiations and the transmitters of HIS Glory for the healing of all Souls, and unto the Redemption and Restoration of the whole world.

May you be moved in this hour to say to HIM: "LORD, here am I: send me! send me!"

I know the Message to be HIS, not only because HE has told me, but because I know it from HIM in realization. May you rise to HIS motion upon you, within you, and reveal it through you. May you henceforth be able to say with the Master:

"Unto Thee, O my Father-Mother, do I now consecrate myself as Thy Servant, for Thy Holy Mystery of the Passion of Thy Redeeming Love."

*   *   *   *   *   *

O Wondrous One! Most Holy and ever Blessed Father-Mother! May it be with us Thy Children that each in the power of the inspiration of this hour, may know that Thou callest him to be Thy worthy vehicle for the revelation of Thy Glory, and the healing of all Souls.

Ever Blessed be Thy Most Glorious Name!

THE BOOK OF ISAIAH
PART TEN

THE DAYSMAN OF ISRAEL

*Wherein it is shown in what relationship the
Master stood to Israel; His Divine
appointment to be Daysman; some-
thing of what that Office implied
sacrificially for Him and the
Divine World; and how
He stood for Israel
as their High
Priest and
Mediator.*

CONTENTS

O Lord God of Sabaoth! What majesty Thy Holy Purpose reveals to us! What a wealth of Love Thou outpourest upon Thy Children as Thou blessest them back into the Vision, Life, and Consciousness of Thee, that they may know Thee again even as they did when this world was clothed in Thy magnetic light, and all its spheres were resonant with Divine Gladness!

Then did Thy Sons upon the Earth shout for joy and sing the Songs of Zion.

Adorable One! Oh, that Thy children could again hearken fully unto Thy Voice, and respond with the alacrity of the ancient days in sublime sacrificial consecration for life and ministry in the service of Thee!

May Thy Holy One be so realized by them that they will awaken fully to the consciousness of Thine ensphering, Thine overshadowing, and Thine indwelling.

O Radiant One! Ever Blessed be Thy Glorious Name!

THE DAYSMAN OF ISRAEL

This is a very intimate theme. They are all intimate in a way, but some seem to be more so than others. I ask you to prepare the motion of your Being to transcend all the personal realm, even though you may have to glimpse something of its outer manifestation and the shadows that have flitted across its threshold.

As the second part[1] is dependent almost entirely on the realization of the first, and as the first, historically in the great ages and from the Heavens, is of primary importance, I will now speak more of it unto you.

THE MASTER AND ISRAEL

Great ages ago those Sons of GOD who came in later times to be known upon the Earth as the Children of Israel, were asked to undertake a mission to this world. The Master known as Jesus Christ, was intimately related to that race. He was not of the same order, nor of the same Household. But in later ages there sprang up between them, through office and ministry, a relationship most intimate. Children whose spiritual generation, growth and evolution were upon another system than this, were given into His charge that He might be their Leader, Teacher, and Shepherd, and be as their Elder Brother. They thus became His children in a spiritual and celestial sense. As the relationship grew and deepened, they came to know Him by other terms and names.

It was, therefore, not surprising that He should be

---

[1] The Master as Redeemer of Judah. p. 241.

asked to be the vehicle unto them of a series of manifestations in different ages, wherein there was conveyed to
them fuller revelation of many of the things they
partially knew, with a higher call to serve yet more
inwardly in the Heavens.

It was thus it came to pass that, when they were
dwelling upon the Solar Bethlehem, He was the vehicle
of His LORD unto them; and at times He was such in a very
special way.

* * * * * *

The time came when the Sons of GOD now known as
Israel, were asked to undertake the office of Mediatorial
Teachers and Interpreters unto the elder children of
Judah, who, be it understood, are the offspring of the
Planet-Soul. So the Sons of GOD set out on their spiritual
pilgrimage of beautiful ministry.

The relationship between the Master and them was not
broken; nor was it in any real sense interrupted, though
He had oft-times to minister elsewhere, and then only
indirectly to them. When they came to this world and
dwelt upon its Bethlehem, which at that time was a home
of loveliness, He was still used as the vehicle of the Divine
World for communication unto those who had become
His children and His brethren; for they were His sheep
in the Angelic and Celestial Realms.

It was thus that He became from time to time the
Messenger from the Divine World during such periods as
are represented in the Old Scriptures under the terms of
Adam, Enoch and Moses. These are, however, Divine
Names, and are always to be thought of in relation to the
ETERNAL. When we speak of the Messengers it must ever
be remembered that a real Messenger of the Inner World
is only a Servant, even though in consciousness and
actual operative ministry, his dwelling-place for great
ages has been within one of the spheres of the Divine

World. When he comes forth as the Messenger he comes as a Servant, however great he may seem to be in his consciousness of the Eternal and Universal Mystery, and in the degree in which his estate is expressed in embodiment and revealed in the exquisite beauty of Divine and Celestial, Angelic and Human childhood. Though a high Messenger he is always a Servant—one who is as if he had nothing, whilst through his consciousness of the Ever Most Blessed ONE he possesses all things.

THE LAW OF SACRIFICE

Now, when the great change took place through the betrayal of this world and the fall of members of her Hierarchy; the descent of the Planet in Celestial estate through an interference with the polarity of the substances of her Kingdoms; with the resultant utter prostration (in the sense of spiritual fall) of all her children; a new order of ministry on behalf of the Sons of GOD had to be instituted by the Divine World. They could not be left, because they were involved in the débâcle. They could not be left without the ministry which they needed in a most special manner. They could have been taken out of the world; but that would have been to have left the world the poorer. For they were the children who knew the Heavens; who understood the life of the Heavens; who were able to interpret Angelic manifestation and reveal it unto the children of this world for great ages after the Fall. They were able to be even as HIS Angels upon the Earth-planes unto the children of men, through their love and their wisdom.

*　　*　　*　　*　　*　　*

It is the Law of the Heavens to make sacrifice. It is the sublime exposition of the Eternal Love. When such an event as overtook this world in its great descent had matured, those who had come laden with the riches of the Heavens to reveal the treasures of GOD and transmit these as heavenly knowledge, whilst also making manifest that they were of the Divine Love and Wisdom, themselves gradually became impoverished. For the conditions of the Earth were such that its miasma began to tell upon the Sons of GOD.

It is not easy to express, and it would be less easy for you to apprehend, all that is associated with the tragedy of that descent and the conflict which arose in this world. We speak in general terms of the Travail of Israel through the ages; but how little even those who have had the Message restored to them in these days, have yet come to realize what that Travail was, and all that it signified for the Children of Israel and for the Heavens.

Those who had brought about such a great disaster within the kingdoms of this world, had wrought that change by means of affecting the intermediary realms first, through changing the magnetic status of the elements and substances. Then the outer planes took on the effects of the altered magnetic conditions even unto such a concrete manifestation of them that the outer became as changed as the intermediary world. The inimical forces were great within the elements which had been so changed that they could not fulfil their original purpose. For these hurtful forces were begotten of high intelligences within the intermediary world. They were the creations of the activities of those who were opposed to such manifestation of Divine Love and Wisdom as the Sons of GOD had given upon the Bethlehem of this world. Those at enmity with the Divine Will, laboured to defeat such a manifestation.

THE OFFICE OF DAYSMAN

In the midst of their labours, Israel became more and more smitten by the awful conditions that had arisen.

Thus it came to pass that the Heavens changed their ministry from time to time to meet the needs of the Children of Israel. And then the Divine World made a request of the one who had been Mediator unto Israel for many ages before the great descent, which testified of the intimate relationship he bore to Israel, and revealed the exquisite beauty of the ways of the Divine Love and Wisdom. That one had been the vehicle of manifestation upon the Heavens unto those Sons of GOD. He had continued to be the vehicle of the FATHER-MOTHER through many ages subsequent to the great descent. And he was chosen to be the vehicle of a new order of ministry: it was contained in his appointment to be the Daysman for Israel.

What is meant by a Daysman will become apparent as we proceed. It was a Divine appointment. HE Who calls all HIS children, and raises them up to fill high office when they are able so to serve HIM, called the Master.

It is well to remember that all learn by service. Even those who are as little children, learn through serving on the Earth-planes. And the same applies in all spiritual growth. Everyone learns through service, and not only through knowledge. Knowledge is light thrown upon the mind; but service is the acquisition of riches in the heart and the Being. We grow enriched as we give. We become crowned with our Divinity in the measure in which we express it as love and devotion, and in beautiful ministry. All the great ones have attained through service. Even those who reach the realms of the Divine World, reach those realms through service.

And all true ministries are of Divine appointment. No man can make himself a Prophet; nor can any academic centre. That is where all the ecclesiastical authorities and schools have been wrong in their outlook. They have imagined they could manufacture in their Theological Seminaries, a Prophet. *A Prophet is fashioned and illumined by God.*

Nor could any ecclesiastical centre of tradition create a Seer. *A Seer is a Soul who is hoary with age.* He is not simply a clairvoyant. He is one who is crowned with the wealth of ingathered riches of attribute throughout great ages. He is able to look into the Inner Worlds and endure the visions beheld there, and understand their meaning.

Nor can man make himself a Priest. No earthly authority, ecclesiastical or secular, can make a man a Priest, or a woman a Priestess. Priesthood is the crown of Seership, as Seership is the crown of the prophetic faculty. It is the acquisition of such power of mediation as will enable the individual to be the vehicle of Divine potencies, and the possessor of the Divine attributes necessary for Revelation, and even for Redemption.

The appointing of the Master to be the Daysman for Israel, was from the FATHER-MOTHER. When HE calls Who is the LORD of Being, HIS Servant responds. It is the depth and the height, the breadth and the length of Being realized as potency and expressed in power for service, which qualifies for such high and sacred Office. And such qualification is made manifest when the whole Being responds with joy to the call of the FATHER-MOTHER.

THE BURDEN OF THE OFFICE

What was the service that He was called to as the appointed Daysman for Israel? He was to be, as in the past, Leader, Shepherd, Teacher, and vehicle of revelation for the FATHER-MOTHER, unto His brethren; but He was also to be so representative of the motion of the Heavens, that He would stand between the Sons of GOD who comprised Israel, and the inimical forces that sought to utterly overwhelm them. There would never have been an Oblation but for the fact that these opposing forces had gained such domination in the intermediary world, that something had to be done to preserve Israel and save this distraught world from utter disaster.

*   *   *   *   *   *

How little the children of men who worship in Sanctuaries and believe many things concerning the LORD of Being, and such things as have come in historical theology to be associated with the Master as to His nature and His Message, realize what the Divine World was and is in nature, government and purpose, and what it became in attitude and ministry unto the Children of Israel and the needs of this world!

As Daysman He had to make great sacrifice. But in the Divine World, sacrifice is a joy. It is accounted a sacred thing and an honour. It is an act of sublime consecration; the yielding up of the Being unto HIM Who fashioned and endowed it. If HE Who is the giver of every good and perfect gift makes us rich in our Being, it is that we may give back in blessed service for HIM whensoever and wheresoever HE appoints. Even Life itself is given that we may use it; first unto the realization of HIM, and then for service to help that same realization to come to some of HIS other children. There is no loss in sacrifice. But there is Eternal gain; and this obtains though the sacrificer may be put under limitations, and have to lay aside estate, and descend from realms he loves, leaving the form of ministry that has been an inexpressible joy, to undertake ministry of an altogether different order.

For the Master it was a new undertaking. The Office of Daysman was verily of a different nature from that of the vehicle for Manifestation. He had once been the

Shepherd of a glorious people, the Leader and Interpreter of Divine revelation unto them, as the FATHER-MOTHER commanded.

To be Daysman for these, meant that He must needs come between them and the play of inimical astral-occult forces. Light will surely break soon upon the consciousness of many as to the real nature of His mediatorial relationship to Israel in the Heavens; and how it came to pass that, as Mediator, He did not mediate on behalf of Israel *unto* the FATHER-MOTHER to effect any change in the Heavens or in HIM Who is the Regnant Presence there; but that He was Mediator *from* the FATHER-MOTHER unto Israel, effecting the necessary changes within the elements of the intermediary world which afflicted them. For these inimical forces smote them, filling them with spiritual Soul-pain, and with profound sorrow, oft-times with an anguish the Earth could not have understood even if it had witnessed it, or heard the groaning of the suffering Sons of GOD, whose spirit was often well-nigh broken.

THE PERIL OF THE WORK

To be Daysman for Israel was, therefore, full of peril. It was so even prior to the Manifestation. Has it not been said unto you that the opposing forces had to be met? That the conditions had to be entered into? That the powers of the Air had not only to be changed, but broken? That the principalities had to be overthrown?

The Work was that of the LORD Regnant. It could not have been borne by the Servant, except as the venue through which there were poured forth electrical forces from the FATHER-MOTHER. The Master was the vehicle. He had to move as the Divine World commanded. He had to act as the Spirit led Him amidst the wilderness conditions which had been created within the intermediary Heavens of the Earth, as well as upon the outer planes.

All this was prior to the Manifestation. These things took place in the betrayed intermediary world; for there great declension had taken place, and even descent. Crushing burden-bearing had been introduced. When He was asked to become the Daysman for Israel, even in the days of the Manifestations named Moses and Elijah, not to speak of others, He had to meet many of those forces as He approached the Bethlehem unto which he had to descend in order to convey revelation unto some of those Elders of Israel who were able to rise to receive the Divine Mystery. Even then the mission was a ministry of peril.

How little you understand this Mystery of the Travail begotten of the Betrayal and the conditions which arose in this world, as the Divine LORD ministered through HIS Servant unto HIS servants Israel in the midst of their suffering! So tremendous were the opposing forces in the intermediary world when the Manifestation known as the Christhood (with which you are familiar), was projected, that it had to be kept secret. Therefore do not for a moment imagine that when the Master came to these planes, there was a great blare of trumpets, or that every one was aware that a Divine event was taking place. That was not so. *He came in secret. He had so to come.* The Heavens had to overshadow, guard and protect those who preceded Him. And when He came, a heavenly invisible cordon had to accompany Him. And they had to do so during the Manifestation. There were no Stories concerning His miraculous coming and birth, such as came to be recorded. (You will find in the "Logia" that such Stories were told by Himself as Celestial and Divine Mysteries and Angelic Revelations.)[1] It was only in the midst of His Ministry in the days of the Manifestation that

[1]The Logia, or Sayings of the Master.

the enemy discovered through those who were followers
of the Message He brought, who He was, and set about
to defeat the Manifestation. This latter they did accomplish in part through causing to be changed the wonderful
Teachings He gave to His intimate friends. For although
the Gospel Stories are beautiful in their way, yet notwithstanding their beauty, and the fact that the western world
has had them for over eighteen centuries, the western
world is still quite in the dark concerning the character
of the Messenger known as the Master, the nature of a
Jesushood and the mission of a Christhood. It has learnt
practically nothing of how a Soul can come into the
estates of Jesus, Christ, and the LORD; nor how a Soul
becomes a Son of GOD in high realization of HIM Who is
the Eternal Mystery of all things; nor how all Souls
share that Mystery in the secret place of their Being.

LIGHT ON HIS SORROW AND GRIEF

Now from this unveiling of the ancient relationship of
the Master to Israel and His position as Daysman, you
will be able the better to understand the cause of much
of the sorrow which He had in the days of the Manifestation. I refer to sorrow which was apart from that of the
Gethsemane which broke upon Him in the latter days,
as He realized all that would have to be accomplished.
There was always a latent sorrow in Him, even from the
early years of the Earth-life part of the Manifestation. By
His spiritual estate He was a chalice of Divine Joy in
His inner Being; yet He became the Man of Sorrows. The
sorrow was not because He had to lay down His earth-life.
In purpose He had done that before He came. Nor was it
because He had to enter into the awful states represented
in the intermediary world by the outer darkness and the
pestilential fires begotten of misdirected passion. He
sorrowed because of the operations of those enemies who

were seeking to overthrow the Will of the FATHER-MOTHER
and defeat the Manifestation. Therefore, from time to
time He warned His intimate ones of this danger. He
counselled them to live divinely; to be wise with the
wisdom of the Spirit; to guard unto the uttermost the
Treasures of GOD which had been committed unto
them.

Towards the close of the Manifestation ministry, when
He discovered the intensity of the activity of those who
were opposed to such a Manifestation of the Christhood
from the Divine World; who were determined to destroy
the vision of that Christhood so that those for whom it was
made manifest and unto whom the Teachings were given,
should not be able to rise up into the realms of consciousness signified by so Divine and glorious an estate, He
Himself became smitten. As Daysman He was the
magnetic centre for the inrush of the inimical forces.
They crucified Him, not simply on the Roman Cross,
which was as naught compared to the crucifixion of the
FATHER-MOTHER'S Message to Him and through Him;
they crucified Him when they misrepresented Him, and
miraged His Teachings beyond recognition.

Hence His sorrow. Well might He pray—

"*O, my Father-Mother! This world hath not known Thee.*"
Well might He say to those who came to confound Him
when they asked upon whose authority He made such
statements concerning the ETERNAL ONE, that though
they claimed to be the children of Abraham, yet, had they
known Abraham, they would also have recognized Him
and the Message which had been given Him to declare.

*   *   *   *   *   *

As Daysman for Israel during the several Manifestations from the Bethlehem, He became the centre of attack
by the opposing forces that were active in the intermediary

realms, though not in the acute way in which He had to realize that position during the days of the Manifestation as He moved amidst the Galilean Hills, the highways of Samaria, and the cities of Judea.

HIS RELATIONSHIP CONTINUES

Now, with such an inner relationship between the Master and the Sons of GOD, and the continuation of that relationship through the great ages which have passed wherein He remained the Elder-Brother of those whom the FATHER-MOTHER had given to Him to Shepherd and bring up as His celestial family, rear them into higher states of consciousness, and lead them into fuller vision of the Sacred Mystery, it was most natural that that relationship should abide. The Message of the Manifestation was unto the finding of His Brethren. The Oblation was to make it possible for them to come back into the High Realms—Angelic, Celestial, and in a measure Divine. These are all Divine; but when we speak of the Divine World it expresses a more intense form of realization.

During the Oblation He could not consciously contact any of them. He did not know them; they did not know Him. He was a veiled and lonely sojourner amidst a dreary land of awful states with which He had to deal. The relationship was not suspended; but the consciousness of it had to be suspended from the time when He passed away in Galilee to take up the burden of the Oblation. His consciousness was only suspended—*for consciousness never dies*. Just as your own consciousness is suspended during the night, so was His. When you lie down to rest the outer vehicle, the physical and mental go to sleep; but your consciousness does not die, it is only suspended in those parts within the vehicle of the mind in its lower capacity, and in the outer vehicle. But the moment you wake, your consciousness returns, and you remember what preceded your rest. You may even remember what had been taking place during the night-watches when your consciousness had been operative elsewhere. Sometimes a veil is immediately passed over between the inner and the outer, so that you cannot remember. Sometimes you may get glints and gleamings of things that have been seen and heard by you during the night-watches. You will understand, therefore, how consciousness is unbroken in its nature and in its power. It is Eternal. It is of the Eternal. Yet it can be suspended in its operation.

It was thus that the consciousness and memory of His friends was suspended. Indeed, had His consciousness been fully operative, He could not have endured the burden He carried. It was a part of the sublime sacrifice that had to be made. In the laying down of His Life there had to be the laying down of that consciousness which can look out and remember everything; for He possessed such. It had to be laid down in the sense of being veiled, to enable Him to bear the burden of the Cross of carrying out the procedure whither He went in the oblatory service. Nor could the restoration of that consciousness be endured until the Oblation was accomplished, all the generations (His incarnations) had been fulfilled, the Forty Lives lived, and the burden that weighed them down, borne.

What such Relationship Implies

But there had to be the return to that consciousness with the completion of the Oblation; and with it the restoration of the old relationship with Israel and all that such relationship implied for Him as the Daysman for Israel, and for them as the Sheep of the Fold over whom He had been appointed Shepherd. It could not be otherwise.

That Israel is now awakening and arising unto an

individual and communal manifestation of the Christ-hood, is most obvious. The Sons of GOD are coming back to re-possess the land of their Celestial Inheritance of the ancient times. And with this return, great recognitions are coming back to them, and sublime realizations are becoming within them. In that return of all Israel as the Sons of GOD who were the Ancients or Christs in this world, and the return of Him who was appointed as their Daysman, there is also the return in Him of the consciousness of the intimate relationship He holds to all Israel, and the necessity for the whole body of the Christ-hood to be restored.

*   *   *   *   *   *

Now, as in the ancient days, even long before the Fall was fully accomplished, there was such an intimate relationship established between Him who was appointed Daysman for the House of Israel and the community of the Sons of GOD who were manifesting, that there could be communication between them by magnetic-electric power in the spheres where they were and where He was. And owing to this intimate relationship it may be under-stood how it came to pass, as they descended further and further in their state in the midst of the fallen Earth, that the Heavens felt sympathetically and magnetically their going down, and were filled with their pain, and felt the motion of the sorrow which overtook them, and the bitterness of the anguish of their travail, and how, because of their great need, the Oblation was projected. And it may likewise be easily apprehended that, because of that intimate relationship they sustained to Him, He was chosen as the vehicle through whom the Oblation could be accomplished by the LORD of Being, for the restitution, the return, and the regeneration of all Israel.

*   *   *   *   *   *

Now such a relationship of the past which was continued through great ages, implies, that in every awakened and arising Israelite, there shall come back the consciousness of that ancient relationship, so that to Him who has been the Daysman, and who will remain the Elder-Brother of Israel and be always Shepherd and the vehicle of Divine Revelation unto them (so long as the Divine Will so appoints), must be restored that old relationship between the House of Israel and Himself.

And through the restoration of that old intimate relationship in high consciousness, it must be borne in mind that He once more feels all that is taking place in every Son of God represented in Ancient Israel; because all are members of His Flock. Thus also comes it to pass, that the measure of His Return is also the measure in which He feels the Travail of Israel within Himself, as that Travail is adumbrated magnetically upon Him and received unto Himself through the play of the electric forces projected from all the travailing, sorrowing, pain-stricken, heavily burdened Israelites.

* * * * * *

What is the meaning of Daysman unto the uttermost Regeneration of all Israel, but the Mediatorial Office wherein the one appointed Mediator receives the magnetic emanations from every member of the Ancient Christhood who is returning, and ministers unto them by means of Divine electric forces unto the transmutation of the elements within them? His relationship to the Sons of God in the Heavens, was and still is most real. The relationship upon the Earth is also most sacred and real. Would that every Son of Israel could realize this! For in the realization of it, there would also be understood the relationship of each member to the corporate body; and there would be realized how one member cannot be smitten without all the other members suffering. And it would likewise be understood and realized that, in the degree in which all the members are smitten, so is the Daysman.

*   *   *   *   *   *

Concerning the Redemption of the Land of Judah, such an event depends entirely upon the measure of the Return of the Sons of GOD. For they have to accomplish that other part of the Redemption of the Earth. They are to make up that which could not be accomplished as a dual ministry during the days of the Oblation. Because it must be fully understood that the Oblation was the Planetary part of the great work. It was Cosmic. It was not only full of Cosmic operation from the Solar Body; it had to deal with Cosmic forces from other systems. The Sons of GOD have to deal with those forces as they are found in accommodated state in the individual and communal life, by giving beautiful manifestation of the Christhood and right direction to all those who desire to be children of love and wisdom. The awakening and arising of the Sons of GOD to their ancient racial consciousness, will be sufficient to hold them in the remembrance that the Redemption of the world is dependent upon the arising of all Israel, and the various branches becoming unified as a race of the Celestial Christhood. And as members of that family of Christs, it will be recognized by each one how important it is that the full Regeneration of all Israel should be accomplished. For only through such a triumphant arising can all be once more united in HIM Who is the living Vine, of Whom we are branches.

May all remember their intimate relationship to the Heavens, and praise the FATHER-MOTHER for HIS kindness, HIS wonderful Love, the glory of HIS Wisdom

expressed in the ways of His going on their behalf throughout the ages and revealed through His Servant whom He
appointed Daysman for His Israel and the vehicle of the
Divine Love as it received into its very Heart the deluge
of the opposing elemental streams unto their transmutation
for the healing of the Heavens of this world, and the
bearing back upon the Bosom of His Love, the whole
Household of Ancient Israel, and also proud Ephraim,
but with his pride changed into the spirit of a little child!

THE BOOK OF ISAIAH

PART ELEVEN

THE MASTER

AS THE

APPOINTED REDEEMER OF JUDAH

*Showing the double capacity of the Priest-
hood of the Master, the sad state of
this world and all its Children,
how the Head of the Planet
suffered and travailed, the
nature of the Redemption
for the Planet-Soul
and all her
Children.*

CONTENTS

237

Lord God of Abraham, Isaac, and Ya-kob-El! In Thy Majesty Thou fillest all Thy Heavens, and stoopest to make manifest Thy Glory unto the Sons of this Earth.

Thy lesser children bathe in Thy Radiance though they do not yet know whence it proceedeth; and thus partake of Thy bounty, though they have not yet beheld the vision of the Divine Giver.

For Thou scatterest the gifts of Thy Love wheresoever Thou treadest, and makest known Thy Goodness through the great Gentleness of Thine approach.

Thou hast saved the Earth in the day of her great distress, and defended her from the full effect of the calamity that overtook her; in the Majesty of Thy Love Thou hast purified her Heavens and redeemed them, and opened up the way for all her afflicted children to be restored to the Home of Eden, healed of all their woundings, and re-garmented in beautiful robes of true Childhood to Thee.

Thou hast made possible this day of their Awakening and their Redemption; for Thou hast travailed greatly by means of the Oblation for their recovery and restoration to the Heavenly Household.

In their Home-coming they shall surely sing Songs of Gladness, and make melody in their hearts unto Thee.

And they shall hear of Thy marvellous works on their behalf, and turn with thanksgiving unto Thee.

Then shall the whole Earth resound with heavenly laughter and joy, and in the fulness of Life make manifest Thy Glory.

And Judah shall, once more, be a Land of Delight.

Amen and Amen.

THE MASTER

APPOINTED REDEEMER OF JUDAH

A FEW weeks ago I was moved to speak to you on the subject set forth in one of the passages of the Book of Isaiah as it has been recovered, on "The Master as Daysman for Israel and Redeemer of Judah," as it is intimated in the prophetic writing,—"Behold I appoint him, my Servant, who shall be Daysman for Israel and Redeemer of Judah." In that unveiling it was necessary to confine the unveiling to the first part, "The Daysman of Israel." This evening I would carry you with me whilst we look at the second part, "The Master as the appointed Redeemer of Judah."

With a brief introductory word which will be in the form of a résumé of the previous address so that you may be able to gather up and correlate what was there revealed, with what may be said this evening, I would unveil the subject to you under these five aspects:—

> The Outlook of the Master:
>
> Counting the Cost:
>
> The Great Adventure:
>
> The Work accomplished:
>
> The Work yet to be accomplished:
>
> The Redemption to follow the Oblation.

Those of you who were present some three or four weeks

ago, may be able to recall the address on The Daysman of Israel, and remember the relationship which the Master had sustained to Israel when as a Community of the Sons of GOD long ages prior to the Manifestation, and prior to their own advent upon the planes of this world, they were shepherded by Him. You will recall how, as one mediating within another sphere, He Himself had grown up before the Divine Love and Wisdom and attained to such realization of the Presence as endowed Him with the consciousness which enabled Him to be appointed to mediate, in the special way that was necessary, unto those Sons of GOD who afterwards became known as "The Community of Israel," and the "Christs of GOD," upon this world.

You will remember that He was appointed Shepherd and Leader, the Interpreter of the Will of the FATHER-MOTHER for ministries unto those Sons of GOD, and how during the ministry of ages there grew up such an intimate relationship between them that they became His children in a celestial sense; and that He became their Elder Brother through identification with them in their life, their experiences, and their own ministries, as He mediated unto them yet more fully of the Mystery of the FATHER-MOTHER.

You will also recall how He spake of those over whom he had been set as Shepherd, as his sheep even in the days of the Manifestation, and therefore great ages after they had been appointed to come here for ministry, thus revealing that the relationship between them and Him continued.

In that intimate relationship He was appointed from time to time, as they required special revelation, the Messenger of the FATHER-MOTHER. It was thus He came to them as Adam, the first Divine Messenger to the Children of Israel—though Adam is usually confounded with the beginning of the Human Race on the Earth.

The Adamic Race, as those of you who have read the Teachings will know, was composed of the Sons of God. The races of the Earth became mixed up with the story of the Adamic Race. In later ages He was sent to the Sons of GOD under other names. But they were all Divine names. Even the word Adam is Elohistic. So is Moses. Under this latter term He revealed to them anew the Laws of GOD as those Laws were laid deep in the foundations of their own Being; and in relation to their own experiential life; and how those Laws were operative in the Planetary Constitution; and likewise in the Celestial Spheres, which they had known but of which they had lost the memory through their dwelling upon the distraught planes of the Earth, ministering to the fallen children, and sharing the burden of their travail.

He also unveiled to them how He came to them in other forms of manifestation upon the Solar Bethlehem, and afterwards, how He was appointed Daysman. And you will remember (and it is necessary for you to understand this), that a Daysman was not simply a Redeemer, but a Divine Mediator. He was one who stood between two different positions.

In this interpretation of the Office, you will see where the Ecclesiastical Authorities and Divinity Schools went astray when they thought that the Master, as Daysman, had to stand between GOD and Humanity; whereas He was appointed to stand between the Sons of GOD whilst they ministered on the Earth-planes, and the inimical forces that played upon them from the fallen intermediary world. For He became like a vortex, in one sense, acting for the time being like the Vortexya of Israel to defend them, and to cause the inimical influences to take a different direction; for this was His work as Daysman, though at that time the work of the Oblation had not begun. Such an one having been appointed as Mediator unto the Sons of GOD to help them even upon the planes of this Earth amidst their travail, and to share sympathetically their sorrow and their pain, how natural it was that He should also be chosen to be the vehicle of the Manifestation for Israel in order that they might have a representation of the glorious Christhood estate in which they had once dwelt; to be followed later by that further redemptive process on their behalf by which He became their Redeemer during the ages of the Passion of the Oblation. And though He knew them not any longer, yet He recognized something in them as He met them on the way, and they recognized something in Him as they met Him on the way. They all sensed something strangely intimate, He of them, and they of Him; but they knew not each other to enable them to designate who they were, and what they had been to each other. They had no true recognition. Indeed such could not have been endured by Him during the ages of the Oblation; therefore, the Divine Wisdom veiled Him deeply; and veiled them sufficiently to prevent them from recognizing Him in the travail.

THE OUTLOOK OF THE MASTER

You know that the Oblation was primarily borne for Israel though it was not their burden. It was the Karmic burden of the Planet which kept them down, prevented them from arising and regaining their ancient Christhood estate wherein they could walk and serve in the consciousness of the ensphering and overshadowing of the Holy One.

Primarily, the Manifestation was for the Recovery of Israel. The Master came to seek unto the finding of His sheep. They were those spoken of by Him as the lost sheep of the House of Israel. He came to gather them together into the Fold which once they formed.

You will observe how these Parables take on new meaning. And wherever new meaning may have fallen upon them during the past years of our ministry, still greater light has yet to fall upon many of them. In them when fully unveiled, you will see the more intimate inner relationship of the Master to the sheep of the Fold over whom He was made Shepherd.

Before He came, and when He came, He had to look out and recognize all He had passed through as Daysman for Israel in the Intermediary World when He defended them from the onslaught of the enemy whose inimical forces sought to undo any good that had been accomplished, and to make impossible the arising of the Christhood upon the planes of the Earth. When He came in the days of the Manifestation, it was most natural that He should be so appointed to come to seek His own. He knew them by name. He recognized them through the spiritual relationship. He knew them through the inner vision, and drew them as those who had been of the ancient Fold.

There were also those who were not of that Fold, but who were most noble and beautiful, whom He met on the way, and whom He had to call. He knew His own sheep. And although they did not know Him, for most of them were veiled, yet they came to recognize something in the Message and the manner of its presentation.

When He looked out on the world, could any one for a moment imagine what His thoughts became, and how the streams of His emotion were affected? When He looked out upon the world He saw the state in which it was, and knew from experience how tremendous were the inimical forces which were playing upon all the House of Israel directly, and indirectly preventing the Solar Ministries from restoring the Planet and its Kingdoms. He saw the tragedy that had befallen the Earth and the evil outworking of it, and He wondered whether it would be possible within the time appointed, which had relation to the Celestial arrangements, to accomplish the Redemption of the Earth as well as the Return and re-ascension of Israel.

Whatever traditional thought you may have held in past years concerning the Master, never imagine for a moment that His Life was free from pain, sorrow, and travail. Though such things were not revealed then through Him, or by Him, yet at times His most intimate ones saw Him sorrow. There were occasions when His sorrow was so deep He had to go apart from them for aloneness and re-cuperation, that He might indraw the Divine Life-stream, and know in fulness for a time, the Overshadowing and Indwelling Power.

He was aghast when He saw the conditions; and these latter made Him question in His heart whether it would be possible within the given time to bring the Land of Judah back. For remember this, that the Laws of GOD are operative Divinely, Celestially, and Angelically, as well as in the Human state, and generally in the Planet's spheres. And there are certain things that can be accomplished only when the Celestial positions are such as to enable the work to be effective.

As He looked out He wondered—"Is it possible even by means of the Oblation, to redeem and restore the Earth within the given time?"

COUNTING THE COST

He had to count the cost. No man undertakes a great work without counting the cost. That does not mean counting the cost of the individual sacrifice to be made—though such will pass before his vision and be weighed in the scales of the ministry. It was not a personal cost. It was not the cost to Him individually. It was the cost involved in the Divine Passion.

Oh! that all could understand the Divine Passion as it should be understood, as surely it will be understood some day by Israel! In that day, the understanding of it will be quite impersonal. It will even cease to be merely individual. Indeed it will become so Cosmic, so Divine, that all will recognize in every part of it, the LORD ADONAI in the motion of HIS Eternities through the Divine and Celestial Heavens and the heavens of this system; also through the Solar body, and all who had to share something of the pain and the sorrow of the world's distraught condition.

Oh, ye who would pass by! The day will come when ye will cease to pass by; when ye will open your understanding to the realization of that which the Divine Love and Wisdom accomplished for this struggling Earth, and all the Souls lost upon it.

When the Master counted the cost of the Burden, it was the cost in relation to the great Passion of the LORD. To think and to know that HE Who is all Loveliness because HE is the Perfect One, should have to find such a way for the blotting out of the world's evil; for the transmutation of the fallen elements; for the restoration of the Earth's fallen Kingdoms; for the healing and the redemption of all the afflicted children of men, and the return of that once most glorious Community of Souls who were the embodiments of Love, the radiators of Wisdom, the revealers through their embodiment and ministry of the Son of GOD as HE had been realized in their own childhood to the FATHER-MOTHER!

Such was the outlook in the Master's vision. Can it be realized? The question was ever before Him. There were many things that He spake which had to be veiled, and many that had to be left unrecorded. But even in such Sayings as have been recorded in the Logia, you will find passages where there seems to be a questioning in His

245

own Being concerning this very matter. Yet He said to Himself, as He had occasionally to say to His intimate ones—I came to do the Will of HIM Who sent me and to accomplish HIS work. It is mine to do it, and to do it full of the great hope that HIS Passion will have the grand resultant.

THE GREAT ADVENTURE

Then came the Great Adventure. I have so named it because each life was an adventure. It was atmosphered in Mystery. It rose; it accomplished an arc of the circuit; and then it set as it rose, full of the Mystery. Every life, every one of the Forty Incarnations, was full of the consciousness of the Mystery, without any definition of what it meant. It was full of an inward motion that could not be defined. There was always a strange impulse to go in a way of service that had to be recognized as one that might bring sorrow. There was the urge to pursue a path that of very necessity raised the Cross at every cross-road, and indeed caused its shadow to be thrown along the whole pathway between the cross-roads. The inward motion was to accomplish something that was not revealed, and which had to be done without being understood.

It seems impossible to realize that it was so. To many it will appear incredible. Are not all the ways of the FATHER-MOTHER, even concerning your own life seen from certain standpoints, incredible? HIS Paths are in the Great Deep. HIS Wisdom is beyond searching. HIS ways are not the ways of men or women. HIS outlook is Universal. And it is so even when related to a particular world. And it is even so when HIS energies are centred upon one Soul. *All His Ministry is Cosmic.* HE works for the enrichment of all: HE never gives to one unto the impoverishment of another; nor labours for the exaltation of one through

the humiliation of another. HE works unto the enrichment of all, though all cannot receive that which HE pours
into the chalice of the Being. HE works cosmically, even
when HE deals with one Soul. And how much more fully
is that true when HE operates within an Israelite; indeed,
when HE deals with one whom the world's guile has
influenced, and has to empty the heart and the mind of
that guile so as to restore the Being. *God's ways are perfect.*

The longer I live, even on these planes, the more
conscious am I of the perfection of HIS Love and HIS
Wisdom. There never could be in my thought the dim-
mest shadow concerning HIS ways in the perfection of their
loveliness and their wisdom.

So, in the Great Adventure of the Oblation, the Master
in each Life had an arising, a meridian, and then a setting,
as He fulfilled His Mission by following the path necessary
for the accomplishing of the Great Work appointed unto
Him to do, and thus completed in each Life the full circuit
of the Arc. When His pilgrimage is beheld from the Inner
Worlds, it does appear to have been marvellous how it was
done. And this is true not only when related to the Master.
It is marvellous when seen in relation to the whole of the
Mystery, from the Master upward to the LORD ADONAI
Who accomplished the Passion through Him. It is marvellous
how the exquisitely beautiful relationships were sustained
from the Divine World when the Master was let down into
the vortex of the awful conditions within the Planetary
Heavens to become the centre of magnetic attraction, and
the venue for the electric Solar Force necessary for the
annihilation of *the graven images*, and the changing, the
purification, and the transmutation of the elements. The
base was in the Divine World of the most sublime but
mysterious triangle, the inverted apex of which rested in
the Soul of the Master. Through that triangle the Solar

World poured its redeeming force. And there was in the Great Adventure, a revelation of the most exquisite beauty of arrangement made by the Divine Love and Wisdom.

By this means, great things were accomplished. Some of these may now be unveiled; and also that which has yet to be done, and on whom the responsibility rests for the doing of it.

THE WORK ACCOMPLISHED

You think of the Oblation only in relation to the covert way in which it has had to be presented, as something borne by the Master in a very special way as He functioned and worked within the Astral and Occult realms, bearing the burden for Israel and for Judah; of the Divine passion bearing Him on; of the urge He never could resist; of the power that never let Him drown in the great sea, though He had many things to do which filled His Soul with sorrow unspeakable, the power that carried Him through the deep waters, poisonous with the foul elements that had been introduced into them; of the transmuting forces of the Solar body which operated through Him unto the purification of those waters, and the restoration of the upper seas of the Planet.

But as you think of these things, think also of these further things accomplished as tokens of the triumph of the Divine Love in and through Him—the Passion borne; the Intermediary Kingdom purified; the Planet's Heavens restored; the rehabilitation of Angelic Life upon their circles; the restoration of the Angelic intercommunication between those on the upper circles of the Solar Angelic World as it is now, with those in the Angelic Kingdom of the Planet.

These things have been accomplished. And in the work

the Kingdom founded by Esau[1] has been overthrown; the seat of the inimical powers has been changed; the spirit that dominated the Heavens of the Planet has been cast out; and the false regnancies have ceased. Thus, in the healing of Esau; in the changing of his kingdom; in the purification of the Planet's Heavens and the making possible the ascension of all the House of Israel to receive again high illumination and enter into communication with the Angels and the Saints who are in the Solar Heavens; in the overthrow of all those who were enemies of the Christhood Manifestation, and the establishing of the Kingdom of Heaven upon the Earth, crowned with the restoration of the Planetary Heavens and the regnancy of Ya-akob-El the Planetary Angel who has begun to take on something of his ancient glory, there is made manifest what the Oblation has achieved.

There is joy within the Divine Realm of this world to-day. The effect of the Oblation is manifest upon Israel; and also upon Ya-akob-El, for the kingdom of Esau is changed.

Not only so; but also as the result of these things, the sphere of Lucifer has been affected so deeply, that it has now become possible (if the Redemption can proceed uninterrupted), to restore the Planet's balance, and with it, the Elemental Kingdoms of the Earth. These are not the kingdoms over which men reign; they are the Kingdoms of the Planetary Angel, Ya-akob-El. It may seem of little importance whether you know anything of the Angel of the Planet; or the realm that once was the seat of the regnancy of Esau; or anything concerning Lucifer, the Angel of the Planet's outer spheres. These names have passed before your vision and been adumbrated upon your audient chamber as the Teachings have been unveiled

[1]See the volume on Ezekiel in which this subject is specially unveiled.

to you. But you think individually and personally, rather than in relation to the Cosmic whole. It may be you think of Life within the circumscribed area of your own communities and nationalities. You think of your own race—the race to which you belong on the Earth-planes— perhaps in a way that leads you to forget that you must also think of and care for other races, because they belong to the great spiritual family of the Divine Love. You must needs think in a Cosmic way of those who are administrators in the Intermediary Worlds; of all the children of the Earth; and likewise all the children of Luna. For all these are to be affected by the Redemption, and are, therefore, dependent upon the arising and ministry of the Sons of God.

That is the work you have to do. Through the restoration of the regnancy of the Planetary Angel; the change by the Oblation of all the Intermediary realms, and the effect of such a change upon Lucifer, the Angel of the Seventh Sphere of the Celestial Hierarchy of this Planet; there has been provided a fulcrum for leverage of a Cosmic nature towards the accomplishment of the full Redemption of all the children of the Planet, including those of Luna.

The Oblation was meant to be a Planetary, a Celestial, a Divine Work. It was neither personal nor individual, although a Son of the Highest had to be used as the vehicle and become the vortex for the inrush of the inimical conditions; and also the venue through which the Solar energy could be exercised unto the changing of the whole Intermediary elemental world.

THE WORK YET TO BE ACCOMPLISHED

What more is there to be accomplished? As you look out on the world and see its states, you sometimes think it is utterly hopeless. You imagine the Redemption seems as far off as ever, because you cannot see beyond the outer places. But that is not so. It is nigh at hand. If your face is always to the ground, you will never see the glory of the Sun either rising, ascending to his meridian, or in the splendour of his setting. If that be so on the outer spheres, how much more so is it true in the Inner World of your Being. If you see the World and Life only from your own circumscribed area, then you cannot understand how it can be accomplished in the individual, the communal and the national embodiments.

To see the way of the LORD in the Planet's Household effecting the Redemption of all, you must lift up your faces to the roseate hues of the Dawn that is breaking. You must be great in the purpose of your Being, whilst never forgetting any necessary service on the personal plane to the one nearest you, nor to many others, nor to yourself. You must be Divine! You must try to be impersonal in your allusions and interpretations, and never forget that you are an individual unit of the Cosmic whole, even whilst you hold the high and deep consciousness of a child of the Great Mystery, one who has HIS Mystery hidden in the Principle of your Being. If you so think and act with your face to the Divine Orient, then you will take on the likeness of the Divine Fashion in your attributes; and you will behold all things in HIS Light, and witness HIS tremendous redeeming agencies and processes in the World. You will recognize HIS Cosmic operations. You will cease to be merely individual. You will think communally and nationally in relation to the human race; and ultimately you will think in relation to the Cosmic whole. In that Day you will relate all to HIM Who is the First and the Last; the beginning and the consummation of all our Being, the Planet's Life, and the Celestial expositions. You will live henceforth in the consciousness of HIM. You will realize that HE is the ALL; that HE is in all; and that all is meant to be for HIM. For all are to be the embodiments of HIS Mystery.

The Redemption to follow the Oblation

There is still much to be accomplished. The Daysman
of Israel was appointed to find the Sons of GOD and
shepherd them. The Message has come to do so. He was
also appointed to be Redeemer of the realm of Judah, the
Planet-Soul, whose bondage to fixed states was to be
broken. And He was to unloose the bonds of Lucifer and
set him free. Thus was the captivity of Ya-akob-El to end
triumphantly.

So are the bonds broken which have held the Household
of Israel in captivity throughout great ages. The bonds
which have held the children of the Planet in captivity
have now to be broken. These are of a different order from
those that held Israel. They are traditional. They belong
to the bondage of beliefs, superstitions, unrighteousness,
iniquity, injustice and inequality. You have now to do
this work and contribute to the breaking of all bonds of
evil. The Redemption of the Heavens has been accomplished. The bonds of the captivity of the House of Israel,
the Sons of GOD, have been broken. Lucifer is again free.
Ya-akob-El is free. You yourselves have been freed. Do
you feel that you have entered into liberty? Have
you the freedom of that Life which is none other than that
of a Son of GOD? Have you no consciousness of the
operations of the Redemption in you, and the effect of
such a Redemption upon you? Hear you not the Voice of
the ETERNAL ONE calling you to recognize that which has
been accomplished for your Redemption and Arising, and
also for your Ascension? Are you awakening and respond-
ing more and more fully to the Voice of HIM Who speaks
from the Eternal World? Have you no consciousness that
this Message has been sent to you for the purpose that
in your arising you might consecrate all your Being for
the awakening and uplifting of this world? Have you no

consciousness that, if you have found the Power of Truth, if you have seen it and felt it, then you must walk in it; and that if you walk in it, you cannot do so without affecting others, and compelling them by the constraining of Divine Love revealed through you, to recognize that it is the true way to the FATHER-MOTHER? Have you received this Message of Liberty that speaks of Eternal Peace, to keep it unrevealed, unspoken, unacted?

No, verily; for you have received it that you may make manifest that you are children of Peace because you are children of Divine Love; children of Compassion; children of Pity; children who would reflect HIM Who loves all and hates none, Who blesses all and never passes by one who can receive HIS blessing.

*   *   *   *   *   *

Great things are being accomplished as the result of the greater things in the Cosmic sense which have been accomplished. Great things lie ahead for you to accomplish, and you are called upon to do so.

That which the Oblation was never meant to accomplish is appointed unto the House of Israel as Sons of GOD, to fully effect. It is the Redemption of this world, not in the Cosmic way of the Oblation, but in the practical sense of every-day life. It is the healing of the Peoples; the changing of their traditions and their thoughts concerning social customs; the purifying of them in all the ways of their going; the relating of pity, the exquisite pity of compassion, to the majesty of Divine Love.

Remember this in your ministry, that it will be effective only in the degree in which a genuine spiritual atmosphere permeates it. I oft-times grieve that the Societies that are formulated to teach the people the purer way of diet and true humaneness, and to make manifest true compassion and pity, so often close their doors to everything spiritual. Many are merely dietetic traditionalists, and halfway-house compassionists. The principles for which they profess to stand are oft-times bound with the thongs of Tradition as severely as with the thongs of Theological thought.

If you would redeem the world, you must be the thing you profess. If you love, reveal it. If you are a child of compassion, make it manifest. If you are a child of the All Beautiful ONE, embody it. Let your wings of pity be spread over the needy and the defenceless everywhere, Humanity and Creatures.

If you would bear back the children of Judah to a sane, healthy and lovely life, teach them through your embodiment the beautiful way of love. If you would help back the children of Luna—those marvellous Celestial minds of a certain order which are related to that wonderful and glorious world (notwithstanding that it may now seem to be in a state of apparent impoverishment because of all it had to give up to keep this Earth alive in past ages, and save it against the day when the Divine Passion could redeem it)—then make manifest to such that ye are the children of Divine Love and Wisdom.

I would have you always be as little children in your mind and heart. I would have you always be lowly. The truly great must be lowly. Whilst I would always have you be of humble spirit, yet I would have you be great in Love, Wisdom and Power. This Message from HIM commands it of you. I would have the Divine potencies of your Being so active that they would become revealed in your embodiment.

How blessed it would be to have poured forth from you, GOD's power! The Deific forces within you set in action through HIS ensphering! To realize sublimely HIS overshadowing Radiant Cloud, so that your auric outflow on entering a room, would make the atmosphere spiritual, and those within it to be conscious of the Divine Awe—as if a Presence had come within!

Make your own home a scene of Angelic ministry. Wherever you go be ensphered by the Cloud of His radiance that your ministry be always Angelic. In all that you do in your life-service, be a revelation of Angelic ministry. Even in your hours of great burden-bearing, when you are carrying your own burden and also the burdens of others, be a manifestation of HIM Who took the burden of the fallen world upon His Heart.

For thus will your auric glory become the expression of His own. No day will be without HIM. No hour will be without HIM. No minute will be without HIM. Your whole life will be lived in the consciousness of HIM. You will walk in the consciousness of His ensphering. You will serve in the consciousness of His overshadowing. You will seek to realize in your consciousness the Light and Power of His Indwelling.

Ye children of the FATHER-MOTHER, if ye so recognize HIM and be His vehicles, how greatly the Heavens will rejoice! They are rejoicing; but how much more will their joy be intensified, increased and multiplied!

Everyone who rises and consecrates himself and herself may say in this hour—

"O my Father-Mother! My life is thine. Thou gavest it to me.

"Everything I have that is truly Spiritual, Divine, Deific, is of Thee; is from Thee; is enriched and upheld by Thee.

"I am Thine henceforth.

"I would live only in Thee; not for myself, but for Thyself;

"For Thou gavest me Thyself. Thou madest me Divine.

"And that which of Thyself Thou gavest me, I would give in service for Thee unto Thy children."

If we had such a daily consecration, the increase, though it might seem small at first, would grow larger and larger; for there would be the coming of the children who are meant to hear His Voice through this Message, and share in the Return and Consecration. The hope that fills the vision of our heart, the realization of which we know is to be, would come nearer the realization day by day. It would be hastened. And it would be a helping of the LORD to hasten it in our time.

You *will* all come, every one of you! You *will* put away every littleness and meanness you would be ashamed of, if they were exposed; you *will* chase away every shadow that has stolen across the threshold of your mind, or your heart, or your Inner Sanctuary! You *will* put away everything that would prevent the fulness of HIS glory shining within you and revealing itself through you unto the healing and redemption of the children of Judah and Luna, ánd through such healing and purification, the Planet's Kingdoms and all the Earth's elements!

You *will* all come back again into your ancient Celestial Christhood and Divine relationships!

And what a time of joy and rejoicing it will be when all Earth's shadows flee away, and you are once more manifesting the Cosmic Christhood, and delighting in the consciousness of the Inner Angelic, Celestial, and Divine relationships!

Ever blessed be His Glorious Name Who is our Father-Mother.
All praise be unto Him; all honour; all the dominion,
For all is His.
Of ourselves we have nothing; yet in Him we have the Eternal Riches, even unto the full knowing of Him.

* * * * * *

Most Glorious One, our Father-Mother, we are Thine.
Keep us near Thee evermore.
May we gain the power to make our Oblation upon Thine Altar.
May we attain the sublime Life wherein our whole Being makes perfect Sacrifice to Thee.

THE BOOK OF ISAIAH
PART TWELVE

THE FIVE CITIES OF EGYPT

Wherein is unveiled the mystical meaning
of the terms, Egypt, Assyria and Israel,
and how these are to be unified;
what the five Cities of Egypt
were and are; how they
may be won to speak
the language of
Canaan and
serve God.

CONTENTS

O Father-Mother! Unto Thy Holy Presence would we come with the sacrifice of Praise and Thanksgiving.

The Sanctuary Thou fillest with Thy Glory, and Thou callest us to enter within its Gates and be one with all Thy Hosts in their Adoration of Thee.

The motion of Cherubim and Seraphim draws us to Thy High Altar of Worship, Oblation, and Service, till our own motion of Being becomes unified in Thee.

In the Mystery of Thy Love for us, Thou hast made us to be as Sanctuaries for Thee wherein Thou mayest abide and reveal Thyself unto us.

Within us Thou hast placed the Mystery of Thine Ark of Covenant and Testimony with the Mercy Seat of Thine Oblatory, from which Thou dost nourish us with the Bread and Wine of Thine Own Flesh and Blood.

Thou openest all the Gates of our Being, and dost make them lift their Heads in the Worship and Praise of Thee;

For Thou hast caused the Doors of the Eternals to move that we may look into the Heart of Thy Holy Heavens and behold the revelation of Thy Radiance.

May we grow more worthy to be so honoured, more beautiful in our manifestation of Thee, and more like Thee in our Fashion and Service.

O Adorable Father-Mother! We would be altogether ever Thine!

Amen and Amen.

THE FIVE CITIES OF EGYPT

IN the Message of Isaiah there is a remarkable passage relating to Egypt, Assyria, and Israel. It is found amidst a strange mixture of spiritual and earthly things. It has been so changed from the original Scripture that it is difficult for anyone to perceive the profound teaching couched at the heart of it. It is like a precious gem which has been heavily veiled, and whose glory has been altogether hidden. As it stands, the light reflected and refracted has to find its way through a leaden atmosphere.

Yet the passage contains a string of perfect pearls of truth. It reveals the effect of the redemption of mankind, the result of the full healing of life, the equilibration of the polarity of the nations and the Planet, and the Celestial regnancy of Israel. It indicates and unveils in part the mysterious attributes of the Human Soul; and it even discloses the Mystery of the Divine World within the individuated Being. In its original setting the truth was stated in mystical terms; but those scribes into whose hands the Message came, understanding not the masonic significance of the terms and the real mystical teaching of the passage, were unable to rightly interpret it. They gave to it historical and religious interpretations of a racial order by dwelling upon the outwardness of things, thus making Egypt, Assyria, and Israel relate only to the Earth's races, and inter-communion between them. But, as we shall see, the real meaning of the passage is entirely spiritual, with a deep Cosmic significance; and the terms Egypt, Assyria, and Israel are like masonic passwords into great Mysteries.

ISAIAH'S USE OF CRYPTIC TERMS

The Prophet Isaiah wrote of the Soul. His Message was concerned with GOD in the Soul. He spake of the Divine World and its Purpose. He chronicled Messages concerning the Sons of GOD and their travail in this world. The healing of the Earth and all her planes and kingdoms as the outcome of the travail of the Divine World, was unveiled in marvellous ways. His Message was concerned with the coming Redemption of the whole Earth; the healing of all the elements which had been changed, hurt and misdirected; the transmutory processes by which those elements would be re-instated; and the resultant of the exaltation of the whole world to purer and happier conditions.

His Message is luminous with the glory of GOD. He beholds the Messengers upon the mountains. He sees that radiant morn which was the prophecy of the perfect day that was to be when even the dark places would be lit up, the valleys exalted, and the plains of the earth clothed with the radiance of the glory of the LORD.

He thus heralded the age in which harmony would come back to the Earth through the purification, restoration, and repolarization of all her elements. He sang of the time when all the antagonistic elemental conditions would be healed, and balance once more be restored. He spake of the return of the Christhood communities; of their march from the land of great weariness and sorrow to that land of supreme joy and perfect equipoise which once they knew. The light of his Message fell upon the path of their travail; and through its magnetic potency it changed that path from one of dreariness, loneliness, sorrow, and anguish, to one of great delight, angelic companionship, and sublimest realization. He described the transformation of the wilderness conditions so vividly that the very process of their change could be witnessed; and of the desert conditions he predicted the blossoming forth into the rose of Divine Love. For him the world thus became transformed from one garmented with impoverished raiment to one enriched because then clothed upon from the Heavens. He saw the wasted substances of the Earth touched from the Divine World, re-enriched and restored to their primal state. For him in that coming age the world would be a redeemed home for the children, and the triumph of the Divine Love and Wisdom made manifest. The Earth herself was again to be beautiful for situation; and her Jerusalem, or Spiritual Household, was to become a home of wonderful angelic ministries for all the children of men. Of the Holy City of Zion he often sang; that City whose streets were paved with gold, w hose walls were bejewelled with the gems of Divine virtues as described by the Seer; of its sacred Temple, or House of the LORD; and of the radiance with which the City was flooded from the Presence of the LORD Who was its Sun.

*   *   *   *   *   *

Closely allied to the realization of all these things were the Five Cities of Egypt; the commerce of Egypt with Assyria, and of Assyria with Egypt; and the directing and blessing of both through the regnancy of Israel.

In the exposition of the Mystery lying at the heart of the Five Cities referred to, we shall have to look at several things which are intimately connected with each other, though they seem quite separate. These are like separate stones in one sacred house: some stones belong to the pillars and some to the arches, and some deal with the exalted vaulting of the Temple of Being.

*   *   *   *   *   *

"In that day there shall be Five Cities in the land of Egypt which shall speak the language of Canaan."

Thus is the Mystery introduced. And in that day, it is said, the Egyptians shall come to Assyria, and the Assyrians shall pass down into Egypt and, ultimately, they shall become as one; after which Israel will become a third factor in the commerce, with the result that GOD shall bless them all; and there will follow the restoration and realization of great harmony between them.

Thus we have presented

Five Cities in Egypt which would speak the language of Canaan,

The association of Egypt with Assyria, and Assyria with Egypt,

The relation of Israel to Assyria and Egypt,

An implied Theocracy through Israel.

THE LAND OF EGYPT

In ancient symbology the land of Egypt represented the outer realms of manifestation, and also the field where the services of generation were rendered. And later in the Mysteries, it came to have a particular application to the vehicle of manifestation.

Descending from *the within* to the outer field of service, the Soul had to know limitation; for the vehicle through which it would make manifest would necessarily have to be accommodated to the realm of the manifestation. Therefore, the operations of consciousness would be circumscribed by the vehicle. This would be the case even in very old Souls, to some extent, and especially during the period of their unfolding into manifest life of manhood and womanhood through the vehicle. Only when they had come into the full possession of the vehicle with the power to dynamically raise all its constituent elements by processes of transmutation to operate within the realm of consciousness from which they had descended, could they dwell in that state of consciousness, and thus be free from the limitations ordinarily imposed upon Souls functioning on the outer planes of manifestation.

Thus the land of Egypt became for the Soul the vehicle through which it had to make manifest and serve within the outer planes of this world. In the unfallen days, to go down into the land of Egypt was quite safe, because the Planet's elemental kingdoms were all exquisitely balanced. The Atmospheria, or belts of atmosphere which were the spheres and scenes of various orders of ministry, were pure, magnetic, harmonious, exhilarating, and life-giving. Even the Christ-Souls were able to descend to the planes adjacent to them for purposes of manifestation and ministry unto the children of this world.

At that time Joseph—I-O-Seph—was ruler in Egypt, and his regnancy in the Earth was glorious. For I-O-Seph represented the Mystery of the Sign of the Cross at the heart of the world's manifestation, and the regnancy of righteousness and equity within even the elemental kingdoms; for the manifestation of righteousness within such kingdoms implied that the Planet's standard, or spiral, was in perfect estate; and equity represented the perfect balance of all the powers inherent in the Planet, so that all worked together for good and the perfect exposition of the Divine Will.

But it was quite different when the false Pharaohs arose and Egypt knew Joseph no more. For, whilst Joseph represented the Divine Presence in His world through the centrifugal and centripetal operations expressed in the Macrocosmic Cross; the false Pharaohs represented the materialization of spiritual qualities and quantities, the dominance of fixed conditions, and the compulsion exercised by those conditions upon the Soul to make it obey the Pharaoh.[1]

Thus it will be revealed to those who can perceive, what was the inner significance of the story of the bondage of Israel in the land of Egypt, with all the suffering endured by them, and their deep travail during the ages of their dwelling upon the outer planes of manifestation wherein they cried, oft-times, unto the Heavens for liberation. The bondage of Israel in Egypt; their affliction by the task-masters, or materialistic powers; the slavery to which they were subjected by the chief servants of the Pharaohs; and their deliverance by a GOD-sent Messenger, is a history of Soul joy and sorrow, pain and anguish, despair and hope, prayer and liberation, such as the ordinary readers of the Old Scriptures wot not of.

There is a Mystery contained within the heart of the story of Israel in Egypt and their deliverance, which, in the profundity of its meaning, exceeds the interpretations given by any of the Divinity Schools. It stands to this day as a story like a precious mirror of intimate and valuable Divine Revelation, which has become broken into frag-ments and scattered, yet each fragment still retaining something of the original power of the mirror to reflect the light of the Divine glory, travail, deliverance and redemption, of which this story speaks.

As will be presently seen, the re-conquest of Egypt, its unification with a redeemed Assyria, and its basking in the glory of an Israelitish or Christhood regnancy, meant the redemption of the body in all its powers, the restora-tion of the field for the service of generation to its primal

[1] For "The Mystical Meaning of the Pharaohs," the reader is advised to consult the Author's volume on The Message of Ezekiel, pp. 121-134 and 222-227.

pure estate, and the exaltation of the land of the outer manifestation to that degree of spiritual power and glory wherein it would become one with the Divine Will.

THE LAND OF ASSYRIA

Like Egypt, Assyria historically represents a great outward history and a remarkable religious expression finding exposition in the heart of ancient Babylonia. The Assyrians were accounted great in conquest, for many of them were earthly warriors. But they also had their great sculptors, and their sculpture was mighty in form and embodiment, and was akin to that which obtained in ancient Egypt.

But mystically, Assyria was a symbolic expression, and contained a hidden meaning. Whilst Egypt represented the outer realm of manifestation, the field of generation, and the vehicle through which the Soul functioned on the outer realms; Assyria represented the whole of the intermediary realms between the land of Egypt and the Angelic Kingdom. It was the land wherein the mind operated. It was the kingdom of formulated ideas. Those things which were to become manifest on the outer planes, were first conceived and formulated within the Kingdom of Assyria. Herein it was true in relation to the Soul, even as it was stated in the Proem of Creation in the Old Testament in relation to creation, when it is said that GOD created every tree, the shrubs, the herbs and the fruits, before they were manifest upon the Earth. So in the Human Soul's growth and evolving into higher consciousness, the realm of Assyria contains the field for the conception of ideas and the formulating of these— which may be called a process of mental generation—into concrete exposition. In the particular sense, Assyria represented the mind in its unfallen days when it had the untrammelled capacity, according to the order of Soul and degree of attainment, to operate between the Angelic Kingdom and the land of Egypt. The mind is the vehicle of the Soul's creative energies. Thus it enables the Soul to function through the higher understanding, or pure reason, within the Angelic World, and through all the lower degrees of the Assyrian realm even unto the land of Egypt, and administer as well as create, unto the fulfilment of the Divine Purpose. It will easily be conceived, therefore, how it came to pass that the Assyrian mind was great in power, in office, in field of ministry, with commensurate responsibilities.

In the fallen days Assyria became a land of inverted mental electro-magnetic states. As the Pharaohs in the fallen state represented the inversion of the life-forces, and the dominance and oppression of the taskmasters of impure desire, so Assyria represented the dominance of mental powers and the oppressive effect these had upon the Children of Israel. It was thus that, when the Assyrians went to battle against ancient Israel, overthrew their cities, made captives of the people, destroyed the Temple and took away all the precious vessels, the mystical story of the travail of Israel was raised from the outer life, or realm of Egypt and the Pharaohs, to the theatre of mental activities. For the conquest of Israel by Assyria, the destruction of their cities, and especially the destruction of their sacred House, with the loss of all the sacred vessels of the Temple, transferred the travail of Israel from the outer to the mental planes. The effect of the Assyrian oppression was to close, for long ages, the very gates of the Angelic Kingdom, so that unto Israel there could be no open vision of Spiritual and Celestial things. For, when the mind of the House of Israel was brought down from the realm of pure reason and understanding, with the consequent closing of the doors of the Intuition, the bondage and captivity of Israel became complete. In the mystical sense, the Assyrian dominance brought the mind of Israel into slavery amidst materialized conditions and false gods.

It will now be perceived what was the dual effect of the bondage in which Israel found themselves in the land of Egypt and the kingdom of Babylonia. For, not only were the great limitations of the fallen outer kingdoms of the Earth, with all the materialistic impositions of the Pharaohs, felt by Israel, but also that greater bondage of all the powers of the mind, from the field of objective vision, correlation and administration, to that of the Angelic World and the glories of its life and ministry; and together with these may be added the unspeakable spiritual loss of the powers and possessions named the sacred vessels of the Temple. For these latter had relation to interior states, potencies, and realizations.

THE LAND OF ISRAEL

The term Israel stood for the Divine World in the Soul system. To be an Israelite indeed, was to be one who had not only overcome amid the fallen conditions, but who had, long before the great Descent took place, attained to Angelic and Celestial heights. To be an Israelite indeed was to be the possessor of *Issa*, the Holy Spirit operating in individuated embodiment; *Ra*, the Eternal Light, or Lord of the Radiance, and, therefore, one whose whole Being was lit up with Divine resplendence; and to possess *El*, the LORD GOD of Sabaoth in high realization of HIS glorious Immanence in the Soul. Thus the Israelite was the Son of the HOLY ONE, the possessor of HIS Sacred Flame, HIS Radiance, and HIS Shekinah.

The land of Israel was that of the Christhood regnancy. It was possessed by the Soul when the LORD was *the*

Regnant ONE within the Sanctuary. It was, therefore, the land of vision, of Angelic communication, of Angelic fellowship, of Celestial illumination, of Solar World relationship, and of Divine communication.

The land of Israel was therefore named in the Mysteries —*The Inheritance of Canaan*. It was designated a land flowing with milk and honey. But these terms were of Divine significance. They were related to the Divine Life-stream, and the efflorescence, or sum of all the fruitage gathered by the Soul in its journey Zionward. We know that in the materialization of the Mysteries, Canaan was taken to represent the small parcel of land now named Palestine, and which became the home of Jewry. *But the real Canaan was a land of Celestial Mysteries, and for the Soul it represented a state of consciousness and a glorious inheritance.* It was the land wherein the full nourishing power of the Word of GOD obtained and prevailed, and wherein the quintessence of all the flowers of Divine manifestation was received, partaken of, and the enrichment thereof entered into.

It will be readily understood from this that the language of Canaan was nothing less than that of the Divine World. And as all things are built up upon signs and symbols, so the language of Canaan had the signs and symbols of the Angelic and Celestial Heavens. By means of these signs and symbols was the Word of GOD expressed. The language of Canaan was the language of Divine Love and Wisdom spoken within the Inner Heavens, and interpreted through all the Heavens of Divine manifestations. Thus, the language, when it had to be spoken for communicative purposes, was used by Israel who understood it; and the Divine ideas, concepts, and purposes, were translated into the language accommodated to the mind or land of Assyria. The language of Assyria was also built up of signs and symbols. When the message related to the land of Egypt it was transmitted through the land of Israel into that of Assyria; and then from Upper Assyria, or the realm of the Understanding, to Lower Assyria, or the realm of objective vision; and here again the language was accommodated to the realm, with suitable signs and symbols.

From all these it will be seen how intimate was the relationship between the Divine World, Israel, Assyria, and Egypt; and how the same message given unto Israel had to be transmitted in an accommodated language of signs and symbols through the spheres to the land of objective vision; also how it came to pass that in the fallen days these languages of the three great kingdoms became mixed. For it was thus that an impure form of Occultism arose wherein the heavenly signs and symbols took on a limited, mental meaning; that the inner vision became lost; and how that which was only of the lower field of intelligence and understanding, became confounded with spiritual realities and Divine events.

Through this influence, great was the fall of the ancient language of Canaan. For it actually came to pass that Israel, in the midst of their captivity to Egypt and Assyria, lost the memory of their ancient tongue, and spake for great ages in the language of Assyria and Egypt. To restore the ancient language for Israel by re-awakening in their memory some dim remembrance of their past, the Messengers and Prophets came.

* * * * * *

It will now be readily perceived what lies hidden in the expression—"In that day there shall be five cities in the land of Egypt which speak the language of Canaan." For, when Egypt is redeemed, Assyria exalted again to its true estate and realm, and Israel have fully restored to them the glorious vision and high consciousness of the Presence, all the powers of Egypt will be at one with those of Israel, and they shall speak with no uncertain voice the language of Canaan. In that day the LORD of Love will indeed be able to say—

Blessed be Egypt, My People; and the powers of Assyria, My handiwork; and Israel, Mine inheritance.

THE FIVE MYSTERIOUS CITIES

What were the Five Cities of Egypt which, in the great day, were to speak the language of Canaan? A city expresses a state. In mystical language it signifies the unification of the powers of the Soul and the inter-communal service of all the attributes. It is this particular aspect with which we are at present concerned. Those Five Cities represent the five senses with their centres and their powers. The five senses are usually thought of as having relation only to the outer vehicle. They are accounted constituent parts of the body. They may be named—the sense of vision, of audience, of taste, of discernment or sensing, and the sense of feeling. As Egypt represents the realm of generation in the outer kingdoms of manifestation, it is not unnatural to associate with Egypt the five senses, since they are regarded chiefly as powers of the body.

Now, notwithstanding the fact that so many who strive to unravel the mystery of evil imply that the Fall of this world was through the desire-body, students of these Teachings of The Order of the Cross will understand that the Fall was Planetary; though all the Planet's children and the House of Israel became involved. In the débâcle that overtook all the children when the great Descent was fully accomplished, all the senses became affected, from their source to the outer realm of their expression.

The effect of the changed Earth conditions upon the senses as these latter operated within and through the vehicle of the body, was disastrous; for they were all brought into bondage to the prevailing conditions, and more or less became slaves of the changed electro-magnetic powers. In this way the mind became subject to the powers of the body, or Egypt; and the spiritual man found himself in captivity within the Occult and Astral-Occult realms. Under those circumstances the Five Cities or senses that were in the land of Egypt, could not speak the language of Canaan. They spoke the tongue of the Egyptians, or the fallen Astral realms.

THE CITY OF VISION

The five senses named have not their origin in, nor are they circumscribed by, the land of Egypt. Nor is their potency confined to the kingdom of Assyria; they are of the nature and constitution of the Soul. In the land of Egypt they make manifest the secrets of GOD in the Soul. For vision is an attribute of the Soul itself. It has its correspondence in the various vehicles. These are related to the different planes. Upon all the planes the vision can be so correlated that the life of the Soul upon all its kingdoms of realization becomes one. It is harmonious and unified.

It is through the attribute of vision that the Soul cognizes, recognizes, and perceives unto realization, the Sacred Mystery we name the FATHER-MOTHER. When that attribute is deeply disturbed upon any of the planes, or within any of the degrees of its manifestation, a veil is drawn across the inner vision. Then the mind sees not and understands not; and, finding itself surrounded by darkness in the intermediary planes, it moves downward and outward until it comes to relate its attribute, chiefly if not wholly, to the outer vision.

In the fallen state the mind can use the attribute unto great hurt of itself and others, through the misinterpretation of the things observed, its failure to relate them to the Divine, and to correlate them to the Divine Kingdom within itself. Under such circumstances the City of Vision, in its particular and general experience, could not possibly speak the language of Canaan. It would not understand the signs and the symbols of such a language. The objective world with its wonderful elements and forms, would have little, if anything, to say of a Spiritual and Divine order; for the inverted vision would give only a materialized world, and not a spiritual home containing Spiritual, Celestial, and even Divine qualities and quantities of most precious elements. But when the attribute of vision is healed, so that the vision is true, and all things are understood in their spiritual nature and relationships, then the language of Canaan becomes spoken. The sense of vision, from the outer to the inner, becomes an avenue through which the Soul commences to acquire Divine riches, revealing the Divine Love, and upgathering the Divine Wisdom. For the language of Canaan in relation to the City of Vision, implies that from the outermost to the innermost, and from the lower degrees unto the highest degrees, Life is one sublime whole in the Eternal Mystery of the LORD of Being.

THE CITY OF AUDIENCE

As with the City of Vision, so is it with the attribute of hearing. The audient power in us belongs to the constitution of our Being; and in nature it is transcendently higher than the power to hear upon the outer planes the latter's sounds and articulations. Also in quality it is much greater, because it is a faculty through which the Soul can give audience to the Voice of the Eternal.

In the unfallen days when the Sons of GOD came to this

world, their City of Audience, or the faculty through which they could hear Celestial voices and motions, was intact. Through great ages it had been built up until its potency was such that one of the Gods could communicate through it a message from the ETERNAL. Amidst the fallen conditions, and owing to changed atmospheric pressure, occult and spiritual, the audient power gradually lost something of its potency and its capacity to differentiate sounds in general and intonations in particular. The result was a great loss to the Sons of GOD in their relation to the Celestial World. For their power to receive in audience from the Celestial Realms was so greatly lessened, that what was communicated had to be re-transcribed into the tongue or language of the Occult World. Herein this great loss to the Sons of GOD added to the labour of the Celestial World. For, however beautiful the language of the Occult World might be in its signs and symbols, and in its interpretation of these, it fell far short of the language of the Heavens.

It will now be the more readily understood how it came to pass that the language of the Intermediary Realms of Upper and Lower Assyria, and then Upper and Lower Egypt, mystically understood, failed to express truly the inner meaning of pure symbolism, and the spiritual qualities and quantities of the Soul and its manifested life. For it came to pass, when the inner audient power had lost something of its Divine potency (sufficient to prevent it from being able to receive directly from the Celestial Realms), that even Israel, and especially some tribes of Israel, became enmeshed in the net spread by a deteriorated occultism, and thus the language of Egypt came to relate only to outer powers and principalities. For the materializing spirit that grew up in Egypt as the result of occult dominance was very great. Even the realm of the

Gods was brought down. The potencies of the Soul, being changed into occult forces, soon became magical only in their uses as the Soul lost the power to hear the voices of the Lower Angelic Kingdom, since its audient powers were reduced to correspondence with the metallic intonations of the Occult and outer Kingdoms.

Great was the fall of the City of Zion in the Christhood, when it ceased to retain the open door of its audient chamber for the approach of the ETERNAL and HIS Message through one of the Gods. And great was the disaster which overtook this world when its Heavens became as brass, and the purported messages from the Gods and the Angelic World, were nothing more than the intonations of the language spoken by a fallen occultism and a benighted Egypt.

To the earnest students these things may reveal how it came to pass that in both Assyria and Egypt, the Gods were reduced to elemental forces and gross embodiments. And by all such it may be readily apprehended how even the Souls of men and women amid the fallen states and the dominance of material and Occult powers, and the loss of true religious vision, came to worship the powers of the air and the degraded creature forms. For the children of the Earth in the day of their terrible dread—a dread intensified in them by self-seeking sorcerers, magicians and priests, prostituted the Divine qualities of their Being in acts of worship and adoration at the altar of those elemental forces and barbaric powers.

THE CITY OF TASTE

This passing vista of the tragedy of the Earth in relation to the City of Audience within the Soul, will emphasize the significance of the meaning of the expression—"In that day shall five cities in the land of Egypt, speak the language of Canaan." For, in the Day of the Redemption of this world and all its children, the healing of the sores of Egypt and the restoration of the powers of Assyria, with the Regeneration and the re-endowment of the dwellers in the land of Israel, the language of Canaan shall be understood by Egypt and Assyria and all the Children of Zion.

Kindred to these is the meaning related to those other three Cities spoken of as Taste, Smell and Feeling. With a clear understanding of the attribute of Vision, and that of Audience, those of Taste, Sensing and Feeling, will be readily understood. These latter have undergone similar changes to those of Vision and Audience; for they also were caught in the maelstrom of the contrary streams set in motion during the great Planetary débâcle. The effect of the loss of taste for Divine Things, even in their lower degree as beautiful childhood ministrations on the part of the Angelic World, is obvious even unto this day in men and women. How few hear the cry of old time—"Oh, taste and see that the LORD is good." And how rare it is to find, even where earthly education has played impor-tant parts, a Soul who has an inherent taste for Divine things; or, if it has such a taste or desire, how rare it is to find the undamaged quality of the attribute by which a Soul recognizes and knows good, and rejoices in the milk and honey of the land of Canaan!

THE CITY OF DISCERNMENT

Of similar import is that of the history of Sensing, usually related in a circumscribed way to smell. But this latter expresses only the inhaling form of the sense. How few there are whose power of Divine Sensing has been left unharmed! How many there are in whom it has been utterly broken! Where the potency is still active the attribute is directed to the outer plane life, where the Divine qualities of it are shed upon material things. Even

277

many of the Ancients who had the power to inwardly sense Celestial approach, and know the touch of the ETERNAL, are no longer functioners upon mystical planes, but merely occult students of signs and wonders, sensing histories in stones and jewels; in metals, silver and gold. How great has been the fall of this one-time wondrous City! It has been brought down, its walls overthrown, its remaining potency misdirected; from being a City garmented in robes of bridal beauty, clothed with the power of Truth and the Light of Life, to be used as an adulterous force in commerce with things altogether astral, occult and material. For, real adultery is the bringing down of Divine qualities and potencies to have commerce with the fallen realms, and the making of their activities the means of pleasure and unhallowed gain.

In that day when the Vision, the Audient power, and the Taste, are fully restored again, and all barbarism ceases, even in the least degrees of it as expressed in the habits and customs of peoples and nations, then this glorious Divine quality of Sensing the meaning of things Spiritual, Celestial, and Eternal, will also be redeemed and brought back in life's service to the realm to which it originally belonged. In that day, from the Inner Worlds to the outer Kingdoms of manifestation, according to the order of the Soul and the degree of its unveiling, or evolution, and the realm where it is functioning for service, there shall be a true sensing of the meaning of all things.

THE CITY OF EMOTION

The fifth special attribute of the Soul, which may also be designated a City of Egypt, is that of Feeling. Feeling and touch are sometimes used as synonymous. We can sense through the touch, and through the touch we feel. But the attribute of Feeling contains elements profoundly deeper than those experiences which come through the touch. We can *feel* pain, sorrow, intensified anguish, without being touched by anything external to ourselves. We can feel deeply the emotion of great joy, or the exaltation of a great hope, quite apart from anything objective to ourselves. It is true that feeling passes from the innermost of our Being to the outermost vehicle in and through which we become conscious of touching objects, or of being touched. A highly sensitized creature feels; and the higher its order the more deeply is it conscious of feeling. For feeling is not only in the vehicle, but in the consciousness. It is not simply in the nerve centres, but in the Soul's consciousness. Thus when a Human Soul feels great pain, sorrow, anguish, joy, exaltation, hope, it is feeling these in the Inner Sanctuary of the Being, though the communicating avenues belong to the various vehicles —the outer body, the astral body, the mental body, the ætheric body, and the higher spiritual body. Love produces intense feeling when, as the magnetic pole of the Being, it is most active; and the feeling can be felt from the Sanctuary of the Being right through the Soul, heart, and mind into the body, which latter becomes affected by the magnetic currents set in motion from the innermost.

The feelings set up by the spirit of negation where the negativing action has to do with the manifestation of Love, the damming of its streams, the suppression of the beautiful outflow of those streams and the negation of pure and noble desire, are ultimately painful and disastrous, for they change the natural sense of the attribute. The feelings set up by the inversion of the Love-Principle, its perversion in the uses of it, and its subversion from the manifestations of its original purpose, lead to that degree of negation which ultimately becomes active as hate. Now, hate is not in the body, but in the mind; and where such negation obtains and prevails, the mind, and even the heart, come to lose the power of tender, compassionate and all-pitying feeling. The mind can become callous. Even the streams of the lovely, Divine heart in the Soul, can become as earth-streams that are frozen by the cold blasts of winter.

With such a conception of the attribute of Feeling as a Divine quality of the Soul, carrying man on to the very threshold of the Divine World and enabling him to share in the Divine burden of service, and even travail, there will be readily perceived the infinite nature of the loss to the Soul of the quality of perfect feeling. And it will be understood how, when the great Descent was fully accomplished, and Vision and Audience, Taste, and Sensing were so deeply hurt that they were like those who give themselves to warfare and find themselves amidst the conflict semi-slain, that the noble, Divine attribute of Feeling was like a river whose natural course was deflected, and whose waters were scattered until the channel of the Soul's feelings of love, compassion and pity, justice, righteousness and tender mercy, became almost dried up. For it was the loss of those senses, culminating in the suppression of Divine Feeling, that perpetuated the fearful conflicts amongst the nations and races, peoples and tongues. And it was through that same loss of Divine potency in the Soul, that mankind made war upon the creatures—hunting them, persecuting them, oppressing them, wounding them, and slaying them—a barbarism whose long, deep shadows have persisted through the ages, and which lie heavily upon the threshold of the nations unto this day.

It will also be apprehended what the redemption of this City of Egypt will mean for humanity; what it will mean for the individual life; what nobility of outlook it will bring back to the mind; what glorious realizations it will restore

within the Human Soul when the inherent qualities of
Divine Feeling have their way, so that Love, compassion
and pity; equity, righteousness and truth; power, tenderness and gentleness, hold sway. How changed the world
will then become, because humanity will be changed! The
races and the nations, the peoples and the tribes, shall learn
the art of war no more. All conflicts on the outer planes
shall cease. Man shall attain to his Divine dignity once more.
The creatures shall cease to be afraid of him. They shall
learn to trust in him and regard him as their friend. What
a new world it will be when these Five Cities of the Soul,
which have their correspondences in the land of Egypt,
are all redeemed and exalted to their true estate of life
and service in the individual, and in ministry for all !

THE TEMPLE OF BEING

Whilst these Five Cities represent the five primary
senses operating through to the land of Egypt, they have
also a further meaning. They are related to the five
courts of the Temple of Being. In their innermost meaning
they are not only masonic, but they are profound. They
are like five citadels reaching from great elevation down
to the plains.

Speaking of them as Courts of the Temple of Being, the
lowest in degree would be that of the Court of the Gentiles,
or the sphere wherein the common things of the daily
round exercise the mind and engage the life. This is said
to have been the Court specially trodden down by the
oppressor. For he changed the entire nature of life's daily
service, in its purpose, its venues, and its activities. He
levelled to the dust the pure, simple, beautiful forms of
life and services in the daily ministries, and changed
peaceful occupations into activities which led to strife,
and even warfare.

Even the Court of the Gentiles was once one of

harmonious activity where the simple services of life were rendered with selfless purpose and joy.

The fourth, or outer Court, of which the Court of the Gentiles was the outermost part, was that wherein the service of life found expression in the various Arts, where the children of men made their sacrifice and impressed it upon the work of their hands. It was the Court of the daily Burnt-Offering. For both men and women, the body was consecrated with all its powers for the service of the Most High; a consecration that was ratified from the Heavens through the renewed energy received for yet greater ministry. The language of the Arts was an interpretation of the language of the Heavens. But the oppressor laid the whole Court low. His powers overthrew the Altar, destroyed the nature of sacrifice and changed entirely the holy purpose of Art as the reflected exposition of the substantial, Divine ideas made concrete, formulative and creative. And he made the Court a dwelling-place for all that was strangely out of harmony with the Will of the Heavens. He even entered in through the veil of the third Court and threw down the Altar, and scattered the Incense upon the ground which was within the Censer, and, for a time, took the Censer away with him.

As the outer Court in its dual aspect represented the field for the creative and formulative activites of the mind, so this third Court spake of the heart and its sacred Altar of prayer, devotion, aspiration, blessing—all these proceeding from childlike trust in the unfailing goodness of the Eternal Love and Wisdom. And, having accomplished so much, the enemy took away the Golden Candlestick with its miniature lights which spake of the glorious ONE in HIS ministries through the ELOHIM, and left the sacred chamber without the Light that spake, in its degree, of the Presence of the most Holy Mystery.

And, still not satisfied, the enemy took possession of the most sacred Mystery of the Table of Shew Bread, which was none other than the accommodated expression of the most Holy Substance of GOD as the ETERNAL MOTHER.

It is said concerning that Shew Bread, that of it none but the priests might eat—signifying those in mediatorial ministry. For only those who are appointed Priests of GOD in the Middle Court of the Sanctuary, could possibly understand and partake of the Substance of the Divine Mother, even in its accommodated form. With such heart treasures originally contained within the Middle Court of the Being, but overthrown by the enemy of Souls, can it be wondered at that the truly spiritual children have aspired and prayed, and burnt their incense in a chamber from which the light had been taken away, leaving dark uncertainty? For thus for ages the children have prayed without knowing how to pray, nor whom to pray to, and without the Divine assurance that real prayer always brings the blessing. And in the craving of the children for the Light, and their hunger to touch and receive of the accommodated Mystery of the Mother Substance of all things, even through outer ceremonial and material symbol, we have the testimony of what they once possessed, but so tragically lost.

THE LANGUAGE OF CANAAN

And when we come within the veil of the next Court, where the highest symbol of GOD's Presence is to be found, we enter through the Understanding and the perceptions of the Intuition, into the Queen's Chamber, or Temple of the Soul itself; for the Soul is the Temple of the Spirit. There is still something beyond, but it is the realization of all that is resident within the Temple of the Soul. Within that most Holy Court we have before us the City of Heres—the City of the Sun. For the recognition through the Vision of the Ark of the Covenant, and through the Audience of the Voice from between the Cherubim, dynamically raises the Soul into the conscious estate of the Cloud of Radiance which is said to overshadow the Altar of Oblation, out from which the ETERNAL speaks. For the City of Heres is none other than the inherent light of the Divine in the Soul, realized by the Soul through the action of its magnetic pole in response to the Divine overshadowing, wherein it comes to share the Divine resplendence. For thus the LORD becomes its Sun, its shield, its gracious garment, its sublimest realization.

Even into this Court most sacred, this City most hallowed, the enemy would have made his way, but for the shielding operations of the LORD of Being, Who, by the manifestation of HIS potencies, could say to the oppressor—*Thou hast come thus far; come no further, lest thou be destroyed also.*

Herein is implied a great mystery which we may not unveil any further. But it will have been made manifest to the pure-minded and earnest disciple of the LORD of Love, how it came to pass that through the oppression of the enemy, the Soul lost its inherent consciousness of the Presence, and consequently its power to operate correctly through the other Courts of the Temple of Being. Here further light will be thrown upon the meaning of those Five Cities in the great day speaking the language of Canaan. It may be apprehended what would be the significance in the daily life, for its ordinary services to be rendered with pure desire and lofty motive. It may be perceived by those who have vision, what it would mean for the whole world of Art in every department, and Science in all its branches, to be purified, exalted, illumined and redeemed from all that is gross and fallen, material and self-regarding. And, to the truly mystical Souls, will become obvious the changes that would be effected in the whole round of life, if the heart were redeemed with the mind, and the flow of its most sacred emotion were a continual prayer unto the Heavens, the offering of sweet incense unto the FATHER-MOTHER; if the Lamps of the Sanctuary were again lit so that light could fall upon every plane by which the Soul could see its way; if the most Holy Shew Bread of the Divine Substance could be partaken of once more by the Soul for mediatorial service unto many.

And to those who once were of the ancient Christhood, and were designated Sons of GOD, it must assuredly become apparent once more what is meant by the Ark of Covenant and Testimony, the Altar of Oblation with overshadowing Cherubim, and the Cloud of Radiance transmitting the vibrations of the Voice; and all that it signifies to be once more reinstated a Son of GOD, a citizen of the Sun, a dweller within the Cloud of HIS Radiance.

Thus, when all that is of Egypt, Assyria, and Israel, speaks once more the language of Canaan, then all service on the outer as well as the inner realms; all Communion of Souls; all Art and Science; all Philosophy and Religion; will speak the true language of Canaan, the language of Divine Inheritance. The signs and symbols on the outermost, though accommodations, will nevertheless be as pure and as true in their degree as those of the innermost; and so shall it be with all the intermediary realms.

Thus Lower and Upper Egypt, Eastern and Western Assyria, and all within the borders of Israel, shall speak the language of the Soul which GOD taught it through HIS servants and mediators when it was still unfallen. In that day the Divine Humanities shall also find expression from the innermost to the outermost through Embodiment; through Mediation; through Religious interpretation; through the Ritual of the Soul; through Philosophy in its interpretive teaching; through Art reflective and formulative; through Design; through the motion of Music; through Science as the world unveils itself to the mind; through the inter-communion of peoples, of tribes, nations and races; and through the daily service of the common task and the duties that lie nearest to hand.

And in that Day shall the Divine Man who holds the Five Cities in himself, be made manifest as a concrete embodiment and exposition of the sacred Mystery of ADONAI. For all the powers of Egypt are GOD's people; all the potencies and forces of Assyria are as the horses and chariots of GOD; and all the Divine qualities of Israel, with the attributes of the Gods for service, are the most sacred gifts of the Holy Substance of the ETERNAL MOTHER, and the most Holy Mystery of the Spirit of the ETERNAL FATHER. And herein will be made manifest the oneness of Egypt with Assyria, and Assyria with Israel, and Israel with the Gods, and the Gods with the LORD, the GOD of Sabaoth, and the triumphant accomplishment of the Redemption and the Regeneration through which there shall be restored once more the glorious Theocracy of the ancient days when GOD, through HIS Sons, reigned throughout the whole world.

THE BOOK OF ISAIAH
PART THIRTEEN

THE CITY OF THE SUN

*Wherein is shown the true meaning of
the mystical term Zion in its
individual and communal
relationship to Israel ; the
superstructure of the Holy
City; its foundations;
its powers and its
attributes for
service in
the Sun.*

CONTENTS

O Resplendent Adonai! In what tongue may we find terms to adequately express our deepest thought concerning Thee, and the motion of Thy Deep Waters within us!

How Glorious Thou art in Thine apparel of Ineffable Light, even when Thou revealest an aspect of Thyself as in our wonderful Sun!

There, glorious things are spoken of Thee by all who have come into the Vision of Thee and learnt in part the Glory of Thy Sacred Mystery.

Thou hast endowed Sol with the Potencies of one who is to be for Thee amid the Celestial Splendours of the Universe of the Father-Mother; and even unto all who serve within the Realm of Sol hast Thou bestowed the Power to reign with Thee.

For Thou hast made the Sons of God to image Thee, that in bearing Thy likeness they may reveal Thee.

O splendour Transcendent! We would ever Adore Thee.

Amen and Amen.

THE CITY OF THE SUN

IN the book of Isaiah the term Zion holds an important place. Sometimes it is used as if it were a personification of someone. There are references also which seem to indicate that it signified in the Prophet's vision, an exalted state of life and consciousness. It is spoken of as the Holy City, and the City of the LORD. There is likewise a reference wherein is conferred upon it the dignity of a mountain. Its citizens are designated Children of Zion; and it is implied that at one time they were arrayed in beautiful garments. There are also clear indications that the glory of the City had been eclipsed; that its walls had been thrown down; that its inherent spiritual splendour had been dimmed; and that from its exalted state it had been brought down to the dust, or a state of great humiliation. There are also clear indications that all its inhabitants shared its fate.

Throughout the prophecy, even in the imperfect form in which it appears in the Old Testament, we can glimpse what Zion stood for in the Prophet's vision, and the great hope which filled his Being for the final full restoration of the City and all its inhabitants. The Redemption is associated with the bringing back of Zion. All its citizens are again to know the LORD in the day of the Regeneration. The Servant of the LORD is closely related to Zion in the Prophet's vision; and, in some mysterious way, the City of Zion and all its children are involved in the Travail of YAHWEH. It is because of this vision that the Prophet declares—"For Zion's sake I cannot keep silent." Then we have also his appeal—"Awake! Awake! O Zion!" Likewise he calls—"O Zion! Get thee up into the high mountain!"

NAMES BELONGING TO THE MYSTERIES

Ere entering upon the interpretation of the inner significance of Zion[1] and the Children who belonged to it as the holy City of GOD, it might be of interest to many to see how the sacred Mysteries, held as Divine Secrets by ancient Israel, came to be related to outer events, situations, places, towns and villages. Many of the places named in the Old Scriptures had terms applied to them which originally belonged to the Divine Mysteries. Such terms as Lebanon and Sinai, Horeb and Pisgah, Carmel and Gilboa, Hermon and Moriah, originally contained within themselves meanings of Divine Secrets. There is a sense in which it may be said that they became preserved as Mystery-terms through being related to earthly mountains and hills; and that we are the richer for the preservation. Nevertheless, with the passing of the real Israel as a great people who, as the Sons of GOD, taught the Angelic, Celestial and Divine Mysteries; and, with the schools in which they taught these things, gradually becoming the possession of occult teachers who belonged to the Jewish race, the inner significance of the terms became lost. In this way all the sacred names of Spiritual, Celestial and Divine exalted states, found themselves circumscribed in their meaning and applied to local hills and mountains. It was in this way that these mountains and hills came to be regarded as sacred.

---

[1] There are many references to Zion in the Old Testament, of which the Psalter contains thirty-nine, Isaiah thirty-six, and Jeremiah twenty-one. Wheresoever the reference is made, importance is given to the place or state. Such a consensus speaks for itself.

The same process took place in relation to terms which we find in the sacred Records applied to villages, streams, cities and parcels of land. Notably amongst these latter there stand out—Beersheba, Penuel, Bethel, Bethlehem, Jericho, Bethany and Jerusalem.

Jerusalem gradually became the centre of Jewish life—religious, social and political. Walls were built around it with gates and towers, and terraces with many lovely dwelling-places upon them. In the upper part of the city there was a plateau which was named the City of Zion, lying to east by north; and within that City, it was said, Solomon built his Temple. It is believed also that the Temple had its foundations within and its superstructure upon, the Mount Moriah which was associated with the Abrahamic sacrifice of Isaac.

It is, therefore, not unnatural both for Jews and Bible interpreters who are unaware of the masonic significance of all those terms, to apply them simply to the outer situations, places and cities, when they meet with them in the prophetic writings. Here scholasticism and tradition have the astonishing power of veiling the perceptions and keeping closed the door of the intuition. They seem to hold their devotees in a world whose glory is eclipsed, almost totally. The worshippers at the shrines of scholasticism and the superstitions of tradition, see nothing in the terms beyond their physiographical, historical, and outward religious associations.

JERUSALEM AND ZION

But the terms Jerusalem, Zion, and Mount Moriah, are full of Planetary, Solar and Divine significance. For the Jerusalem meant in the real prophetic vision, related to the Spiritual Household of the Planet as a beautiful City of GOD, with its bulwarks and towers of righteousness and equity; its gates into a life which was, verily, a song of praise unto the Creator of it. The beautiful terraces were none other than the planes of the Planet; and the palace-homes were the dwelling-places upon those terraces, or planes, of the various orders of children of the FATHER-MOTHER. For the true sons of Judah were none other than the children of this Planet; and the whole Household in the unfallen days was a concrete embodiment of the Jerusalem which is Above. In those far-off days it was truly a City of GOD, full of HIS peace, and radiant with the exquisite beauty of a real childhood before the LORD of Being.

The holy City of Zion that seemed to be within the confines of the greater Jerusalem, was, nevertheless, apart from it. It had its own walls, towers and gates. It was a Celestial City. The term Zion mystically signifies a special Solar revelation and manifestation. Celestially it was the citadel in which Christ dwelt, and through which He manifested. But here Christ is no man, but a Solar, Cosmic exposition of ADONAI. The Children of Zion were those who were related to Christ and to the Christhood manifestation. They were, therefore, Children of Zion the City of the Sun. They represented a community of Souls in high spiritual estate, sharing in large degree the Solar Cosmic Consciousness. They were, therefore, the Body or Vehicle of the LORD for a concrete, communal exposition of Christhood in the various degrees in which that high estate was to be revealed, manifested and interpreted unto the children of Judah.

THE TEMPLE OF SOLOMON

The Christhood, as a concrete revelation of ADONAI, took the fashion of the Temple of Solomon, and was built within and upon the sacred Mystery of Mount

Moriah. Such a Temple was the most magnificent this
world has ever had reared upon its threshold. It was
rich with the most sacred vessels of the LORD of Being.
Its pillars and its gates were of Divine attribute. Within
that sacred Temple, in the innermost court of it, abode
the Shekinah, or relative embodiment of the Sacred and
ever most Blessed Mystery of ADONAI. And within that
most holy House Seraphic ministries were rendered from
the LORD unto the Children of Zion. Cherubic worship
of the most glorious ONE was mediated from the Children
of Zion through the LORD's Own appointed High Priest.
For the ADONAI HIMSELF mediated in the hour of the
Children's adoration, worship, praise and blessing.

Upon Mount Moriah, it was said that Abraham offered
up Isaac. It will be found recorded elsewhere who and
what Abraham stood for, and the place he occupied in
the Divine administration of the Solar System. Mount
Moriah is that estate of conscious realization wherein the
Altar for a Divine oblation is reared. It is the Altar of
Ramah, the Lamb of GOD in the centrifugal aspect or
mode of HIS ministry, wherein HIS Divine Majesty is
revealed in sublimest sacrifice. And in all Christhood,
individual, communal and Cosmic, there must needs be,
not only the willinghood, but the actual offering up of the
Being sacrificially for service unto the FATHER-MOTHER.
And though the Abrahamic story in which it is said
Isaac was offered up upon Mount Moriah, has an exposition in every planetary system; yet the story of
Abraham offering up Isaac had special relation to the
part that the Cosmic Christhood, sent to this world as a
community of the Sons of GOD, was called upon to play.
That Cosmic Christhood, built up of the Sons of GOD,
each member of which was like a glorious Divine cell in
such a Body of the LORD, in a unified form became, not

only in individual units as Sons of God, but in the one unified Cosmic life, as Son of Abraham,—a communal exposition of the sacred Mystery of the Christhood.

All the Children of Zion were intimately related to him we speak of as Abraham. They were the true Children of Abraham. Communally and Celestially they were Isaac. And the sacrifice upon Mount Moriah of Abraham's Child of Promise in and through whom all the nations of the earth—the races of Judah—were to be blest, was none other than the sacrifice of the Cosmic Christhood, wherein there was given to this world in redemptive sacrifice the whole Household of Ancient Israel unto the preservation, it was hoped, of the Soul-life of all the children of Judah. They were the preserving salt in the Earth. And in the measure in which, owing to the calamitous conditions which overtook all the world, they lost their savour, so did they suffer the loss of power and conscious realization of the Blessed and Holy ONE Who mediated from between the Cherubim unto HIS own Shekinah or Sacred Presence within them. In the midst of this sacrifice, Ramah was caught up. From first to last it was a Divine Sacrifice.

THE CITY OF GOD

With such an unveiling of the Mysteries associated with Jerusalem, Zion, Mount Moriah, Isaac, and Abraham, surely something will be glimpsed by the reader of that which was meant by Isaiah when he spake of Ierusalem and the Holy City of Zion. And with such an opening of the doors and windows of Celestial story, Solar and Planetary, the need for, and the purpose of, the Redemption will become manifest.

* * * * * *

The Holy City as a centre of spiritual thought, activity, and revelation, occupies a prominent place throughout the whole of Jewish and Christian revelation. The closing scenes of the Apocalyptic visions are associated with the Holy City. The City of GOD has been the quest of the true pilgrim through all ages of spiritual story. The finding of that City has been the Divine urge within all who have sought to know and realize GOD as a near Presence. The older a Soul is, the deeper are its yearnings to contact the realm of Revelation wherein it may find realization. Though the mind in its lofty moods may rejoice in the world of manifestation which it contacts in outer vision and touch; and though it may learn many things from the objects which it beholds, contacts and handles, yet these things never satisfy the yearning of the pilgrim's spirit. He seeks for a City wherein it will be manifestly revealed that its Founder and Maker is GOD. For such a pilgrim there could be no abiding satisfaction in less than the finding of the realm of the Arcana Celestia where the High Priests of Divine Mediation unveil the sacred Mysteries of GOD, the Soul, and the Universe.

It is because of the microcosmic superstructure of the Holy City within the pilgrim himself that he seeks for its Celestial and Divine correspondence. That microcosmic City within the pilgrim is none other than the Holy City of Zion. For Zion has a relative and individual relation to the Soul, as well as a Solar and Cosmic significance. The superstructure of Zion in the individual reveals the Divine Mystery of Soul fashion; and this is manifested in the auric splendour begotten of Divine action within the pilgrim as the Sacred Breath is wafted through all the planes, or atmospheres, by which his Being is en-sphered, as the most Holy Mystery we name the Spirit of GOD moves down and up the exquisitely beautiful and marvellously constructed Spiral of the Being.

To ascend the Holy City of Zion is, therefore, an

ascension taken by the pilgrim. By ascension is meant an entrance, by means of an evolutary act, into a higher state of consciousness wherein there is increased vision and intensified realization. Such an ascension on the part of the pilgrim is the *becoming* within him of the sacred Mystery of the Son of God. When it is recorded in the prophetic writing that the City of Zion is beautiful for situation, it is this spiritual estate that is referred to. And to possess Zion as an inheritance, is to enter its gates and be of its citizenship.

The City's Superstructure

To follow the analogy of a city encompassed by walls and towers, or bulwarks, we have presented in the Apocalypse a vision of the City with twelve gates. Now, in the superstructure of the Soul there are twelve gates, or avenues, of ingress and egress; and in a mystical sense, three of these look towards each of the four dimensions.

In occult philosophy these gates have been spoken of as the Twelve Labours of the Soul. And in the Greek myth of the Twelve Labours of Hercules, there is a Celestial significance.

In a racial sense the twelve are related to tribal potency and service.

In a Celestial sense they are related to Mazzaroth, or the twelve signs of the Zodiac.

In the Divine World they are related to the Twelve Attributes of the Eternal.

The attributes of every Human Soul are twelve, corresponding to the inherent Mystery in Tribal, Celestial, and Divine numbers. Each attribute is a gateway by which the Being enters into experience, acquires knowledge and vision, and gathers into itself increase of potency. And then the gate becomes a venue through which it makes its egress, or goes forth to serve.

Each attribute thus becomes an avenue of spiritual

commerce for the enrichment of the Being and the manifestation of that enrichment in some service of life.
Each gate, through its relation in a spiritual sense to
Celestial and Divine things, becomes a precious pearl.
It is a treasure fashioned in the great Deep of the Divine
Mystery. Each one of the Soul's twelve attributes
expresses in some degree the holy Mystery of Being which
we relate to the FATHER-MOTHER. If human attribute
be something that seems to grow up with the physical
and mental states of the individual life, it is only apparently so; for its potency is always present in the
spiritual individual. From the first it is a latent potency.
In the Souls who have greatly evolved, all the attributes
have acquired a measure of Divine estate. A pearl,
whatever unhappy associations it may seem to have
when related to the fallen conditions of the world,
belongs to the Divine Elemental Kingdom, and is built
up of the most exquisitely beautiful elements surpassing
anything the human mind could conceive of. Every
attribute of the Soul is pure in its original elements and
fashion, and partakes of the nature of Divine Attribute,
the Soul itself being in the likeness of GOD. All the
attributes, having such a quality both as to substance
and fashion, are sacred and must ever be held sacred,
even though the use of them may have to be amidst
elements which are not conducive to the revelation of
the inherent beauty of their exquisite texture and
fashion.

This may help the reader to understand the significance
of the Apocalyptic vision of the Holy City with its twelve
gates composed of twelve precious pearls. And when it is
known that the pearl is the symbol of treasure gathered
out of the great Deep, and, therefore, the Divine victory
of the Soul in its acquisition, the real meaning of the

Soul's Twelve Labours may be glimpsed, if not fully apprehended. For it is through its attributes it acquires, ingathers, stores up in its treasure-house of potency, memory and vision. For the process of ingathering through acquisition, is also the process of the Being's expansion in consciousness towards the fuller realization of the meaning of being a citizen of the Holy City of GOD. And upon the mind of the reader there will dawn yet more fully the significant meaning of the gates of that City never being shut by day; and the fact that there is no night within that City, nor the darkness which falls upon all things where the Sun shines not, and the Stars of Celestial embodiment adorn not the Heavens, and the Moon of an illumined understanding sheds not her beams.

THE MYSTERY IN EVERY SOUL

The citadel of Zion is, therefore, a holy Mystery in every Soul. It is that most Sacred Mystery of the ETERNAL LORD of all Being Who is present in all the Stars and all Systems, the realization of which makes of the individual life a vehicle expressive of the Body of the LORD, in its degree; and, unto those who have attained, gives the Nirvanic consciousness of absolute oneness with the FATHER-MOTHER. The streets of such a City are paved with the gold of the Eternal Love as that Love crowns the twelve foundations, or primal principles of the attributes. In such a City, the LORD GOD Presence within the consciousness becomes the Temple built upon this Hill of Zion. For, when the Soul realizes Nirvana truly, it lives in the consciousness of an all-ensphering by the atmosphere of the Divine World, and overshadowing of that Royal Arch of HIS accommodated Universal Mystery, wherein the Soul feels itself dwelling in the Universal, and becomes filled unto all fulness. And the degree of its Divine capacity will also be the degree of embodiment for Him, and the manifestation of the life begotten of the Sacred Substance and Holy Spirit of the Father-Mother in profound, sublime and resplendent Immanence.

* * * * * *

The mystery of Zion deepens when we recall the description given in the Apocalypse, wherein it is stated that its foundations were made up of the twelve most precious stones, and that the City lay foursquare. The twelve foundation stones upon which the City is built, each of which represents a precious gem, signify the twelve combinations of Divine Elements out of which each attribute is created and formed. In the process of the combination of these elements a radiant centre is formed, and that becomes the magnetic pole of the attribute. By means of this latter the Soul gathers into itself increase of those elements which endow it with power. And that radiant, magnetic centre also becomes, when active, the distributing centrifugal force by means of and through which the Soul serves and ministers.

Each attribute thus becomes an exposition of the Sacred Mystery of the Father-Mother as He is present in the Divine Elements as the Eternal Living Force. In this way the Human Soul in its substances and potencies becomes built up of the first waters, so that each attribute is, verily, a most precious gem. When perfectly polarized, its radiant centre has centripetal and centrifugal motion, by means of which it receives and gives. And, in perfect estate and balance, the magnetic centre of each attribute immediately responds to the Divine Will. Here the Divine Will is for the Soul the Centre of all things.

* * * * * *

The Divine Fashion of the Soul thus becomes an ever

deepening Mystery; for it is part of the Secret of Being. GOD's secret is in it. It bears within itself a replica of that same secret as is found expressed in the Divine Fashions which obtain in the inner realms of Celestial Systems.

The Divine Standard on which there are mounted the Insignia of the Eternal, is none other than the Spiral of Being to which all Divine magnetic streams flow and from which they again proceed, all potencies are related, all the planes are attached. This Standard is the centre that holds the Divine magnetic secret by which the Soul draws to its own centre and holds when it wills, and from which its centrifugal force proceeds as electric power by which it gives and creates.

Within the Standard there are seven very special potencies which we have to call nerve-centres that are most intimately connected with the Insignia of the Eternal. These are centres of receptivity and procedure, and are subject to the sacred Mystery that crowns the Standard or Spiral. By this means the Soul acquires power to move its seven planes or atmospheric circuli, as it desires. It can move inward and outward, upward and downward, to the extent of the circumference of the field of magnetic action generated by the Divine uses of its potencies.

The Soul may thus be seen to be a citadel—a Divine fortress, a replica of Celestial and Divine World Mystery.

MAN MAY BECOME AS A GOD

Such a vision of the nature and constitution of the attributes of the individual Soul, surely reveals its inherent divinity, and how it becomes possible, through its latent potencies becoming active, to grow up into the estate wherein its attainments make manifest that it is a Son of the Gods, and even a Son of GOD. And such an estate interprets some strange sayings found in sacred story wherein it is reported that Moses said unto the Children of Israel when acting as Messenger unto them from the LORD of Being—"Said I not unto you that ye shall be as Gods?" For the full realization of all the potencies which make up the attributes of a Human Soul makes that Soul Divine, clothes it with Divine power, makes of its auric activity a reflection, in embodiment, of the Divine Resplendence, crowns its fashion with the splendour belonging to a Son of the Gods, and then exalts it to the realm of divinity, wherein it not only beholds the Cloud of the Radiant Mystery, but enters into it, as it is said Moses did on Sinai and Horeb, and the Master on the mount of Transfiguration.

Furthermore, when it is said that the City lieth four-square, a most sublime, Celestial and Divine Mystery is indicated. It is a picture presented in geometrical formation of the holy meaning of the square and the right angle. The square is reminiscent of the Macrocosmic Cross and the Tetragrammaton. It relates to righteousness and equity. But righteousness and equity are more than qualities which may be expressed in human or Divine action when they are thought of as goodness and justice. The LORD of Love and Wisdom is ever good, and HE is always just. But in HIM these are more than ordinary qualities revealed in and through HIS attitude towards, and HIS action on behalf of, all HIS children. They are the principles which lie in the very heart of HIS own Sacred Mystery as that finds exposition upon all the Kingdoms. For righteousness and equity relate to perfect balance. And wheresoever perfect balance is found, there will be expressed GOD's righteousness and equity.

In the foursquare City of Zion we have expressed the exposition of the righteousness and equity of GOD upon the four great Kingdoms. And in the four Triangles within each square we have revealed the motion of the four Eternities throughout the four Dimensions. In such a perfect City the Presence becomes the Light of all things. That Presence is enthroned upon the magnetic centre of the Being; and around the Presence are arrayed, sitting upon their own thrones, the twelve attributes. These latter in their dual mode of centripetal and centrifugal motion, express the Twenty-Four Elders, or crowned potencies, around the Throne of the ETERNAL. For, the Holy City of Zion, built up into such a perfect exposition of the Holy Mystery within the Soul, and through the manifest Life, is a microcosmic revelation of the Solar Mystery in its veiled Divine Realm.

It may now be seen that there is a Divine reason why the most Holy City should be named Zion, the City of GOD; a reason for its association with the Sons of GOD, and its application to ancient Israel; and likewise how it came to pass that the Message which is signified by the name Isaiah, should have had special reference to that Holy City, and the need for its redemption, restoration, re-exaltation and manifestation. And, surely, in one and all of those children who great ages ago were known as the Sons of GOD, the motion of the real Message termed the Prophecy of Isaiah, will cause the waters of Eternal Truth to lap the shores of their consciousness, and speak to them again of what they were in earlier ages; what they became; what they have been throughout great ages of travail; and what now they are once more to become so that the Solar glory may flood their Being, and that they may become once more, not only the Divine Inheritors of the Presence, but the revealers of that Most Glorious ONE; and the interpreters of HIM in and through the service of their lives, so that they shall be again as the Sons of GOD walking upon the planes of the Earth.

O my Father-Mother, may the services of Thy Servant be effectual in leading many of Thy Sons back to the Homeland of Zion, and into the Holy Sanctuary of Thy Dwelling.

May the unveilings of Thy Glory as revealed in Thy Purpose, come to them as the Revelations of Thyself as the Divine Isaiah.

May this Message be unto each Son of Thine, the Voice from within the Temple where the Ark of Covenant and Testimony is once more revealed; and may they know it to be none other than The Divine Burden of the Spirit of Yahweh.

And may this sublime Revelation of Thy Holy Purpose be the Herald of the Coming of the Lord-Presence, and the full Restoration of Zion.

Amen and Amen.

THE BOOK OF ISAIAH

PART FOURTEEN

THE TEXT AND NOTES

CONTENTS

CONTENTS

FOREWORD

The Text of the Sacred Book of Isaiah as presented in this volume, has been *recovered* by the Author in the process of the recovery of the Story of the Sons of GOD known in ancient times as The Adamic Race; The Patriarchs; The Houses of Abraham, Isaac and Jacob; The Children of Israel and Zion; and the true nature of the Christhood of the Master Ioannes, known to history as Jesus Christ; and the mysterious Oblation associated with that other Mystery named The Sin-Offering which was made for the Redemption of this world.

The Notes accompanying the Text are meant to aid the reader to the better understanding of the cryptic nature of the prophetic Message, and to interpret many of the Masonic Terms in which the Cosmic Drama is presented. For, it must be recognized that many of the signs and symbols which belonged to the language of the ancient Mysteries known to and understood only by the Sons of GOD, were applied to *mountains, hills, valleys, cities, villages, districts, peoples and nations;* and, through the use of them in the prophetic Message, naturally the meaning could be discerned by the Sons of GOD who alone of all the races upon the Earth, knew them.

It must therefore be remembered that, as only the Sons of GOD knew the Mysteries of the Celestial and Divine Worlds, all Divine Messages were sent to them. It was thus that all the true Prophets spake to the House of Israel concerning their own past as the Sons of GOD, their then present estate, and the Divine Will to be accomplished by the Heavens on their behalf.

It is in the Light of this Knowledge that the Message of Isaiah may be fully apprehended and finally understood; for it is the Masonic Book of The Cosmic Drama of the Oblation enacted for the Return of the Sons of GOD and the blotting out of this world's Karma, and the Redemption of all its Children.

I

The Vision of The Lord

I saw the Lord:[1]
He was enthroned on High, and His Glory filled the Temple.[2]
Around the Throne stood the Seraphim:[3]
Each of them had six Wings:
With twain each covered his Face;
With twain he covered his Feet;
And with twain he did fly.
And each unto the other thus spake in song:—

"Holy, Holy, Holy, is the Lord of Hosts;
The Heavens are full of His Glory;
And the fulness of the Earth also manifests His Glory."

The Veils dividing the Thresholds moved,[4] *for the Voice*
of Him from within the Sanctuary spake;
And the Temple was filled with His Radiance.[5]

Because of the Glory of the Vision, I was as one who is
overwhelmed;[6]
For I felt as if my praise of Him were uttered by unclean
lips, and that I dwelt amongst a people whose ways were of
the unclean:
For I had looked upon the King, the Lord of the Heavenly
Hosts.[7]

Then flew unto me one of the Seraphim:
In his hand he bore the Sacred Flame, which in appearance
was as a Glowing Stone;[8]
From out the Fire upon the Altar had he taken it:[9]
With it he touched my Lips, and spake:—
"Behold! Behold! The Mystery of His Love!

It is thine to know; for it hath touched thee and made thee whole."[10]

Then, from within the Sanctuary, spake the Lord;
The sound of His Voice[11] *was as when many waters meet;*
And He said unto the Hosts of the Heavens[12]*:—*
"Who will go down for us? Whom shall we send?"
And my Being was uplifted unto Him, and I spake, saying, "Send me! Send me!"[13]
And He said, "Go then to the People as the Servant of the Lord."

I

NOTES ON TEXT

[1] This vision is of Cosmic significance, and is in harmony with the Message which the Prophet had to proclaim. The Book of Isaiah is a Cosmic Drama. It begins in the Divine Heavens, embraces those Heavens, unveils the first act of the Oblation after it had been projected in response to the motion of the ETERNAL's Purpose, and then deals with this System in its recovery.

The vision was transcendent. The Servant was called up into the Divine Heavens where he beheld the informulate assume form, and appear in fashion like an individuated Being transfigured and regnant. The exalted state and sublime vision are beyond description.

[2] Here the universal Nature of the ETERNAL is indicated. Though the full vision had to be apprehended through the Divine Realm of the Being, yet what was beheld and seen had been reflected into the Sanctuary from the Universe wherein the ETERNAL is Regnant. His Glory filled the Temple of Universal Being. This most stupendous Vision was brought within the realm of the Prophet's Being, so that he witnessed the Drama as something taking place within himself, yet apparently objective to him.

[3] The Seraphim are Beings of high order. They are the counterparts of the Cherubim, and are the centrifugal agents of Divine ministry. They are the distributors of the Divine

Bread and Wine, being the Vehicles of Divine Conveyance to the Soul. Whereas the Cherubim are the agents of conveyance to the ETERNAL ONE of the Soul's gifts in sacrifice. By means of them, the Being reaches the High Altar, and is upborne in consciousness to the realm of the Regnant Presence; for they overshadow the Oblatory in the Divine World.

⁴ Each Court of the Temple of Being has its own Threshold, whether the Temple be that of the Human Soul, the Solar Embodiment, or the Divine World. And between the Courts, dividing them from each other, there is a veil. As the Being passes in consciousness and state and, if commanded to do so, in presence, from Court to Court, the veils are parted. The Initiate rises from Glory to Glory, till he stands before the REGNANT ONE.

⁵ This refers to the Auric Splendour of the Holy Presence. When the Glory of the LORD fills all the Heavens it is witness to the Fashion of the ETERNAL in HIS manifold embodiments, HIS Wondrous Works; but when HIS Radiance is beheld, it is the Vision of HIS Auric resplendence.

⁶ None could realize the effect upon the whole Being of such a Cosmic Vision unless it had been experienced. The vastness of it and the grandeur, the intensity of it and the radiance could not fail to overwhelm any Soul, even a great Prophet. In the hour of greatest Revelation, there are times when even the Seraphim veil their faces before HIM Who is unveiled. To be overwhelmed by such an experience was sign of neither weakness nor sinfulness; on the one hand, it was the Majesty of the Vision, on the other, it was the tremendous effect upon the consciousness of the contrast between the Awful Purity of the SUPREME ONE and his own limited state. He felt as if he were impure in that Presence. Everyone, from Human Soul to Archangel, feels like that in the midst of HIS Auric Resplendence.

⁷ Some there are who think they have had visions of the King of This World, and so a Planetary Cosmic Vision. But this glorious unveiling was more than that. It is even more than a Solar Cosmic Vision wherein ADONAI is beheld as the Divine Man clothed in Solar Radiance. The Vision is akin to that of the ADONAI walking amid the Seven Golden Candlesticks, followed by that of the ETERNAL regnant amid the Hierarchies around the THRONE in the midst of the Thrones. The Presence was the KING of all the Kings, and LORD of All.

⁸ The White Stone of the Sacred Mystery—the Philosopher's Stone of pure Wisdom illumining the mind; the Knight-Templar's stone of pure Devotion and Consecration upon which his name is written; the Mystic's Stone of Heavenly Wisdom which becomes Sacramental Bread; the Divine Initiate's Gift from the Presence in the hour when he becomes one with GOD.

⁹ The Altar of Living Fire speaks of the Baptism of Eternal Energy. When the Being receives that most Sacred Gift, he is henceforth lost to himself, and becomes the Vehicle of ADONAI. He is henceforth a Son of GOD upon the Divine Kingdom, and can be vehicled through for a Divine Christhood Manifestation.

¹⁰ Made thee completely a Son of the Highest. It was an exaltation from Celestial Sonship to the Divine Realm, and the higher transformation and transfiguration of the whole Being.

¹¹An effect of the motion of the ETERNALS moving at HIS Command.

¹²A glimpse of the Nature of a Divine Assembly, and an indication of how a Soul is called by the FATHER-MOTHER for special Divine-World service. It was in this gathering of the Gods and Sons of GOD that the Servant was chosen to be the Vehicle of the Oblation.

¹³ Though simply expressed, this is no ordinary Call and Consecration, but the giving of the whole Being to be sacrificially used in the Sin-Offering and Oblation.

II

YAHWEH'S ANOINTED ONE

Jehovah hath caused me to move within the Spiral of His Holy One that I might speak of His Word.[1]

It is of His anointing that I am able to proclaim His Message.[2]
His Word is glad tiding unto all who are meek in spirit.
With His Message He hath sent me to give its healing unto the broken-hearted and to bind up all that has been bruised; for it is the Balm of Gilead unto every wound.[3]

Through His Anointed One He shall give liberation unto all who were of the Captivity.[4]
Even the prison-houses shall be opened that those who are in them may find deliverance.

It is the Day of the Lord that is to come. It is the Advent spoken of by the Heavens when the Secret of God might be revealed concerning the Redemption of the Kingdom of Ya-akob-El and the Restoration of all Israel.[5]
. The Day of the Lord is the set-time for the re-establishing of Zion.[6] *In it shall be accomplished the healing of the cause of all her sorrow, and the re-appointing of her sons and daughters to the priestly service of their Lord.*[7]
In that Day the vestiges of their former glory shall give place to that estate of realization wherein they are once more those who are anointed with the oil of gladness for Temple Service:
The heaviness begotten of their captivity shall pass away; for in their Priesthood they shall know once more the Divine Joy and Gladness of Praise.
Again shall they become the Cedars of God's planting, and reveal the glory of His Presence with them.[8]

They shall be re-named the Priests of the Lord, and be known as the Ministers of the Lord God.

The courts of the Gentiles within the Sanctuary shall also be glorified; and all the Gentile powers shall be enriched for the service of the Holy One.

* * * * * *

Now will I delight greatly in my Lord; for my Being is rejoiced to know His Name.

With the garments of Salvation hath He clothed me, and with His Righteousness hath He upheld me;

He hath adorned me with the Jewels of His Holy One, and ornamented me with the precious stones of His Breastplate: upon these hath He written His own most glorious Secret Name.[9]

II
NOTES ON TEXT

[1] Herein is expressed in a few cryptic words one of the most profound Mysteries associated with a Soul's ascension to the Divine Kingdom. It is the Whirlwind of Eli-jah. Sometimes it becomes the Cloud of Radiance upon the Sanctuary; on other occasions *it is* Eli-jah's Chariot of Fire. To move within it, whether as in the Cloud or Chariot, is a tremendous as well as a transcendent experience. The Son of the Celestial Spheres who is called up on to the Divine Kingdom to be a "Son of the Highest," must, on his way, needs pass into the Cloud of Spiral motion and be caught up by it; and then unto the Chariot of Spiral Fire and know the Eternal Mystery, and be endowed of GOD.

[2] The Divine Messenger is always an Anointed One. He is illumined, inspired, and empowered from the ETERNAL ONE.

[3] Gilead relates to the House of Comfort. To a fallen world it becomes the House of the Physician. "Is there no Balm in Gilead? Is there no Physician there?"

But the Heavens Comfort and Heal by means of the Truth. For the Initiate the Truth is enrichment and acquisition; for the afflicted, it is the power for healing and restoration. The

Message of the Messenger is the Truth; it brings health to all the Being.

⁴ The reference is to those Sons and Daughters of Israel who found themselves enslaved by the powers of the materialistic systems designated by the mystical term, Babylon. These were to be found by the Message of the Messenger and know Divine deliverance from their bondage. Even from the prison-houses the captives were to be set free; for those places of confinement for Israel relate to the constricted conditions amid which the captive Sons of GOD had to live and serve.

⁵ Here there is the foreshadowing of the Secrets to be unveiled and revealed concerning the Planetary Constitution, the Hierarchy, the Fall, the Oblation, the Redemption, and the restoration of the Planet and the Household of Israel.

The Mystery of Ya-akob-El and his Travail; that of Lucifer in his fall and restoration; and that of the Sin-Offering-Burden, with the rebuilding of the City of Zion, are all portrayed. And these are culminated in the glorious rehabilitation of the entire Solar System, through the restoration of the Sons of GOD and the healing of the Earth by means of their manifestation and ministry.

⁶ Zion is the Glorious Christhood Community of the Sons of GOD. Later Notes will give fuller explanation.

⁷ The *set-time* for Zion to be restored is another form of the expression "the fulness of time." Its interpretation is found in the Manifestation and Oblation. The former could be given and the latter be accomplished only when full arrangements had been made in the Celestial Realms as well as in those of the Divine and Angelic. For it was necessary to have all the Celestial Bodies directly affecting this World in such positions as would enable them to contribute their ministry to the Great Events.

The *set-time* for Zion was therefore the period arranged for by the Divine World wherein the Manifestation could be made, the Earth's Heavens changed and purified, the intensification of Solar and Angelic ministries become possible, and ultimating in the finding and restoring of the lost Sons of GOD to the estate of their ancient Christhood and Priesthood ministries.

319

[8] These were and are the Cedars of Lebanon, Trees of GOD's planting. They were and are the Children of the Cross, who once were the expositions upon this World, of the Sacred Mystery of the Cross. They once formed a community of Souls in Holy Priesthood for the LORD, and were as Divine Kings in their regnancy. They bore upon them the Signature of the Divine Name which they revealed in their Way of Life and Service. In their lives the Courts of the daily life and service were pure; and all their Earth-powers were so consecrated to the LORD that these made manifest HIS Purity and Glory.

The Manifestation and Oblation were, in due time, to bring back to Earth such Blessed Ones and Blessed Ways. Hence the insistence of the Divine Call to Israel.

[9] Herein is cryptically revealed the endowments of the Servant who was the chosen and appointed Daysman for Israel and Redeemer of Judah.

To know GOD's Secret Name is to understand through the Being's realization, the deep Mystery of ELI-JAH and that of JEHOVAH.

The Jewels of HIS Holy One are the Attributes of Divine Christhood. They are the twelve precious Gems upon which the Holy City is built, for they are its foundations. All Christhood is reared upon such foundations. They represent qualities and quantities of Divine Potencies.

The added gift from the Divine LORD of the precious Stones of the Breast-Plate has profound signification. It gives a glimpse to the Initiate of the nature of the Priesthood of the Servant of the LORD, and his relationship to the House of Israel; for the Twelve Stones on the Breast-Plate had the names of the Tribes of Israel, and these were covered by the most sacred Urim and Thummim.

III

An Address to Israel

O House of Israel, ye Ancients of the ages whom the Lord God chose to perform His Will towards Judah, through rendering priestly service within the House of Ya-akob-El![1]

Hear ye the Word of your Lord!

"Though ye once had the ears to hear Me and understand My purpose, yet now ye understand not;

And though ye had the eyes to see and perceived greatly unto the knowledge of My Will, yet ye are now veiled so that ye realize not.

I, your Lord, would heal you unto the opening of the eyes of your understanding, and the unveiling of your vision, that ye may again look upon the Beauty of your Lord within My Sanctuary, and the restoring of your heart's emotion till it moves in unison with the motion of the Heavens of My Dwelling."[2]

*   *   *   *   *   *

Behold now, O Israel, what the Lord hath purposed to accomplish for you and the whole House of Ya-akob-El, including the land and the inhabitants of Judah![3]

For, through His Servant whom He shall send unto Ya-akob-El He shall change the cities of Ierusalem[4] that were laid waste, and restore the Houses within Ya-akob-El to be once more Houses for the Children of Judah, and cause all the desolated places to become again like the Garden of God.[5]

III

Notes on Text

[1] The Community of the Christhood known as Israel was related to the Ancient of Days, and its members were

often referred to as the Ancients. They were not of the House of Ya-akob, but of the House of Joseph or I-O-Seph. They were sent to the House of Ya-akob whose head was Ya-akob-El in order to render ministry through that House, unto the House of Judah. This latter was the Household of the Earth, the members of which were performing their growth and evolution of a Planetary order. It was the Sphere of the ministry of the House of Ya-akob. This House represented the triple administration by the Hierarchies over whom Ya-akob-El presided. There were and there are representations of the Divine, Celestial, and Angelic Hierarchies for the government of the Earth, the administration of her Kingdoms, and the culture and enrichment of all the Planet's Children.

[2] The deplorable loss of power, vision, spiritual wealth, and Divine embodiment is here revealed. Those who had been in Christhood had even lost the power to function in the Christ-realm. They had no longer the vision and consciousness of the Presence. Their audition chamber was so changed that they could not hear the Divine Voice with any degree of certainty, so great had been the betrayal of them.

This is the introductory part of a Message from the Divine World, pregnant with hope and healing. Bye and bye the full significance of it will become obvious.

[3] The Oblation had been projected; operations Divine and Celestial had begun; the Vehicle of it had been appointed; the nature and effect of it might now be partially unveiled and proclaimed. The House of Ya-akob-El was involved, for the Seventh-Sphere Angel of the Celestial Planetary Hierarchy had fallen into the snare of the Betrayer, and, as a result, all the outer Kingdoms and Planes of the Planet had been brought low.

[4] "The Cities of Jerusalem," relates to the various communal states upon the Planes of the Planet. The whole of the Spiritual Life of the Earth had been devastated.

[5] The restoration of the Houses within Ya-akob-El implies the restitution of the Zones and Degrees through which all the Children of the Planet must pass in their growth and evolution. Even within the Planetary Heavens were *many mansions or dwelling-places* of the FATHER-MOTHER.

IV

The Voice of Adonai
unto
Those Who Govern

O ye Heavens of the Earth, hear ye now the Word of your Lord!

Give ear all ye who are dwellers therein![1]

The Lord Himself hath spoken and His Word is to be made manifest.

The children whom He did create He hath also nourished; He brought them up to know the way of His commandments.

But those who rebelled against His ways, came unto them. The enemy smote them, taking them away from the land of their inheritance, till they remembered no more the One Who had so blessed them.

They became laden with iniquities; for they were made to be as evil-doers by those who sowed the seeds of evil in their midst. The enemy sought to destroy the works of God by alienating His Children from the paths of Righteousness.[2]

Though their ox still knoweth its owner, and the ass the crib of its master, yet the children have forgotten the goodness of Yahweh.[3]

Even the House of Israel hath been so smitten that its members have forgotten that they were the Ancients of God, a segregated people consecrated to the service of their Lord.

Why should ye be so stricken, O House of Israel?

Why should ye longer share in the ways of those who increase the revolt upon the Earth?[4]

Ye have been stricken from the crown of the head to the soles of your feet; there is no part that hath not been smitten.

Hear ye now the Word of the Lord, and bend no more beneath the yoke of the rulers of Sodom, nor be ye as the peoples who go down into Gomorrah![5]

"Unto what end do ye increase your sacrifices of the creatures' lives unto Me?

I delight not in the slaughter of the bullocks, lambs and he-goats.

The offering up of the sheep and the rams is a source of grief unto Me.

Who commanded you to sacrifice the creatures and eat their flesh?

It was not from Me that such command reached you, nor from My servant, The Messenger.

Those who took you down into bondage wrought this evil thing upon you.

Such sacrifices pollute My Temple; they are the oblations of the Vain.

Bring no more such offerings into your Sanctuary: it is sacrilege.

Let your Lamp burn upon a purified Altar, and your Incense ascend as true Prayer.

Let your Lunar and Solar Festivals be accompanied by the sacrifices of the pure Mind and Heart, that I may bless you in your Sanctuary.[6]

Therefore put away every evil thing, and cleanse your ways from all blood.

Then when ye lift up your hands in prayer, ye shall know the motion of the Spirit.

If thus ye respond to My Word so that ye walk again in the path of My Law, it shall be well with you.

Ierusalem shall also be restored unto you, and become once more the Holy City wherein Righteousness is made manifest, and Equity becomes regnant.

And within her Gates shall Zion[7] again be rebuilt, and all her sons and daughters shall serve before their Lord.

The Word of the Lord unto the House of Ya-akob-El, through His Servant:

It shall come to pass in the latter days that the House of God[8] shall be re-established upon Mount Zion in the midst of the Mountains of the Lord which are above all the Hills of Judah.[9]

And all people shall be blest through the outflow of its glory.

Many of these shall say to each other,

"Come with me, let us together go up to the House of the Lord that is upon Mount Zion, for it is the Temple of the House of the God of Ya-akob-El.[10]

He will teach us still more fully the way of Life that we may walk in His Paths;

For from His Holy Place upon Mount Zion doth He send forth His Word unto Ierusalem."[11]

The Word of the Lord shall make clear His judgments upon all evil;

He shall cause the nations to lay down their weapons of destruction, beating their swords into vessels of honour for His service like the ploughshares and the pruning-hooks.

Then one nation shall no more make war against another nation, nor peoples have evil designs against other peoples;

For the whole House of Ya-akob-El shall have learnt to walk in the paths of righteousness, and serve as those who follow the Way of the Lord.[12]

O House of Ya-akob-El! Wherefore did ye forsake those who ministered unto you and replenished you with the treasures they brought from the Orient?[13]

Wherefore did ye account them as Soothsayers, like the Philistines who say and do things to please the strangers?

Your ministrants belonged to a land that was rich in Silver and Gold; and of precious treasures there was no end.[14]

It was a land containing many noble Horses which drew the Chariots of the Lord.[15]

But thy land is now given up to the worship of idols; for the people bow down before graven images, the work of their own hands.

Even the great ones in your midst bemean themselves before their idols, seeking for that which idols cannot give.[16]

* * * * * *

O House of Ya-akob-El! Enter ye the courts of Life by the Gates that lead to the Rock of Ages, and there abide ye, dwelling in the Awe of your Lord.[17]

He alone is great: His Majesty filleth all the Heavens.

Before Him the proud of heart is bowed down, and the uplifted mind made humble; for haughtiness has no place of abode in His Presence.[18]

The day of the coming of the Lord of Sabaoth shall be for everyone a day of true humility; for the proud will have learnt how to be humble, and the uplifted to be lowly.

Even the great Cedars of Lebanon who have known exaltation, shall bow themselves before Him.[19]

Likewise shall all the Oaks of Bashan upon the Hills beneath, when the daily sacrifice is offered, bow themselves before Him.[20]

For when He doth come in Majesty and Power, the Heavens are filled with the motion of His Spirit, and the Earth is made to tremble to her foundations.

* * * * * *

O House of Ya-akob-El!

Enter ye in by the Gate that leadeth to the Eternal Rock, and find those Clefts wherein ye may abide in His Peace in the Day of His appearing.[21]

IV

Notes on Text

[1] Here the Planetary Cosmic nature of the Message is obvious. The Heavens of the Earth represent the various circles of the Atmospheria, and those who dominated them and ruled the Human Race from them. The members of the Lower Hierarchy dwelt there, and these latter are addressed in this Message. It must be borne in mind that the Message relates to a period preceding the Oblation by more than a Naronic Cycle. It was in those Heavens that the influences of the Sodomites prevailed and filled all the Earth with the darkness of Gomorrah.

[2] The way of the betrayal is here set forth. Those who joined in the defection, supporting the one who went out from the Presence in anger, came to this world and smote all its Children, robbing them of their Divine Heritage, and making them forget the Goodness of God. For in this way the enemy sought to destroy the Works of God by changing them into the likeness of things foreign to the Divine Purpose.

[3] The Ox is the symbol of the powers of the body and the Ass of the attributes of the mind. The body knew how to get nourishment, for the physical realms owned it; the mind knew the powers that harassed it, and whence it derived its knowledge of things seen; but the Being had forgotten the Lord. Even those who in part once knew Him, had lost the memory of His Countenance.

[4] Even the House of Israel had forgotten the Presence, who they were, why they were here, and the estate that once was theirs as Divine Inheritance. For the communities of the Christhood had been greatly tried by the conditions. They had been affected by the fallen states of the Planet's children and the Earth's Kingdoms, and they suffered affliction from the Crown of the Head to the Soles of the Feet; for their thought had been hurt and the ways of their going changed. Mind and Heart had been unduly burdened and oppressed until they were even as those who did iniquity.

[5] This reference to the rulers of Sodom and Gomorrah indicates the nature of the later forms of Soul betrayal. They are named "the Cities of the plains." They represented states

of existence upon the Planet's Planes. The sensualizing influences changed all the spiritual conditions, and caused a cessation of Soul growth and evolution amongst the Children of the Planet, and interfered most lamentably with the Life and ministry of the Christhood. Even the Heavens had to be shut up for long ages so that their ministries were put under great limitation. Pandemonium reigned in the Heavens of the Planet, and a Red Sea of passion inverted, belted the Earth.

It was during this awful descent of the children of this World beneath the Human Kingdom that the polarity of the Planet became suddenly changed, causing the "Bow of the LORD" in the Heavens—the second Magnetic Plane—to fall upon the outer planes of the Earth, producing tremendous upheavals on sea and land, and causing devastation in many quarters and destruction amongst the Human Races.

This catastrophe was the event referred to in the Old Testament as the destruction of Sodom and Gomorrah by the descent of fire and brimstone from the Celestial Heavens. "The Bow in the Heavens" which fell was composed of many most sacred Elements and Substances, and contained many precious Gems.

6 The whole of the paragraph reveals the effect upon Israel of the conditions which had obtained. It shows how the priesthood of Jewry had materialized the Mysteries, and misapplied the Sacred Terms in which certain of the Mysteries had been expressed. The Spiritual Sacrifices had been changed and made to relate to the Creatures. The Lunar and Solar Festivals were originally great events in the religious ministries of Israel. They were associated with the advent to this world of the Sun of GOD and the marvellous ministries of Luna.

7 Unto this day it is made manifest how difficult it is to heal the Earth's wounds and restore the Christhood whilst the terrible system of traffic in the lives of the creatures prevails. The shambles and what issues from them are a blot upon the name of the FATHER-MOTHER, and a travesty and mockery of all that Love and Wisdom in Life stand for. To bring Peace and Joy to Jerusalem, and enable the Sons of GOD to arise, make Jesushood manifest, and rebuild the Holy City of the Christhood, there must be a cessation of the dark ways of Sodom and Gomorrah.

8 The Servant of the LORD who was appointed to be the

Daysman for Israel, was also given the ministry of conveying Divine Messages to the Planetary Angel, Ya-akob-El. The Message here is of great significance. The re-establishing of the HOUSE OF GOD upon Mount Zion which was in the midst of the Mountains of the LORD indicates that the Order of the Sons of GOD would be fully restored; for they formed the House of GOD within the System presided over by Ya-akob-El. The Mount Zion was the exalted Christhood manifestation revealed in the ministry of the Sons of GOD. The Mountains of the LORD cryptically expressed various altitudes of vision and realization. The Christhood estates were in the midst of these.

⁹ The Hills of Judah also represented states of Life, vision and realization; but even the most exalted of them were but as foothills to the Mountains of the LORD. Before these latter were reached by the Earth's Children, the former had to be climbed.

¹⁰ The elder children of the Planet known as the Children of the Adoption, had been taught many things concerning the Sacred Mysteries, and it is of them these words are spoken. They alone of all the Earth's Children could have so spoken. They belonged to the House of Judah but were under the administration of the House of Ya-akob-El, of the inner Hierarchy of the Planet. For the Temple of the Lord within the House of Ya-akob-El, was indeed the Temple or exalted state represented by Mount Gerizim in Samaria.

¹¹ Here the above Children of the Adoption recognize that it is out of Zion the LORD doth speak unto HIS Children; for it is through the Christhood HE ministers unto the redeemed of Ierusalem—the whole spiritual Household of the Planet.

¹² This is a general use of the expression to cover all the Earth, and is pregnant with great hope as a prophecy. For all the Planet's Houses are under Ya-akob-El.

¹³ This Divine Lament is most moving. It implies a state of shadows, deepening unto doubt resulting in the rejection of the Divine Ministries. And it covertly reveals the subtle influences of the Betrayer upon the various members of the Hierarchy.

¹⁴ The Servants of the Orient were members of the Christ-hood. They brought with them the Treasures of the Divine

329

East, for they were richly endowed of GOD. They belonged to the Land of Silver and Gold, and all precious things. The coinage of Silver and Gold had no relation to the Earth use of these most precious substances, but rather to the enrichment of Vision, Knowledge and Love. Those sent were Sons of GOD who dwelt in the golden Auric splendour of the Presence, and knew both of the Mysteries represented by Silver and Gold. Because of this, they were the possessors of Treasures untold—the knowledge of Heavenly Secrets.

15 The Horses which drew the Chariots of the LORD were high Intelligences, unfallen Sons of Ephraim. They saddled the Potencies through which the Divine LORD rode through the System. They understood from the Divine World the Will of the FATHER-MOTHER.

16 When great Minds fall the results are disastrous. They become great idolaters. They bow before the creations of their own unillumined imagination. They worship the graven images of their own fashioning. This is true in every sphere, from the Hierarchy downward. It may be witnessed in religious pursuits, in material science, in politics and governments, and in commerce.

17 Incidentally it is revealed that the appeal is to members of the Hierarchy who were influenced by the Betrayer. The LORD of All Being alone is great: and HE alone must be acknowledged.

18 The truly great ones are ever humble. They make no claim except for their LORD. They are of lowly mind and heart.

19 Even those who have grown up upon Lebanon as the Cedars of GOD, bow before HIM, and acknowledge HIM in all their powers and services.

20 The reference here is to the stalwart Intellects or Intermediary Intelligences who serve in the daily sacrifice of powers in the service of Life upon the Planet. In an unfallen World the ministry of these is of great moment in the growth and evolution of the Soul.

21 The appeal is profound. The Gate that leadeth to the Eternal Rock wherein is found perfect equipoise and the ministry resulting from such exquisite balance, is that of the Will. Let the LORD be ever welcomed in the Day of HIS appearing. Let HIS WILL be accomplished.

V

The Angel of the Outer Sphere

"O Lucifer! Ancient Son of the Morning and Day-Star of the Heavens of the Earth![1]

How art thou still as one who hath fallen from his high estate?[2]

Why art thou still captive, lying in the dust of thy humiliation unto which thou wast brought down by him who came unto thee in the Name of the Lord of Hosts?

He brought thee down from thine high estate that he might make of thy Kingdom a heritage for all those whom he took with him, after he went out from the Presence of the Lord.[3]

He said in his heart;—

"I shall make myself great. Unto the heights of God's Heavens shall I ascend and reign above the Stars of God:

I shall yet sit upon the Mount of the Assembly of the Gods, and reign over them from my throne in the North.

I shall ascend beyond the heights of the Cloud of God's Radiance and be even as the Most High."[4]

Yet he brought thee down, O Star of the Morning! To the abyss whither he went, he brought thee down, and filled thy Kingdom of regnancy with the fires of hell.[5]

But My loving-kindness is great unto thee: the healing of My Mercy is upon thee to raise thee up, and thy Kingdom with thee.

Thus will I restore again the Household of Ya-akob-El."[6]

V

Notes on Text

[1] How often Lucifer has been named "The Devil and

331

Satan!" Yet he was neither, though he became the victim of the betraying influence of Satan and the negativing spirit of the Devil. For Satan means the *betrayer*, and the Devil *the destroyer*.

Lucifer was the Angel of the seventh sphere of the Planet, counting from the Within to the Without. He was the Director of those who worked amid the Elements of the outer sphere, and directed the outer flow of the magnetic currents. He was a radiant Son of the Gods, and was specially endowed for the work to which he had been appointed. During his office, he was clothed in Magnetic Light. So he is addressed as the Morning-Star and Day-Star of the Earth.

2 Many had been the efforts made to recover him and lift him up to his original estate: hence the nature of the address to him. How came it to pass that he was still in fallen state? He was betrayed so greatly that he lost his estate and his Kingdom, for the Betrayer led him to do things which brought havoc upon all who were associated with him. It was the primary cause of the fall of the House of Judah; for the magnetic conditions were changed in a manner that led to the fixity of many elements and substances.

3 The Son of the Gods who opposed the Divine Will regarding the entirely spiritual nature and constitution of this one time most glorious system. This hidden-for-ages sad story is uncovered in one of the preceding parts of this volume, the reading of which will aid the earnest ones to understand many things that have hitherto been sealed.

4 The ambition herein unveiled is sufficient to explain why it became necessary for that Son of the Gods to go out from the Celestial Assembly and from the Presence of Him Who presided over it, and even from the presence of the ETERNAL. He claimed to be even as GOD. There is a corrupted reference to that one in the Pauline Second Letter to the Thessalonians. The original Cryptic Logia were spoken by the Master to the most intimate Friends.

5 The Earth has been full of the Fires of Gehenna and the awful darkness of Hinnom for long ages as the outcome of the Betrayal.

6 The Divine World promise is full of hope; and especially so unto those who know what the Eternal Love and Wisdom has been doing through great ages for the recovery and healing and restoration of this System.

332

VI

The Travail of Zion

O Lord God of Israel! Our prayer is unto Thee.

Look upon us from Thy Heavens, the High Habitation of Thy Holiness and Thy Glory!

Behold us who once had Thy strength, and were full of zeal for Thee.

The motion of Thy tender mercies is not restrained; for Thou art our Father-Creator, though Abraham has not yet set his seal upon us, nor the inheritance of Israel again become our possession.[1]

From everlasting Thy Name hast Thou given to us. Thou hast been our Redeemer in the land of tribulation: we are Thine; the Tribes of Thine Inheritance.[2]

O that Thou wouldst open up the Heavens of our Being through Thine overshadowing Presence, that from the Mountains of Thy Glory there may flow unto us of Thy Radiant Power, and the elements of our Being become changed through the transmuting Fires of Thy Holy Energy, that within us Thou mayest make glorious Thy Holy Name, and manifest Thyself through us; even as when Thou didst mighty works on our behalf from the Mountains of Thy Habitation, and there flowed unto us from Thy Holy Presence the streams of Thy Radiance full of glorious power.[3]

Since the beginning of this World, as now it is, when Ierusalem became a desolation and Zion a fallen City in her midst, and the Courts of the Sanctuary were trodden by the oppressor, it hath not been declared to the ear of man, nor hath the eye of anyone beheld, nor the heart conceived and perceived, what Thou hast kept in store to give as Inheritance to all who seek unto the knowing of Thee.[4]

O Lord God of the Heavenly Hosts!

333

Who is to be likened unto Thee in Thy Ways?

Thou meetest in the way of his going the man who holdeth Thee in his remembrance, and who rejoiceth to work Righteousness before Thee.

Thou blottest out the shadows of his iniquities, and healest his dread of Thy just judgments.

Thou, Lord, art the Father-Creator of us all; we are Thy handiwork; out of Thy Substance Thou didst fashion us.[5]

Thus saith the Lord:

"O My People! Be ye comforted! Be ye comforted!

Speak ye My Word unto Ierusalem, that her warfare is being accomplished, that her mistake is being healed;[6] *that when she issues from her wrong states, again she shall receive the double portion as inheritance from her Lord's hand."*

The voice of the Messenger of the Lord amid the Wilderness crieth:—

"Prepare ye the way for the coming of the Lord;

Build ye across the Desert the Highway of God!

Thus, every Valley shall be exalted; the Hills and the Mountains made clear; the crooked ways straightened out; the rough places made smooth;

Then the Glory of the Lord shall be revealed and all Souls shall behold its Radiance.

The Word of the Lord hath declared this!"[7]

"In the strength of thy Lord lift up thy voice and proclaim unto Ierusalem, the Glad Tidings, that the Lord cometh in the greatness of His Power to make manifest His Kingdom unto His people, and how He doth bear rule over them.[8]

Unto all those who look for His coming, to wait upon Him and serve Him, shall be great recompense;

For, in His coming, He doth give the Glory of His Presence:

It is His Inheritance restored unto them.[9]

He shall nourish them through His Word even as the

Shepherd feedeth his flock:[10] for He is the Shepherd of them all.

He shall gently lead those who be still young, bearing them up and carrying them in His Arms;

For in His Bosom dwelleth the Lamb of God." [11]

"It is the Lord Who holdeth the Waters of Life;
In His Hand is contained their full measure:
He meteth them out unto the Heavens;
His span doth encompass them all:[12]

He giveth comprehension unto Souls upon the Earth, that they may have Understanding whereby they may know the measure of His Tierce: [13]

He giveth Balance unto those ascending His Hills, and Power to all who scale the great Mountains;[14]

He giveth the motion of His Spirit unto all, and His direction unto those who seek His Counsel;

He giveth unto such His instruction how to walk in the Paths of His Righteousness, and doth shew unto their Understanding the meaning of all His Judgments;

For He doth fill these with knowledge of His Way."

"O Ya-akob! Why sayest thou
'My way is hidden from the sight of God?'
O Israel! Why speakest thou thus
'In His Judgment hath the Lord passed over me?'[15]
Unto whom do ye liken Him?
Compare ye Him in His ways towards you with those who bear not His likeness?

Have ye not known Him of old time when His Voice spake unto you concerning the Word of His Message?"

Unto the Messenger His Voice spake, saying,
"Cry the Message unto Ierusalem":
And the Servant made request of Him
"How shall I proclaim it?"
And the Voice commanded him to cry—

"*All that is of the Flesh is as the Grass, and even as the Flower of the Field;*

For the grass withereth, and the Flower fadeth away; and thus do the People when the Breath of the Lord faileth to rest upon them and move through them: then surely they are as the Grass.

But when the Spirit of the Lord moveth within them they know Him as the Word, El Adonai, whose Presence maketh them endure for evermore."[16]

*   *   *   *   *   *   *

Behold, O Zion! It is the Word of thy Lord Who standeth sure for evermore.[17]

O Zion! Hearest thou the Glad Tidings?

Arise, then! And come unto His high mountain; from thence shalt thou bear the Glad Tidings, even the Message of thy Lord, to cry unto the cities of Judah, saying to them, "Behold, your God!"[18]

*   *   *   *   *   *

Thy Lord is the Everlasting God, the Creator of the Heavens and the Earth.

From the beginning hath this been revealed to you, even before the foundations of this world.[19]

He fainteth not in the way of His going, nor groweth weary in His regnancy;

He understandeth all His children's needs;

He reigneth upon the Earth's encompassing circles, and filleth them with the Glory of His Presence.[20]

The Heavens move with the motion of His Spirit,

He doth curtain them with His Overshadowing;

He maketh Tents within them for our dwelling.[21]

*   *   *   *   *   *

To His faint children will He give power, and to all weakened in the way, increase of strength;

In Him the young shall grow rich, and those who seemed failing shall overcome;

His might shall be unto all who wait upon Him; on the Wings of His Spirit shall they be upborne:

*As they soar, they shall know no weariness; and none shall faint nor fall who walk in the Path of the Lord.*²²

VI

NOTES ON TEXT

¹ Zion was the Holy City of the Christhood. It was related to the Solar World. The word means the City of the Sun. In the ancient Mysteries taught by the Prophets of Israel, it was within the radius of Ierusalem, but above it. It was the real City of David, and contained the Temple of Solomon. It was the Temple of On—the Sun. Its foundations were Mount Moriah—the Altar of the Abrahamic Sacrifice.

It was the Temple of High Initiates. These were the Illumined Ones, whose heads or Elders were the Illuminati. These formed the Priesthood of Israel; though in mediatorial ministry the whole Nation of the illumined became a Kingdom of Priests for GOD.

This knowledge of what Israel had been will explain the prayer. At one time all of the Household contacted the Inner World in some degree, and knew the strength and blessedness of Heavenly Fellowship, and the Divine Joy of perfect service. And the prayer is characteristic of The Return; for the Recovery of that high estate seems a slow process. Yet the longing of the true Israel is to have once more the Abrahamic Seal upon the Life.

² There is no beginning and there is no end, though changes are manifold and perpetual. Our elements of Being belong to the ETERNAL, and our individuated consciousness was always in HIM before HE gave it us. Here it is revealed that the Prophet of GOD knew the Secret of the Mystery of Israel. For the Elect People had the Divine Name engraved upon them. They were Tribes of the Solar Christhood.

³ This prayer reveals how deep was the understanding of the nature of the encompassing and overshadowing Presence and the energizing effects of the realization of such. And there is uncovered notwithstanding the cryptic form of expression,

the memory of the past tragic experiences passed through, the burdens borne, and the marvellous Divine intervention.

⁴ In this epitome of the great changes that had taken place in Zion and Ierusalem—the Christhood and the Spiritual Household of the Planet—there is a gleaming given of the Prophet's knowledge of the coming Messianic Manifestation and the Burden of the Oblation. Eye had not seen, nor ear heard, nor had the heart even of Israel conceived what the Divine Love and Wisdom had in store for His People.

⁵ This acclamation, full of prayer and ascription, is most moving. The recognition of the Majesty of the ETERNAL, and the distinctiveness of His Ways in the manifestation of HIMSELF unto His Children wherein His Love and Wisdom are unfailingly revealed, searches to the depths of the Soul, and exalts the Being above all the Earth, and even all the Travail of the Ages.

There is also revealed the sublime Mystery, that the Sons of GOD knew that they had been fashioned out of the Divine Substance—the Divine Ætheria, and that they were the Inheritors, as Divine Heirs, of the Eternal Spirit. Nor is it to be marvelled at that the House of Israel, spoke of the FATHER-MOTHER as JEHOVAH, when we know that that most Sacred Name contained both masculine and feminine elements, and represented the Divine Duality—Fatherhood and Motherhood.

⁶ In this cryptic statement there is contained the whole history of the Fall and its result. The Holy City of Ierusalem was the blessed Household of the Planet in the spiritual constitution and estate of all the Human Races, and the various Hierarchies whose members administered its elements and ministered through them, unto all Souls. By means of the Divine Passion in the Oblation, the mistake made by the governors and the children of men, was to be healed, the Earth restored to her Celestial status, and the dual blessing of the triumphant Love and Wisdom to be once more realized.

⁷ The full Restoration is here unfalteringly proclaimed and how it was to be accomplished. By the embodiment of Righteousness and Equity through the triumph of Love, can the Light of Wisdom be made manifest as the Hills of the Soul and the Mountains of GOD—the Soul's Spiritual Uplands, and the Great Altitudes of Divine Vision and Realization. In this way alone can the beauty and wonder of the works of

the FATHER-MOTHER become unveiled and recognized by His Children, and the effects felt of His Auric splendour.

⁸ The *real* Glad Tidings are interpenetrated with the Light of His Wisdom, and interfused by the streams of His Love. The Divine Government of the World and GOD'S attitude unto His Children have been a long-lost knowledge; for those who were concerned with the Betrayal, caused a false view of the Nature and Ways of the FATHER-MOTHER to obtain rule and prevail.

⁹ The religious people of the Prophet's day sought for and expected as reward for their belief and devotion, increased earthly inheritance, or the restoration of some lost possession. But the real gift of GOD is Eternal Life whatever earthly gifts may run parallel to it. And the full realization of Life Eternal is the knowing of GOD as the FATHER-MOTHER through His Indwelling Presence. On His coming to the Sanctuary, the consciousness of His Abiding becomes an everlasting possession.

¹⁰ The Word is the vital Life of the Being of one who has known Christhood. He is the Living Bread and Wine, Sacramental and Eucharistic. By means of such sustenance, the recipient becomes a Living Sacrifice for the LORD—a Divine Mass.

¹¹ The Eternal Mystery of the Divine Love in ministry. It is ever in all worlds, the Divine Passion. The Lamb reigns with the LORD.

¹² The Sea of Mystery is contained in the ETERNAL, and its Waters of Life are poured forth in ministry. GOD'S giving is without measure; yet does HE accommodate measure to the need and capacity of the recipient. Thus are the whole of the Heavens nourished from HIM and held in His embrace.

¹³ This is a most profound statement and has to be expressed in Cryptic terms. That the Soul has such power of comprehension is the sure evidence of the Soul's inherent divinity; for if it can rise unto the state wherein it is able to understand the Divine Mystery expressed in the sign *Tierce*, then it must be the inheritor of deific potencies. And we have sure evidence that this is so. Man is in the Likeness of GOD; and when the Soul attains to the estate of a Son of GOD, it becomes an embodiment of Deity.

¹⁴ The Soul's Ascent is from hill to hill, then from hill to

mountain, and on from mountain to mountain. To be in Balance upon the heights, is to be equilibriated. The power acquired is commensurate with the degrees of Ascension.

15 A glimpse of the state of impoverishment and loss of vision sustained by Israel, and by the Planet's Angel, as the result of the desert conditions which had overtaken the Earth. They were in despair at one period and actually felt forsaken.

16 Something of the Mystery of the Breath is here indicated, and its vital relationship to all Souls. GOD breathed into Man the Breath of Life, and Man became a Living Soul. In that "Saying" there is revealed the attainment by Man of some Divine Estate. *It was an act of initiation.* Man became *Bio-generic*—not only a Planetary Man, but one who had reached a state of Childhood to the Eternal wherein he was capable of receiving the hallowed Mystery of the Baptism of the Spirit.

In a general sense all Souls are dependent upon the Spirit. But it is very specially true concerning the Sons of GOD who had once risen to the high initiation referred to above. These fade away in the sense of the loss of Divine Realization which the Holy Spirit gave them as Inheritance.

17 The "Saying" or Word of GOD—the Substance of Being, is the one sure rock of all the ages. HE is the Rock of Ages. HE never faileth. The Sons of GOD must again trust HIM. HE is the foundation of Zion, its bulwark and its glory.

18Arise! Sons of GOD! Such is the call. And in the arising know again the Divine reality, and be equal to revealing it; for in this way alone may all the members of the Christhood be able to truly say unto all the House of Judah—Behold! GOD is here!

19 Yet another reference to the unfallen days and the high state in which Israel stood and ministered before the founding of this cosmos, or order of things which came to prevail upon the Earth. Herein may be glimpsed that the present order of existence was not in harmony with the Divine Purpose.

20 In the unfallen days it was even so. Through the regnancy of Ya-akob-El, the ETERNAL reigned in righteousness and equity. But through the changed conditions within the Planet's Heavens the Divine World could not minister. But now, because of all that was accomplished by means of the

Oblation, it may be again truly affirmed that the LORD reigneth upon the Circles of the Heavens of the Earth.

21 Within those Circles the children of the Earth have stations to which they go and in which they dwell for a time; but the reference here is to higher Heavens or states for the Sons of GOD.

22 The promise is potent, and the truth of it is assured in realization. The riches of HIS Grace are bestowed upon the sincere Soul who takes flight into the Land of the Spirit. The measure of the Soul's possession of the Divine Spirit is also that of its ascension into the Heavens. In the flight of the Spirit there is no weariness of Being; the tiredness imposed by the conditions of the Earth has no place where only the might of the Spirit prevails.

VII

The Remnants of Israel

In that Day the Lord of the heavenly Hosts shall stretch forth His Arm over the remnants of Israel who may still be dwellers in the countries of Assyria, Egypt, Pathros, Cush, Elam, Shinar, Hamath and the Isles of the Sea, as outcasts from their own land, that they be such no more, but again become of the Assembly of God's people who bear His Ensign unto the Nations.[1]

Then the Assembly of God's people shall, as His Servants, gather together all the Children of Judah from the four dimensions of the Earth.[2]

The pride of Ephraim shall be healed.[3]

Envy shall no more have any place.

In the land of Judah there shall remain nothing that would hurt, nor anything that would be the cause of grief.

The treasures of the Orient shall be gathered together.

The powers of Philistia shall be used for service in the West.[4]

The hand of Blessing shall be upon Edom and Moab: and the children of Ammon shall serve within the land.[5]

The Lord Himself, in the Day of His coming, shall utterly change the Delta of Egypt through the motion of His Breath: the seven streams of the River shall be purified; and these shall be as highways for Assyria, even as the redeemed powers of Assyria shall be for Israel in the service of the Lord.[6]

In the Day of the Lord, when He cometh unto Zion in the fulness of His Glory, the Sacred Seven shall possess the man of God.[7]

They will give him of their Bread, and adorn him with their Raiment.[8]

In that Day the reproach of all Israel shall be taken away; and the Branch of the Lord, in the beauty of His fashion, shall reveal unto all Israel the Glory of the Lord.

In that Day the whole House of Israel shall have escaped from the effects of the bondage they found upon the Earth; and the Earth herself shall have become comely in her fashion, and her Kingdoms be filled with beautiful things that will bear rich fruits for all her children.[9]

Then shall it come to pass that all who are in the City of Ierusalem will be accounted holy, like those who have been dwellers in the City of Zion.

For upon every dweller in Mount Zion shall rest the Cloud of the Glory of the Lord; and there shall burn continually upon the Altar His Sacred Flame, to illume the Sanctuary with His Radiance.[10]

And overshadowing the Shekinah within the Tabernacle, shall the Glory of the Lord abide for ever.[11]

VII

NOTES ON TEXT

[1] The scattered Children of Zion are found in many Lands and many States. Each of the terms signify states. When the polarity of the Mind is deflected, the latter passes into the House of Bondage. But redeemed Assyria is a noble creative state.

When the Passional Nature is inverted—the Love-principle, it carries the Soul down into the Land of Darkness—Cush. But where a Soul is full of Divine Passion, it conquers even the land of Cush.

When the Soul knows the agedness of an Elamite, it has become a worshipper within the Sun, and realizes the Mystery of GOD in HIS Love and Wisdom—the two Rivers of Shinar. They are the very elect ones who of all Israel have retained this Divine Inheritance throughout the ages of Travail in this world.

And these have been as a Fortress of Defence for many of the members of the House of Israel, as the term Hamath implies.

[2] When all Israel has arisen and become again An Assembly of GOD's People, then and only then can be accomplished the full healing and redemption of all the Earth's Children. For nothing less than a corporate manifestation of Christhood will effect the healing of the Nations, and the reconciliation of all Races. For only Love made manifest in action; Compassion, Pity, Righteousness and Equity embodied in their interpretation, will bring back to Humanity the Divine Message that Life is a most Sacred Gift of GOD to be cherished and cultured into the Divine Image, and that whosoever hurts that Life in the Individual, Nation, and Race, sins against his own Soul, and so sins against GOD.

[3] The Great Minds—Administrators, Rulers, Philosophers, and Scientists, with sadly fallen reflections of these in oppressive and oppressing Ecclesiastics.

[4] The Land of those who are as Wanderers and Wayfarers—mental and spiritual nomads, who, until redeemed, never seem to have an abiding place. They are wandering lights. Yet are their powers manifest in the outer Life to be redeemed and saddled for service.

[5] The Land of Personality, Generation and Forgetfulness. In the day of the Redemption the Soul will remember, and the *Outer Life* shall be consecrated even as *the Inner*.

[6] The reference is to an Ancient Knowledge. It was one of the great Secrets of the Illumined Ones. The reader will be familiar with the physiographic Delta of Egypt, and in reading this passage would naturally associate the reference with modern Egypt. But the real meaning is mystical, and the expression is Cryptic, and hides a great and most Sacred Mystery. Later in these Notes, there will be a further reference to the Mystery; but here it may be stated that it concerns the superstructure of the Soul, the dual River represented by the White and Blue Nile, and the Seven Streams proceeding from the dual River. It is of the Divine Kingdom in Man and all Celestial Systems that these speak—of which more bye and bye.

[7] This is likewise a cryptic statement of Elohistic value. In the authorised version of the Old Testament, the Prophet is made to say that seven women will lay hold of one man and ask him to marry them. It is amazing how the most Sacred Truths have been brought down and made personal and

material. For these Logia refer to the exalted attainment of a Soul through the Divine becoming realized in the Sanctuary of Being, wherein the ELOHIM possess every part of the Temple.

8 They nourish that Son of the Highest upon the Divine Substance of GOD's Holy Eucharist, and give him to drink of the Wine which fills the mysterious Chalice within the Tabernacle.

9 A glorious promise of the full effects of the Redemption and Regeneration. In that day the Travail of Israel shall have been accomplished. No longer shall the Sons of GOD dwell and serve in the Land of the Shadows, but in that of the Radiance of the LORD. And the Earth shall share in the Blessing of such realization and embodiment, for all her Children and her Kingdoms shall be restored.

10 What a time of Light, Joy, Peace and Power, when once more the whole House of Israel has become conscious of the Cloud resting upon the Sanctuary, and the Sacred Flame alight upon the High Altar.

11 This is prophetic of the fully recovered state of the Presence within the Guest Chamber; for this latter is the Sanctuary of JEHOVAH.

VIII

The Refashioning of The Earth

Thus saith the Lord:

Behold I will re-create the Heavens of the Earth, and the glory of them shall be so great that the former shall not be remembered nor cast their shadows upon the threshold of the heart.[1]

And ye shall be glad for evermore, and rejoice in that I re-create Ierusalem and have Joy in Mine Inheritance.[2]

The voice of sorrow and weeping shall be no more heard within her Gates.

* * * * * *

My People shall be no more as infants of days; but all shall be as those whose days are fulfilled; for they shall be wise, and build again the House of the Lord, and become once more the dwellers within His Courts.[3]

Their Vineyard shall be planted from the Lord and their Vines bear great fruitage for Him; their Dwellings also shall be as Wine-vats wherein the fruits of the Vineyard shall be gathered, and the Wine pressed forth shall be Vintage of His Love.[4]

Their days shall be those of the Tree of Life, for they shall be of the Everlasting Ages.[5]

Ere the incense of their prayers ascends to the Heavens they shall be heard; for unto their prayer will I make response; and in their sacrifice they shall be blest.

VIII

NOTES ON TEXT

[1] There are quite a number of references in the Books of the Prophets found in the Old Testament to the passing away of the Earth and the Heavens, and the replacing of them by new Heavens and a new Earth. Many have thought the references to relate to the time when everything would be changed—the end of the World. But the meaning is to be found in the fallen state of the Planet's Heavens and the purposed purification of them by means of the Oblation. For the field of the operations of the Oblation was in the circles of the Planet's Heavens. This mysterious Work will be found more fully unveiled in the sections wherein the Sin-Offering Mystery is unveiled.

[2] The re-creation of Ierusalem was the forecasting of the effect upon the Earth of the Oblation, and restoration of the spiritual estate of all her children. For the Holy City of Ierusalem was the whole Household of the Planet as a spiritual system. For Ierusalem had been fallen. It was the dwelling place of those who were enemy to its highest life. Its terraces and palaces had been broken down by the enemy. It had become a centre of strife and confusion. But by means of the purification and restoration of its Heavens, the Earth was to be recovered, and all her children redeemed. In this way Ierusalem would be re-created, and become a Home of joy and gladness for all the children.

[3] The reference is to the Sons of GOD. Through their œonial travail amid the fallen conditions of this world, they had become as those who have lost a great heritage; for they forgot their Divine Heritage and lost the memory of their Lord, and even of the one who had frequently been sent as Messenger unto them. Though the eldest and most advanced Souls upon the Earth, they had become as young children in their vision and realization compared with the high estate which once was theirs.

[4] The Vineyard, the Vines, the Dwellings and the Wine-vats, are symbolic expressions of their estate within the Kingdom of GOD, their recovery of the Christhood, their ministry amongst the Sons of Men, and the most blessed

fruitage. For, in the recovery of the estate of Christhood, they would be again living, manifesting and serving the Divine Love as His embodiments. Even the pain of their travail would be as the pressing out within the Wine-vat of their Being, the Wine of Divine Love.

[5] The Tree of Life signifies, in the most interior Kingdom, the Eternal Mystery of the FATHER-MOTHER. Here that Mystery is unveiled as part of the Inheritance of one who has attained Christhood. For, as Eternal Life is to know the FATHER-MOTHER, so the Tree of Life is the Mystery of GOD realized in such high degree that the Soul dwells within the vision and consciousness of the ETERNAL ONE.

IX

YAHWEH UNTO YA-AKOB-EL AND ISRAEL

O House of Ya-akob-El, hear ye the Word of the Lord![1]
*Ye have been called by the name of Israel, though ye
be still children of the land of Judah.*[2]

*Ye make your vows in the name of the Lord, and affirm
your belief in the God of Israel.*

*Ye speak of yourselves as belonging to the Holy City
of Zion, and of being stayed upon the Lord of Hosts.*

*Yet have ye to learn many things concerning His Truth
and Righteousness;*[3]

For the God of Israel is also the Lord God of Sabaoth.

    *   *   *   *   *   *

*In former times these things were declared unto you;
but ye became as those who heard them not, and even as
those who had never known them.*

*For those who created the graven images and fashioned
idols, took you away from the knowledge and service of
the God of Israel.*[4]

*They dealt treacherously with you in the day when you
put your trust in them.*

*In the furnace of affliction I found you suffering at the
hands of those who put you there.*

*But out from the furnace will I bring you, refined as
gold that has been purified from all dross, and as pure
silver poured forth from the alembic.*

*And I shall thus be glorified in you in the day when
ye become inheritors of the Holy City of Zion,*[5] *and know
yourselves to be children of the Lord, the God of Sabaoth.*

    *   *   *   *   *   *

*O Ya-akob-El! Hearken unto Me, for I would speak
with thee through My Servant.*

349

O Israel, Mine own elect ones! Hearken ye also unto the Word of your Lord which My Servant will speak to you.

As I am Alpha so am I also Omega.

That which had its beginning in Me shall also have its fulfilment in Me.[6]

By My Hand were the foundations of the Heavens laid, and the Earth shared in the glory of them.

The Arch of the Heavens was formed by Me, and all beneath it must come together.[7]

For My Word commands that this should come to pass, and that the Heavens and the Earth should again be as one.

I AM that I AM, the Lord God of Sabaoth, hath declared it.[8]

Hear ye, therefore, the message given unto My Servant to speak unto you from Me; for I have chosen and anointed him for My service.

* * * * * *

The Servant of the Lord unto Ya-akob-El and Israel:—

Let the Assembly be called together, O Ya-akob-El![9]

Let all Israel come before the Lord to hear of His marvellous doings.

In the beginning it was not given to me to reveal the secrets of the Lord; but since the time when it was so given unto me, I have been caught up by Him that I might speak of them.

And now the Lord, the God of Sabaoth, through His Holy One, hath sent me that I might speak of those secrets unto you.[10]

* * * * * *

Thus saith the Lord thy Redeemer, O Ya-akob-El; and likewise unto you, O Shepherds of Israel.[11]

"I AM that I AM," doth speak.

The Holy One of Israel is Yahweh. He is the God of Sabaoth: hear ye Him:—

"*I would teach you of My Secrets, and make known unto you the way of my goings for the restoration of thy Kingdom, O Ya-akob-El, and your ancient Inheritance, O Israel.*[12]

"*Oh that thou hadst hearkened unto My commandments, O House of Ya-akob-El!*[13]
For then had My Peace flowed through thy land like the deep, calm waters of a great river.
Then had Righteousness lapped the shores of thy land like the waters of the sea in their motion.
Thine offspring would have been touched by those waters and shared in the blessing of their coming;
Nor would they have been cut off as those deprived of their sustenance."[14]

"*Hear thou this, O House of Ya-akob-El!*
Thou shalt go forth from bondage to the King of Babylon, and be delivered from the false Chaldeans.[15]
In song shall this be told to Israel, and the uttermost parts of the Earth hear it; that the Lord of the Heavenly Hosts, the God of Israel, hath purposed to redeem the House of Ya-akob-El."

*   *   *   *   *   *

O ye dwellers amid the Isles, listen unto the Word of the Lord which He hath spoken unto me concerning you.
He it was who brought you forth from the Great Deep and fashioned you to be His servants.[16]
Through His overshadowing did He guard you, and by the polished shafts of His Bow He defended you.[17]
Of you hath He said unto me, I would be glorified in My servants Israel.

Hear ye, therefore, His Word unto me; for, though Israel be not yet gathered together from the four dimensions of the Earth, even now would I be a dweller in the Presence of my Lord, and be clothed in the strength of the Radiance of my God.[18]

For it is no light service unto which He has called me, even this, to bear the Burden of the restoration of all Israel and the redemption of the House of Ya-akob-El, to bring salvation unto the Gentile lands and cause to shine throughout the Earth, the Light of the radiance of my Lord.

Thus saith He who hath called me to be the Redeemer of the House of Ya-akob-El, and the Shepherd of Israel through the Indwelling of His Holy One whom men have despised and whose ways nations have abhorred though He is always the Servant of all,[19]

The Kings of the East shall once more arise and behold the radiance of the Lord; for the Princes of Israel shall come before His Presence and worship Him.

And the Word of the Lord shall be fulfilled unto Israel through him whom He hath chosen, even His Servant.[20]

Of him hath He spoken:

"In an acceptable time thy request was heard and thine offer of service unto the House of Ya-akob-El received, that the lost Inheritance of Israel might be restored unto them.[21]

Therefore, I will reveal My Covenant through thee which of old was given unto Israel, to raise up the fallen land of Judah, re-establish the reign of Ya-akob-El, and change the Earth's desolation till it regains its ancient glory.

The prison-houses shall then be opened, and those who have been imprisoned shall be set free.[22]

The dwellers in the land of darkness shall be brought to the great Light;

Those who have hidden themselves through dread of the terror, shall come forth to unmask themselves.

These shall all find their way into the pastures which are upon the high places and receive nourishment there.

No more shall My People languish because of their

unmet hunger, nor perish in their thirst; nor shall the fires, with their heat, consume them.

For the mercy of My Love shall heal them; they shall be strengthened and led unto the upper-springs of the Fountain of Living-waters.

They shall be exalted to climb the Hills of Zion, and find their way to the Mountains of the Holy City.

From the countries that are afar off shall they come, northward and southward, eastward and westward, and even from Sinim—the land of Bitterness."[23]

* * * * * *

Therefore, do the Heavens sing for Joy, and call upon the Earth to be glad;

For upon the Mountains of God the Heavenly Hosts are breaking forth into joyful song;

They are telling how the Lord hath comforted His people in their affliction, and delivered them from the land of their sorrowful captivity.[24]

* * * * * *

When Zion thought in her heart that the Lord had forsaken her, the Lord Himself had prepared the way for her Return.[25]

O Zion! Lift up thine eyes, and behold what great things thy Lord hath wrought out for thee!

IX

NOTES ON TEXT

[1] The House of Ya-akob-El in its inner meaning, relates to the three Hierarchies who administer within the various Spheres of the Planet. In its more general meaning it embraces all the Houses of the Planet. In this appeal all are included.

[2] This challenge is to the elder children of the Earth. These became the *Children of the Adoption.* They had grown up into the Jesushood life, and had learnt much from the House of Israel. There came a time when many of these qualified in

their initiations for a fuller fellowship with the Sons of God. These in later ages, with all the Children of the Adoption, were accounted a part of the House of Israel. That is the explanation of their claims in the midst of fallen conditions, and their declension to be even as the children of the Land of Judah.

³ They have always been anxious to be accounted of the stock of ancient Israel. They also have the urge of their awakened Divinity to return to the state of the Life represented by the Holy City. But to do so means the recovered understanding of the Truth, and the restoration of Divine Righteousness. For Truth is the Light of Life, and Righteousness is Life's Balance.

⁴ Here the effect upon them of the great betrayal is emphasized, and incidentally what happened within the Heavens of the Planet. For it was within those spheres there dwelt those who had brought about the descent of Planet and Children, and there they created conditions which made impossible the return of all the Earth's children to beautiful and joyful pure living, and the Children of the Adoption to the Jesushood Estate.

⁵ Here there is the promise of full restoration for all.

⁶ This part of the Address is unto the high Potentate, the Angel of the Planet, and the House of Israel, to restore confidence. It is a glorious statement of the Unchangeable ONE in Whom are all things.

⁷ All beneath the Canopy Celestial of this System must again come into perfect unity; every sphere must be restored in its elements, motion and service.

⁸ The Eternal Wills and Performs. The Tetragrammaton—the most Holy Mystery—shall be restored again within the Heavens of the Earth and the whole of the Solar System.

⁹ The Assembly referred to is the Hierarchy over which, as the Angel of the Planet and Vice-gerent of the ADONAI, Ya-akob-El presided. The various members of the Hierarchy were to meet in council, and there be informed by Ya-akob-El what the Divine World had purposed.

But Israel, as the Sons of GOD, were so bound up in the Planetary history that they were also to be informed. They were to come into such spiritual estate as would enable them to receive that which the LORD of Love had done for them, and the further work to be accomplished on behalf of the Houses of Ya-akob-El and Judah, and also for the return of the House of Israel.

10 The Secrets associated with the Divine Purpose concerning the Manifestation and Oblation had been kept sacred. Any reference to those Secrets was so veiled that only those who knew could possibly understand. The Servant of the LORD knew, but had to be silent. After the Great Assembly, where the vital decision was made and the Burden-bearer chosen, there was a long silence. This is implied in the Prophet's Message. He could speak only when the Heavens so willed it.

11 This form of address discovers the ancient service rendered by the House of Israel unto the elder children of Judah. Even as they themselves had belonged to a Fold of GOD, over which the Servant of the LORD had acted as Shepherd, so they had the office appointed unto them as the Herds or Sheep-gatherers. In their ministry they gathered into groups or little folds, the Children of Judah or such of them as were ready to receive the Mysteries in the lower degrees of interpretation. They became the Shepherds of Israel upon the Plains of Judah.

They were so intimately related to Ya-akob-El, and their ministry a department of His own, that often they are addressed together, as in this instance. Indeed, perfect co-operation between the House of Ya-akob-El and that of Israel, was absolutely essential to the well-being of the House of Judah, and the recovery and restoration of the Holy City named Ierusalem.

12 The Majesty of YAHWEH is tremendous in its effect upon the Soul that is able to hear the utterance in the Inner Realms of the Divine Name JEHOVAH. When the PRESENCE approaches for high realization and proclaims HIMSELF through an exalted ONE as the I AM THAT I AM, the multitude of Sons of GOD and the Sons of the Gods, bow adoringly before HIM. The ETERNAL ONE radiates HIS Glory through all the adjacent spheres. Even there, the great Secrets must have right conditions for their unveiling.

13 There is deep pathos in the exclamation. It was not the noble Ya-akob-El who failed to carry out the Divine Command,

for he loved to do the Will of His Supreme LORD. But members of his Household disobeyed. Nor would they be warned of impending dangers, nor counselled how to avert them. It is the conduct of these that is referred to in this Divine Lament.

14 A revelation of the effect upon the whole of the Planet. The latter was shaken to its foundations, every Kingdom disturbed, all the wonderful Divine Substances and Elements changed in their polarity, and all the nations and races afflicted.

15 Babylon represented the land of confusion, and the Kings of Babylon the regnant mind and will that made confusion and oppressed Souls. The land of the Chaldeans originally represented illumination and Celestial Knowledge. Its inhabitants were the illumined ones. From Ur of Chaldea it is said Abraham came. The false Chaldeans were erroneous teachers and leaders. They claimed Celestial and Divine Knowledge and power, but were not of the line of Divine Prophets and Seers.

In the cosmic sense there is reference here to those who betrayed the Hierarchies and brought down the whole House of Ya-akob-El, by false messages purporting to come from the Divine World.

16 The Isles amid the Great Deep in a cosmic sense signified Celestial stations and states; and in an individual way referred to various spiritual states. The House of Israel had dwelt amid the Celestial Isles, and known the blessedness of the Life realized in consciousness of the Holy Mystery of the Great Deep.

17 The reference is to the Divine preservation given to them amid the Celestial tragedy, when the Hierarchy Members were betrayed to change the direction of the magnetic and electric streams of the Planet. During that most poignant period, the Divine World had to preserve the whole House of Israel by means of special Solar electric ministry.

18 This is the Servant's statement concerning himself. He would have to await the coming together of Israel from the different dimensions of consciousness, to once more take their stand as Sons of GOD; but he would even now be a dweller in the PRESENCE, and abide there.

19 Here it is made most obvious that the Servant of the

Revelation is also the Servant who became the chosen vehicle of the Divine Passion of the Oblation. Even so long ago, ages before the Travail would have to be undertaken, the immensity of the Burden of Redeemer filled the Servant. It was no light thing that he was called upon to undertake, nor even to declare such unto the House of Israel.

20 "The Kings of the East" is an expression embodying the coming of the Celestials or Ancient Christhood. They are the regnant ones who belong to the Orient, or Land of Light. They were the Princes or Elders of Israel, who reigned and ruled for GOD. They will have restored to them their ancient inheritance of the Christhood, and the abiding consciousness of HIS HOLY ONE, and worship and service as in the past. Here also there is emphasized the Call of the Servant, the Work he had to do, and the authority for his Mission.

21 The reference is to the great Celestial Assembly of the Gods and the Sons of the Gods, at which momentous gathering the Servant of the LORD offered himself for such service as the FATHER-MOTHER might appoint. It is a confirmation of his call to the High Office of Redeemer. He had been a Messenger from the Divine World for great ages. Long ago he had been placed over Israel as Shepherd, and Mediator of Divine Mystery unto them. He well knew the one who had been appointed to the Office of Planetary Angel, and Divine Vice-gerent to the triple Planetary Hierarchies. As he was the Shepherd of Israel and Mediator unto the various Tribes, and these were all related to Ya-akob-El as stewards, teachers and interpreters, it was most natural that he should become the Vehicle of the Divine Passion on behalf of them.

22 Though seemingly quite simple and easily understood, it is cryptic and the meaning profound. For the reference is to the liberation of Spirits who had to be shut up—an event that has still to be accomplished. They were of those who wrought desolation upon the Earth. They are the spirits in prison unto whom it was said the Master went to preach. Even they were to share in the blessed deliverance and redemption.

23 The whole of the paragraph is full of promise for Israel. The Hills of Zion are the spiritual estates experienced by the Soul, and the Mountains of the Holy City refer to great altitudes of consciousness.

357

Sinim is cryptic. There is implied in it the bitterness of great betrayal. There were those who went down into the state of Sinim.

[24] The intimate relationship between the Heavenly Hosts and all Israel is most beautiful. The Heavens have joy in the good of the World, and work unto the end that Israel may bring back that wonderful time when Eden was a reality.

[25] What ages of Travail in the Heavens and within Israel are implied here! Though the Return is with us, how very few of Israel have as yet awakened to the conscious realization of these things! Little do they dream of all that the Divine Love and Wisdom accomplished in the past, and is out-working now, on their behalf. Will Zion ever realize it?

X

THE BURDEN OF THE OBLATION

Behold the Servant of the Lord![1]

The Work of the Lord shall prosper through his coming.

The Name of the Lord shall be exalted; for through His Servant, the Children of Zion will come again to extol Him Who is the Most High One.

Many will look upon the Servant with astonishment, for his visage will be marred more than the visage of the sons of men, and his form more than any of his brethren.[2]

Many will be baptized into his sorrow; even those who were of kingly heritage shall be dumb before him;

For they will witness in him that which could not be told them; and they shall learn from him things of which they had not heard.[3]

* * * * * *

Who of his brethren will believe this Message, that unto His Servant the purpose of the Lord hath been revealed?

Who of them hath the open ear to hear and understand all that the Lord shall accomplish for His Children, through the Burden-bearing of His Anointed one whom He shall send?

The Lord shall cause His Servant to bear away the burden which the transgressions of the people did fashion, and thus the way shall be prepared for the coming of Yahweh.[4]

For the Lord shall make of the Soul of His Servant, an Oblation unto the carrying away of the sins of the people.[5]

As the Daysman for the whole House of Israel, shall he be; and as the Redeemer of the Household of Judah.

* * * * * *

Beneath the Overshadowing One shall the Servant grow up; for his roots shall be in God.

He shall be full of the tenderness of Yahweh, and make manifest the great gentleness of His Love.

Yet will many regard him as a dried root of earthly ground, and as one having neither form nor comeliness to make him to be desirable unto the people.

Despised and rejected by them will he be whilst he moves amongst them; for his soul shall be full of sorrow, as one well acquainted with grief.[6]

Unto those who have known him, there shall be, as it were, the veiling of his face;[7]

For his countenance must needs be hidden as he treads the winepress alone.

The scorn of many shall he bear, even of those from whom he shall hope for esteem.

As the Daysman of Israel he will carry within himself great grief; and as the Redeemer of men, he will bear the burden of many sorrows.[8]

It will appear as if he were smitten of God in his affliction.

In the blotting out of the transgressions of the people he will be tormented; his bruising shall be great by means of their iniquities.

In the path of his Travail there shall lighten upon him, the chastisements begotten of sin; yet shall his bruising be unto peace through the healing of the people.

The children of men have all gone astray; like wandering sheep they have gone along a way other than that appointed of the Lord.

Upon His Servant hath Yahweh laid the burden of their return.[9]

In the bearing of the Burden, oppression and affliction shall be his portion;

Yet may this Mystery not be spoken of until the Burden-bearing be accomplished.[10]

Like a lamb which is taken for sacrifice, so shall his Life-stream be outpoured.

In the prison-houses he will make his dwelling; for he must take judgment away from them.

But his generations none shall know.

With those who have made graves of wickedness, shall he lie down; and thus in his many manifestations must he needs pass through spiritual death.[11]

But by his Travail many shall be enriched.

   * * * * * *

When the Lord hath fully accomplished His Holy purpose in the offering up of the Soul of His Servant as an oblation unto the blotting out of the burden of sin, then shall He see of His Travail and be well pleased; for His elect ones shall serve before Him, and the good pleasure of His Will shall be accomplished through them.

For Forty manifestations must be the duration of the Oblation; but when it is finished, the Servant of the Lord shall look upon the path of his Travail, and be assured that the Passion of the Lord hath prevailed.[12]

Then shall be made manifest the greatness of the work wrought in the accomplishment of the Holy Purpose of the Lord of Love;

And His Righteousness shall be re-established amongst His Children, and the glory of His Wisdom once more be revealed.

X

NOTES ON TEXT

[1] This is a call to the House of Israel to look out for the Advent, and recognize the Travail of the Oblation when it took place. And there is revealed the blessed hope that through the coming of the Servant for the Advent and the Oblation, the Divine Purpose would be realized. That Purpose is named, THE WORK OF THE LORD. The Great Work was threefold. It was the revelation through manifestation of the FATHER-MOTHER as testimony of the Christhood, followed by the purification of the Heavens of the Planet and

their refashioning, resulting in the Arising of the Sons of
GOD and the Redemption of all Souls.

² This statement is quite cryptic. In it is contained the
effect of the Oblation upon the Servant. The whole history
of that most tragic history is gathered up into the statement.
The "sons of men" is an expression relating to the Children
of the Planet, to whose estate the one who had been on the
Divine Kingdom in Life and Consciousness, had to descend.
So great would the contrast be for him that he would appear
as other than a Son of the Highest. The sorrow in him
begotten of his burden would be manifest even to those who
had not known him when he was arrayed in glorious apparel.
Even his Brethren—those who had known him in his Divine
estate—would fail to recognize him or think of him as one
of themselves, so changed would he be. And when the time
of the Return took place, after the Oblation had been accomplished, and partial recognition came to them, they would
witness in him, by contrast, a greater change from his former
glory of Life, than that which might be discovered in
themselves.

³ The first part of this sentence relates to the way of the
Sin-Offering Oblation, and the second to the exposition of it
in the days of the Return. The revelation of the *cause* of the
"mystery of iniquity" in the World, the need for the Oblation,
and the path and burden of it, are here veiledly stated.
Those of kingly heritage, who were to know something of the
baptism of his sorrow, were and are the Sons of GOD in the
Earth-spheres.

⁴ Who of all His Brethren were able fully to grasp the
significance of the Oblation? None. Even in the days of the
Manifestation when the Master, as the Messenger of the
LORD and chosen Bearer of the Burden, gradually announced
and unveiled it, few could receive the Teachings He gave.
When He opened up vistas of the path of the Burden, they
were overwhelmed. Even one most intimate friend said it
was beyond his understanding that the FATHER-MOTHER
should permit such an Office to be filled by the Master.

⁵ He had grown up beneath the Divine Canopy of the
PRESENCE, and though He would have to descend unto low
estates, He would dwell within the ensphering of the ETERNAL,

Whose ministry to Him would be accommodated through the Solar World. His roots were in the Eternal Soil, and His Life would evermore be derived from the FATHER-MOTHER.

⁶ Notwithstanding His Divine Mission, many were to despise Him, the way of His life, and the ministry He might be able to render. The consciousness of His Burden of Sin-bearing, though it would be on behalf of others, and of the attitude towards Him of those amongst whom He moved, would so fill Him with the pangs of Anguish that many would come to look upon Him as a "Man of sorrows and one well acquainted with grief."

⁷ During the period of the Sin-Offering Oblation, no one on the Earth planes would recognize who He was, however intimate they might have been in the Heavens. He would be veiled to all His Brethren, and even to the Angelic World. The reason for this latter would be found in the provisions of the Divine Love and Wisdom that those in that most blessed realm should not have to witness the awful tragedy of the age-long Travail. Of all in the Angelic World those only who would be appointed to attend and minister to Him, would know who He was.

And He Himself would be so veiled that He would be unable to recognize any of His Brethren.

⁸ He was appointed Daysman of Israel, because He had been the LORD's Messenger unto them.

⁹ Upon Him was laid the Burden of the Return of Israel, the whole House of Judah, and the Planet. Redemption was a necessity, and it could be accomplished, even by the Divine World, only by means of the purification of the Planet's Heavens by the process of the Oblation, the awakening and arising of the Sons of GOD, the Return of these to the Christhood estate of Life and Manifestation, the healing of the Earth's disorders and the redeeming of all its children.

It was to be the Burden of YAHWEH borne for HIS Children.

¹⁰ The Divine Passion was a Secret of the Divine World. From the time when it was decided in the Assembly of the Gods, to the fulfilment of the purpose of the FATHER-MOTHER in the overthrow of the evil forces and states within the circles of the Planet's Heavens, it was contained within the Archives of the Divine World. It was set forth in the Book that was

sealed with Seven Seals. During the Manifestation, the Master cryptically unveiled its necessity, nature, path and His own part in it. But the little He gave them often overwhelmed them, and the Secret had to be kept veiled and guarded.

[11] No one would be permitted to know the incarnations of the Servant. He would have to be kept veiled, though every Life would be a distinct oblatory manifestation, suited to the Work to be accomplished. And in each of the forty generations or lives, he would know spiritual death.

[12] The triumph was assured. It was not personal to the Master. It began with and was to be continued by the Divine Love and Wisdom. The purpose was that of the FATHER-MOTHER; the power was His; the Passion was that of ADONAI in and through the Servant; and the glory of the Triumph was His alone.

The effect of the Oblation is becoming manifest in the arising of the Sons of GOD and the harvest of Souls.

XI

The Return from Edom

Who is this that cometh up from Edom?

His garments are red-dyed like those who have been treading the wine-vat.[1]

It is he who went down from Bozrah arrayed in glorious apparel, to travail for the people.[2]

In the strength of Him Who is mighty to save, even the Lord of Righteousness, went he down.

Wherefore cometh it to pass that his garments are dyed red like one who has been treading in the wine-press?[3]

* * * * * *

When the Lord appointed His Servant to go down into Edom, it was that he might travail on behalf of the children of men.

He sent him to work in the Wine-vat of this world to tread amid the sour Grapes which they had grown.

These Grapes were the fruitage which they had gathered from their furious ways.[4]

* * * * * *

In this work did the raiment of the Servant become red-dyed.

For the way of his going as he travailed, was unto the Redemption of all who went down into the strange land.

The Day of Recompense shall come in which Zion shall be restored, and the inhabitants thereof made glad.[5]

* * * * * *

I will make mention of the loving-kindness of the Lord;
I will sing the Praise of the Most High;
He hath bestowed upon me, the riches of His grace.

He hath remembered His people Israel;
Great is He in His loving-kindness.

* * * * * *

Of Israel He spake in the day of their affliction—
"Ye are My people, assuredly, though ye have had to
lie down in the midst of evil conditions, and dwell amongst
rebellious children!"[6]
And He became their Saviour.
In all their affliction, He was afflicted; for the Angel of
His Presence was with them, ministering unto the bringing
to them of His Salvation.[7]
Throughout the ages, from generation to generation, He
did upbear them in His Love and Wisdom, that He might
bring them all back to Himself.[8]

XI
NOTES ON TEXT

[1] The Return from the Oblation may truly be described as one of the most tragic parts of it. To descend from Christhood into the various states necessary for the Work of Planetary purification was painful beyond telling; but the awakening and return to the consciousness of all that had been passed through in the processional of the Soul through the awful conditions that had existed within the Atmospheria and Vortexya of the Planet, and what had had to be done to change these, was accompanied by anguish unspeakable. He saw Himself as He had become in the World's Wine-press, and it appeared in contrast to the Christhood estate, as if he could never return to that glorious Life.

[2] Great is the revelation here in these few simple words. Bozrah was the Sheepfold on the Divine Kingdom, where the Servant had been Shepherd—leading and teaching the Sons of GOD comprised within the House of Israel. He went down from the land of Divine Realization to that of Edom, where He was made to forget so that He might endure the Travail of the Divine Passion.

[3] There is anticipation here of the marvel of the Angelic World, and the question many of the Angels asked during the Return. It is not too much to say that hosts of those who had known the Servant in His Shepherdhood, wept when they

beheld Him after the Return began (for they were only then permitted to know Him again). The Angelic Heavens had to be closed during the Oblation so far as He was concerned. He was a stranger and a sojourner in a land absolutely strange to Him; an unknown warrior inwardly clothed in the armour of a Son of GOD, contending with elemental and occult forces and even with not a few who had fallen from high estate, and who had become the channels of these forces. Edom was a very different land from Bozrah, and its inhabitants from those of the Divine Sheepfold.

[4] The earnest student of the Teachings will discover much in these verses. The Church long thought that the Eternal Love afflicted the Master and imposed upon Him the burden of human guilt in order to satisfy Divine Justice. That was a sad perversion of the Truth. The Lord appointed the Servant to be HIS burden-bearer during the operations of the Sin-Offering Oblation. The Servant was the vehicle. Yet the chastisement was not from the LORD, but through the states into which the Servant had to enter. He was sent to work amid the vintage or conditions resulting from the conduct of humanity. The Earth's Vineyard grew wild grapes, and it was the wine of these (mystically understood) which red-dyed the Servant's garments as He laboured in the Wine-vat.

[5] The Recompense is to be multiple. Zion is to be restored, the Children of Judea redeemed, and Ierusalem rehabilitated. It implies the full restoration of the Planet, the regaining of the Edenic Life, and the return of the Ancient Sons of GOD in Christhood manifestation and ministry. The whole world is to be made glad. In anticipation of it, the Prophet-Soul sings praise.

[6] The whole history of Israel after the great Planetary descent is here implied. They had to remain on the Earth though their dwelling had to be amidst evil conditions. The whole became spiritually depleted, spiritually dead and rebellious. Though the Sons of GOD were influenced and greatly tried, they were true in the Inward Life, and cried out for the Vision of GOD, as their literature shows.

[7] Herein is revealed the intimate relationship between the Sons of GOD known as ancient Israel and the LORD of Being. HE not only knew of their affliction, but felt it. He shared their burden of sorrow.

For all Souls this should bring comfort, especially to Israel in these days of the Travail of the Return. For the Angel of His Presence is with every son of Israel to-day. Through that One the Divine LORD ministers unto them.

[8] Here the reference is to all the incarnations which the Sons of GOD have had to experience on the Earth. From one generation to another means from Life to Life. In the far-away ages they came here, and have been kept returning and coming until this day, and must continue to do so until the Land of Judah is redeemed, and Ierusalem restored for her children, and indeed until the LORD of Love and Wisdom bids them return to their Celestial Home.

XII

The Vineyard

*Of the Well-Beloved-One would I sing a song concerning
the Glory of His Vineyard.*[1]

    *   *   *   *   *   *

*My Beloved-One had His Vineyard upon a very
fruitful hill; it was upon the horn of the Olive-Mount.*[2]

*Around it He built a high wall with the stones
He gathered out of it.*[3]

*Then He planted the choicest Vine in the midst of it,
and built Himself a Tower. A wine-press also did He
hew to receive the wine.*[4]

*But when He looked for the fruitage of the Vine,
behold! there were no grapes;*[5] *except some wild fruit that
grew upon another kind of vine the enemy had placed there.*

    *   *   *   *   *   *

*O Ierusalem! Ierusalem! O ye inhabitants of Judah!
How may I judge you concerning My Vineyard? What
more could I have done for it? Wherefore hath no true
fruit been found, but only the wild grapes of low desire?*[6]

XII

Notes on Text

[1] The Beloved One is the ADONAI in the Divine World. The
Vineyard is His, and He is the True Vine. But in every
System He has His Vicegerent as well as many plenipotentiaries. There is a sense in which all these may be Guardians
of the Vineyard.

[2] The Cosmic nature of the Prophecy is once more clearly
discovered here. For the individual, the Vineyard was the
Soul; for the House of Israel it was Zion; for Judah it was the
whole spiritual constitution of the Planet. The Edenic Earth
was lovely. It was a fruitful hill. Those who governed the
Earth had power to see and understand. They were in the
state of vision described as a horn of the Olive Mount. They

had the capacity to look back through great ages, and the gift of vision to perceive the Divine Will in the Planet's ministry unto its children during their growth and evolution. The various Races were so spiritually constituted that they had the capacity and attributes to enable them to rise in manifold degrees of ascension until they reached the state of realization signified by the horn of the Mount of Olives—that is, until they arrived at Cosmic consciousness in a Planetary Degree.

³ The Wall built out of the elements gathered together from out the Vineyard or realm of Soul-Life, referred to the ensphering Atmospheria and Vortexya, with special allusion to the Magnetic Plane.

⁴ The Vine planted was the Sacred Mystery of Divine Life. The LORD of Being is the True Vine. HIS Flesh and Blood are in the constitution of every world and every Soul. Thus, every Planet becomes a Branch of the System to which it belongs, whose Centre or Sun becomes representative of the Eternal Vine. In this way also, every System becomes one of the main Branches of the Vine. Herein is revealed the intimate relationship of all Worlds and all Souls. All are of the Eternal Vine; all have their nourishment from the Vine; and all find the realization of Life *in* the Vine.

The Tower is a cryptic term. It hides the Divine Mystery within the Spiral of Soul and Planet. It is the Container of the Chalice into which the Wine is gathered after the transmutory processes of the Wine-press.

⁵ Those who had charge of the Vineyard had been betrayed. The true Vine of Divine planting had been removed and a Vine foreign to the soil had been introduced. The original Divine Life and Service had been changed on the Planes of the Planet. The true interpretation of the Divine Love and Wisdom as given by the Sons of GOD, had been usurped by another kind of teaching given by those who had been brought to the Earth to effect such changes as would destroy the spiritual system by setting up within the Kingdoms astro-occult regnancies.

⁶ What pathos is revealed here! It is an echo of the Great Lament uttered in the Heavens, great ages before. Yet there was more done to save the Vineyard. The tremendous Lunar and Solar sacrifices were crowned by the Travail of ADONAI in the Oblation.

XIII

Trust Not in Egypt

Those who, in the day of their trouble, go down to the land of Egypt, to put their trust in the Horses and Chariots of Egypt in its fallen state, and think that the horsemen are strong enough to deliver them from the power of the enemy, shall be overtaken with woe.[1]

Such look not unto the God of Israel for succour, nor account His Holy One sufficient.[2]

They think themselves wise, yet they bring only evil upon themselves.

They forget that Egypt as it is, is the land of man and not of God; that the Horses and Chariots of Egypt are fallen powers, and not those created by the motion of the Spirit.[3]

When the Lord doth stretch forth His Hand over those powers, they all fall down before Him; for they cannot stand in His Presence when He doth appear from within Zion, to make Himself manifest.[4]

Unto this end must His Ensign be unfurled in Zion as the testimony before Egypt and Assyria that the Lord is with His people Israel; that Zion contains the Altar of His Sacred Fire; and that Ierusalem is the Crucible and the Alembic wherein His Sacred Fire doth purify the Silver and the Gold, and transmute these for His service in Israel.[5]

XIII

Notes on Text

[1] As explained in other volumes, especially Ezekiel, Egypt had an unfallen history long before it became the Land of Bondage. It was a cryptic term signifying the state of limitation, and especially in relation to the carnate life. Most people in the day of trouble seek their chief help in Egypt.

They relate the cause and the resultant to the conditions of the outer life; and in the lower powers seek for healing, restoration, increase and power. They show that they have more trust in the world-powers, mental and astral, than in any kind of spiritual force. They put their trust in the Mind and physical powers, and in these think to find remedy for all their ills. They seem oblivious of that which is most obvious, that many of the evils in the world to-day have had their origin in the wrong direction taken by the Mind of Man, and the false attribute endowments men have given to the powers of matter. And verily, mankind is overtaken with woe.

² The World has long forgotten GOD. The Nations appear to remember HIM only at such times as they find themselves in great distress. Even then, the remembrance is circumscribed by their own need and self-regard. But the day is surely coming when it will be otherwise with them, and their thoughts of GOD will be noble and worthy, and their approach to HIM free from self-regard and unholy motive.

The GOD of Israel is not limited to the circle of the Sons of GOD named Israel, but to the glorious Life and Service implied in the Holy Mystery expressed as ISSA-RA-EL.

³ It is one of the amazing experiences in national and racial history that, though mankind has suffered terribly for ages through the mistakes of Kings, Queens, Potentates, Rulers, Teachers, and Politicians, wherein these have made war within every Kingdom—Creature and Human and in every sphere of activity—Social, Commercial and Religious, yet the races and nations continue to appeal to the Horses and Chariots of fallen Egypt, and live in dread of war, yet contribute both by desire and means, and even life to its diabolical states and results.

⁴ The day hastens to its close for all who love conflict in spirit and action, when they will have to become changed if they would know the joy of HIS Presence; and also, when all the effects of their Egyptian idolatry shall be consumed away in the purifying Fire of HIS Holy Energy.

⁵ The above is to be effected through the restoration of Zion, and the manifestation of the Ancient Christhood wherein the Sons of GOD shall once more be the revealers of GOD as the Eternal Presence, and the interpreters of HIS glorious Love and Wisdom. In this way shall Egypt be healed of her wounds, Assyria be re-exalted to the Land of Light, and Israel be the exposition of Divine Regnancy.

XIV

THE DIVINE SIGN

O Israel! My people! Do you ask of the Lord whence the Ensign shall appear?[1]

Hear you again the Voice of His Word!

The Lord Himself shall send His Branch to save and bless you, and bear you back to Canaan.[2]

Do you doubt this Word of His unto you that up from the Deeps He hath brought you to exalt you even until you stand again upon the heights of His Dwelling?[3]

Herein His sign is announced to you:—

Behold! A Virgin-Soul shall conceive and bring forth into manifestation, His Son:

He shall be named of Him, Immanuel.[4]

XIV

NOTES ON TEXT

[1] The House of Israel had a difficult time during great ages of their ministry. During the period covered by the Prophecy of Isaiah, the future looked dark indeed and the way most disheartening. Is it to be marvelled at that they lost their vision at times, and felt the miasma of despair upon them? Around them there was paraded a religion that was the travesty of all that they had stood for and taught, though it claimed to be the worship of Jehovah after the manner of the Israelites.

[2] This may seem an abrupt introduction of a new aspect of Divine ministry, under the cryptic term BRANCH. But the Revelation has been gradually working up to this climax. For though the Oblation had been proclaimed, its real nature had been undiscovered. The BRANCH promised was the Servant who was to be the Divine Vehicle of the Manifestation and Oblation. Yet in the Innermost sense, there is implied Divine Mystery. The relationship of the Servant to the Divine World is partially unmasked. He stood in relation to

the Inner World as a Branch to the Vine. He was a Mediator of the ETERNAL unto the House of Israel. Through Him, YAHWEH transmitted HIS Word.

The restoration of the Christhood is indicated in the prophecy that the Branch should be the instrument of leading the Sons of GOD back to the Land of Canaan. That restoration was to be effected by means of the Manifestation of Divine Christhood.

3 The vista of the path by which the House of Israel had been led during the tragic ages of their sojourn and ministry here, is very touching; and also how the whole community of the Christs had been raised out of the Great Deeps of the Eternal Mystery by the operation of the Word of GOD—the ministry of ADONAI in and through the ELOHIM. The Purpose of Christhood is discovered to the Sons of GOD; for to stand upon the heights of HIS Dwelling signified that they had risen to altitudes of realization which enabled them to contact the Divine World in an intimate way, and were capable of becoming the vehicles of spiritual and Celestial Christhood.

4 The Prophecy was only related to the Human Kingdom in connection with the Manifestor. It was not a Human generation and conception the Prophet had in his vision. Christhood WAS NOT OF BLOODS AND RACES; IT WAS THE ESTATE OF A SOUL. The term Virgin was cryptic. It became applied to the physical state of men and women, and in this way lost its Divine significance. Originally the term was used to signify THE PRIMAL SUBSTANCE. A Virgin-Soul was one who had retained the virginal estate of its substances and potencies. Virgin-Soil or Elements, implies for the world-mind, soil that has not been used for cultivation; but the inner meaning relates to what has retained original status—*unfallen elements*. Only such a Soul could become a Divine Christ and be Immanuel. A Soul in lower estate could not have endured the tremendous play of Divine electric force associated with the state of Immanuel. For the term, though used as a Divine Name, means, THE IMMANENCE OF GOD REALIZED BY THE SOUL. To be so named of GOD proclaims such a Soul a Son of the Highest in Estate. The prophetic pronouncement heralded the coming of the Manifestation, the Oblation, and the Messianic reign.

374

XV

THE BRANCH OF THE LORD

Behold! Behold! O Ya-akob-El!
Hear now, and see, O Israel!
Your King doth reign in Righteousness;
All His decrees reveal His Equity;
His Judgments, Princes shall interpret and show forth
the Justice of His Ways.[1]

*   *   *   *   *   *

The one who is His Branch shall be as a hiding place
from evil breaths;
Pavilion of the Lord for those who seek sure covert from
Earth's tempests.
From him shall flow in living-streams amid the arid
places, God's Waters, to make the wearied land refreshed
and give to those who seek, Life's Joyance; till all dwell
beneath the Overshadowing One, the Rock of the
Eternal Ages.[2]

*   *   *   *   *   *

The Light, for those who seek, shall not grow
dim;
Nor shall God's Audience cease to fall upon their
opened Ears, when His Word speaks;
The Heart shall hasten unto understanding Him, nor
falter in response to speak of Him.[3]

XV

NOTES ON TEXT

[1] Both Houses were addressed because they were equally concerned in what was to be accomplished. They were and are distinct Houses. That of Israel took in the Zion Christhood; that of Ya-akob-El embraced the three Hierarchies who were the administrators of the affairs associated with the

375

Planet's Kingdoms, and the growth and evolution of the human races. But they were all inter-related. The ministry of the House of Israel unto the House of Ya-akob-El, was solar. They did not instruct Ya-akob-El, but they were sharers in his ministry and regnancy, as Sons of God in Celestial Christhood. They did not communicate to the three Hierarchies; all instructions from the Divine World were transmitted through the Messenger.

Both Houses are reminded of the KING of all the Kings or Celestial Rulers, and that HIS reign is characterized by Righteousness and Equity. Therefore HIS Princes, the minor Gods, shall rightly manifest and interpret HIM. Such an address to the Hierarchies under Ya-akob-El is full of hidden meaning which they could well understand. Had their regnancy for HIM always been in Righteousness and Equity, the Planet would have been in a very different state. Eden would have continued, and all the Earth's children would have grown up naturally, because true spiritual conditions would have always obtained. There would have been no cycles of spiritual darkness begotten of Soul descent, nor any bestial conditions generated. The lives of the Children would have been full of joy and gladness.

² The Living ONE canopies the Soul who seeks HIS Presence, so must the Branch be as a sheltered place to those in need; for HE must be the exposition of the Eternal Love. The imagery is most beautiful and intimate. To become a Pavilion for Souls is indeed high office and Ministry.

The Branch is also to be the vehicle of Divine outflow. The Branch of the Vine is the channel for the life-stream to pass to all the lesser branches. Divine Christhood is essentially the medium of Divine-Force transmission. The resultant of such ministry is glorious.

³ What wealth of promise there is here! How full of encouragement for all who are seeking the Light unto the realization of its full radiance, and the radiation of its glory! The Branch is to meet the needs of Being, Soul, Heart and Mind.

XVI

THE BIRTH OF CHRIST

In that day shall it be said of Israel:—

The people who walked in the darkness have seen the Great Light:

They who have dwelt amid the shades have had all the shadows chased away;

For the Lord hath caused His Light to shine upon them.[1]

* * * * * *

Now may the House of Israel sing this song:—

Unto us a Child is born: unto us a Son is given who upon himself shall bear the regnancy of the Lord.[2]

Upon him shall be the sacred sign of the Name of the Lord:[3]

Of the Wonderful One shall he speak to us, and be from Him our Counsellor:

The Almighty God shall he reveal as one who knows the Eternal Lord Who is Jehovah, Name ever blessed, the princely giver of His Peace.[4]

The Lord of Sabaoth will accomplish it; in the Passion of His Love He will seal it:

His Word hath He sent unto Ya-akob-El; and He hath also alighted upon Israel.[5]

XVI

NOTES ON TEXT

[1] This passage is related to the coming of Christ. He is the Light of GOD. The Christus bespeaks the baptism which fore-runs illumination, and this latter is the magnetic atmosphere which leads to the full realization of the radiance of Christ. It is quite impersonal, and denotes a state of attainment and consciousness.

The Birth of Christ is the Soul's awakening; and the going forth of Christ on His mission, signifies the manifestation of Christhood by the Soul. To the Sons of GOD in the world's dark night the great Light of Christ has shone. The world shall yet behold something of the glory of that radiance.

² How different is the concept of the Messianic Advent that makes the event one of Soul Realization of ADONAI, from the merely personal interpretation of the coming of the Master! One real manifestation of the Master was in the revelation of the Divine Love in action, and the Divine Wisdom in interpretation.

³ The Sign of the Cross is the most sacred seal of the Divine Name. The one appointed to be Messenger unto Israel, bore that name. He was representative of ADONAI, who is the Eternal I-O-SEPH or Sign of the Cross. The Master was not Christ in His person, but in state was of Divine Christhood. One who knows in realization, Jesus, Christ, the LORD, is the vehicle for and the embodiment of the Divine regnancy. The human element in such an one is only the atmosphere through which the operations of manifestation take place, and the Glory is revealed. Such is always the nature of a Divine Christhood for manifestation upon the Earth. The Vehicle of the ETERNAL LORD as the Indwelling Presence, is the Being of that Son of GOD.

⁴ The Christ must speak of THE WONDERFUL NAME. He does not speak of Himself. His is the opposite of a Pauline claim. In Him there is no room for any claim of His own; the Sanctuary is His LORD's. The Glory of the LORD revealed through Him, is never dimmed by the exaltation of the office as relative to himself.

The true Counsellor ever points the way to the Divine LORD and ever leads Souls thither. He reveals the Divine Love and Wisdom in His own Love and the interpretations He is able to give to the Works of the FATHER-MOTHER, and the Secret of Life. He shows Love to be the supreme possession to be cherished, embodied and revealed, and Wisdom to be the inshining of the Glory of the FATHER-MOTHER and its revelation in all the motion and service of Life. For thus is JEHOVAH, Name ever Blessed, made manifest.

⁵ The Message is that of ADONAI through HIS Servant who has been appointed HIS Messenger and Son of the Most High. The LORD is in the Message. It hath been sent unto the whole House of Ya-akob-El—every member of the three Hierarchies; and the glory of the Message hath alighted upon the House of Israel.

XVII

The Way of The Messiah

Behold My Servant! He is Mine Elect one in whom is My delight and Mine upholding strength.[1]

The motion of My Spirit within him shall cause to be made manifest My judgment, even unto the Gentile lands.

*   *   *   *   *   *

He shall not cry aloud within the city; nor lift up his voice in its streets that he may be heard by passers by.

*   *   *   *   *   *

The Life that is like a bruised reed, he shall not break; the Flame dim-burning, he shall not quench; but he shall make God's judgments manifest, and show forth the Righteousness of Truth.[2]

*   *   *   *   *   *

He shall not fail; for naught shall stay him in the making manifest of judgment, even unto all the Earth, whose Isles shall await his coming to fulfil the Law of the Lord.

XVII

Notes on Text

[1] The Messianic Manifestation is a glorious event. It is characterized by all that we would associate with the coming of a Son of God. The radiance shed upon Life by such a revelation stands in remarkable contrast, in the sublime reality of it, to the false lights that claim to illumine the sky, and the way of agitators and would-be world redeemers. To the enlightened the two could never be confounded.

[2] One in Christhood and making manifest for his LORD will always embody and reveal the Truth as the radiance of Divine Righteousness. He will be majestic in the might of his embodiment of and for Truth, and exquisite in his tenderness, compassion and pity. The Way of the Messiah could not be

that of the agitator, the politician, the dictator, nor self-regarding ruler. He must be like the Love and Wisdom of GOD as these are expressed in Righteousness and Equity, Pity and Compassion.

XVIII

The Liberator

*The Lord, the God of Sabaoth, unto His Anointed One,
even Cyrus whom He hath called to be the Liberator of His
people Israel, and endowed with power to be a Redeemer:*

*Behold the things that shall come to pass when thou
comest unto the Children of Zion!*[1]

*The two-leaved Gates shall open at thine approach, and
the loins of the Kings of the East shall be unloosed.*[2]

*The Gates of bronze shall be broken before thee, and the
fetters of iron fall apart;*[3]

*And I will go before and make all the crooked ways
straight.*

*The treasures that were carried away into the land of
darkness, I shall restore through thee; for the hidden riches
of the secret places shall be thine.*[4]

*Through the wisdom revealed in the service thou shalt
render unto My people, they shall come to know that the
One Who named thee His Anointed, is indeed the Lord of
Sabaoth and the God of Israel.*[5]

*For the sake of My Servant Ya-akob-El, and on behalf of
Mine elect ones, even Israel, have I called thee by name to
become the Daysman of Israel and the Redeemer of the
land of the children of Judah.*[6]

*And for the ministry which thou art now called upon to
render I have sur-named thee, My Anointed One, though thou
didst not know until I called thee by name, that thou wert
so appointed by Me.*[7]

*Yet hast thou known Me to be thy Lord, for thou hast
been in the Spiral of the Sacred Fire of I AM that I AM,
the God of Sabaoth, where thou wast girt around in the
Cherubic mantle of Eli-Jah.*[8]

For it was none other than thy Lord Who clothed thee for the priestly service to be rendered unto Ya-akob-El, Israel and Judah.

And in the day when this service has been fully accomplished, shall the Light of the Glory of My Holy One make glorious the inheritance of Ya-akob-El, and cause the darkness to flee from the land of Judah, and re-clothe in the garments of their ancient Priesthood, My people Israel.[9]

For their Sun shall then set no more; and the Heavens shall be able to pour out in fulness the Eternal streams; and these shall cause Righteousness to be re-established, and Peace to reign through all the land.

XVIII

NOTES ON TEXT

[1] The name Cyrus is cryptic. It has an inner meaning akin to the Greek term for LORD. The name in some Persian forms is related to the Sun. This is most interesting. Though Cyrus is regarded as an historical character, yet mystery surrounds him. He is supposed to have been King of Persia and then also of the Medes, and to have given permission to the Jews, for governmental and political reasons, to return to Palestine. There followed later, two partial returns in Ezra and Nehemiah, the one to restore the Law and the Priesthood, the other to rebuild Jerusalem.

But just as the real Babylonian Captivity was Mystical, so the deliverance from it under Cyrus was of a Spiritual nature. It became most obvious in this passage that Cyrus was the Liberator, Redeemer, and Daysman for Israel.

[2] What profound meaning for all the Children of Zion is conveyed in the promise that, through the Servant Cyrus, THE TWO-LEAVED GATES would open, and the loins of the Kings of the Orient would be unloosed. The Intuition and Understanding were the dual Gates into the Holy City; and the Divine Creative Forces contained in the Spiral of the Divine Man—one in Christhood, were to be set free for Divine Service. Intuition, Understanding, and Creative Force, which had long been in captivity, were to be liberated.

³ The Gates of Bronze and the Fetters of Iron related to the instruments of bondage and affliction. They represented the state of and the oppression within the Planet's Heavens which had become pandemonium, and even hell to the Sons of GOD. The brazen and smiting conditions were to be broken down, and the Sons of GOD delivered under the reign of Cyrus. For Cyrus was not only the Servant of the LORD raised up and sent to the House of Israel for their deliverance by means of the Oblation, but He also represented the restoration of the Christhood through Messianic Manifestation and Redemption.

⁴ The result of the Deliverance and Redemption was to be made manifest in the recovery and repossession of all the Sacred Vessels that had been carried down into Babylon. These belonged to the Temple of the LORD on the Hill of Zion. They contained Divine Secrets, for they were of the Mystery of GOD. They were the sacred possessions of the Soul, and were the inheritance of each Son of GOD.

⁵ This implies that the true mission of Cyrus would be recognized by the Sons of GOD, and that the Divine Wisdom in all the arrangements for the accomplishment of the Deliverance and Redemption with the resultant, would be accepted by them as the further revelation of the Love and Wisdom of the FATHER-MOTHER. One of the great difficulties of a Messenger in all ages has been to get recognition for the Message as the Word of the LORD. He may not seek personal recognition—he would not wish to, but he longs for the Divine Word to be accepted and the Divine Purpose to be understood. For he is the possessor in consciousness of Divine Secrets to be transmitted unto all who are prepared in themselves to receive them and make use of them for the ascension of Being and the Divine Service.

⁶ What wealth of Love has been poured out in living streams upon this world! Who could measure it? What Tierce could hold it? Who could gauge the anxiety of the Heavens for Ya-akob-El and his Kingdom, or count the cost and appraise the pain and anguish of the Vice-gerent?

The purpose of Divine-World action is unveiled. Ya-akob-El and his Kingdom must be saved, the Sons of GOD liberated, and the Earth redeemed. To the service of the Eternal Love there is no end, nor to the revelation of the Glory of HIS Wisdom.

[7] The tenderness expressed here shows how Cyrus was regarded before he was chosen to be the vehicle of the LORD for special Manifestation and Oblatory ministry. He was to be one who could be named The Anointed One. The phrase was indeed Chrismatic. It savoured of the most precious unguent. Yet Cyrus was unconscious of it. He did not know what the Divine World had in store for him. Those who have so attained have not sought great things. Those who have been exalted to the office of Messenger and Mediator, have been of lowly spirit.

[8] The revelation given here is of tremendous nature. To know the LORD of Being in such fulness as to be drawn into the Spiral of Jehovah, sphered in the Cloud of Sacred Fire of the most Holy Mystery of Life spoken of as I AM THAT I AM, and clothed in the Mantle of Eli-Jah, implies Divine Sonship— a Soul who has become one with and the vehicle of, The Beloved.

There is also reference here to the High Priesthood of the Messenger, Cyrus, in the mediatorial ministry to be rendered unto the House of Ya-akob-El represented by the three Hierarchies, to the House of Israel as the Revelator, and unto the House of Judah as the Redeemer.

[9] When the Oblation had been fully accomplished then would the inheritance or regal estate of Ya-akob-El be restored, the Planet's Heavens be fully redeemed, and the twelve Tribes of Israel be re-instated in the Christhood and its Priesthood, and a recovered and reconstituted Earth be the fruitage.

XIX

A CALL TO ISRAEL

Thus saith the Lord, the God of Sabaoth,
He Who created the Heavens and arranged them,
Who fashioned the Earth and all its proceeding powers;
Who has given His Breath unto the People, and His Spirit
to those who know Him:[1]

"*I the Lord have called you, O Israel, to make manifest*
My Righteousness, in the doing of which your hands will
be held in My keeping; and I will give you the Light of
My Covenant, and cause My Glory to shine through you
unto the Gentiles that they may dwell in My Light as
those who come forth from the prison-houses, and are
no longer prisoners of the Darkness.[2]

*   *   *   *   *   *

I AM that I AM, speaketh: Thus saith He;
"*I am your Lord:*
Jehovah is My Name:
It is a secret Name.[3]
The Glory of its Mystery may not be given to those
who know Me not, or who worship graven images."[4]

*   *   *   *   *   *

Behold, and know this, O Israel!
The things of former times again are come to pass;
new wonders also are declared unto you ere yet their
springing forth is come.[5]
Therefore, sing unto your Lord, O Israel![6]
Let the Praise of Him fill your song, till the ends of
the Earth hear of Him.
Sing unto Him, ye who go into His Deeps and seek
unto all fullness of the things therein; who search out
His Isles and make of them sure habitations!

Sing of Him, until the wilderness doth change, and all the cities thereof lift up their voice in Praise, even to where Kedar doth dwell![7]

Sing of Him, ye inhabitants whose dwelling is upon the Rock of Ages!

From the summits of His Mountains make the joyful sound reverberate;

For thus shall His Glory be made manifest, until His Praise shall girdle all the Isles.[8]

XIX

NOTES ON TEXT

[1] THE GOD OF SABAOTH is an impressive Saying. It embraces in its meaning all the Hosts of the Celestial and Divine realms. It signifies that the ETERNAL ONE is the Head of all the Gods and their Systems, and that HE is LORD of all the Lords who reign for HIM.

When rightly spoken, the vibrations produced by the words are far-reaching and profoundly moving. There moves within the Being, the ground-swell of the Great Deep. The name is vibrant with the potency of the Sublime Mystery that filleth all things.

What an honour was conferred on Israel that HE should have so addressed them! And what an honour is continually bestowed upon us that we should be designated, HIS children!

[2] The Divine Purpose of all Stars and their Hosts of ministrants, is manifestation of GOD and service for HIM. HIS Purpose in the creation and endowment of a human Soul, is to find fulfilment in its fashion as it grows into the Likeness of the Eternal in attribute and service. To be a vehicle for the Divine is a high vocation. To be called to receive and radiate HIS Glory, is an immeasurable honour. To lift on high the standard of HIS Righteousness and Equity—HIS Love and Wisdom—is a ministry of Divine Value, pregnant with HIS own Omnipotency.

[3] The innermost meaning of the Tetragrammaton cannot be spoken. We use signs and symbols to try and express it sufficiently for our meaning to be apprehended. But the

inner Mystery remains. *It must be realized to be understood.*
The signs built up into the term Jehovah, are masonic. They
are like Passwords to the sevenfold Degrees of the Mystery.
When in combination they are pronounced as the Sacred
Name JEHOVAH, the vibrations are tremendous. NAME
MOST SACRED!

⁴ The knowledge of the Divine Secret cannot be forced. It
must be discovered along the royal road. Religious idolaters
of any order may not pass through the Gates unto the Celestial
City of its realization. All who worship the graven images of
their own fashioning will fail to find the Secret until they
divest themselves of the burden of their false creations. The
Mystery of JEHOVAH is guarded by Cherubim and Seraphim.

⁵ In so far as Israel knew this Mystery in ancient times it
was again to be uncovered for them, though indeed, the
discovery would be within themselves. And with the *recovery*
by them of something of their Ancient Inheritance, new
wonders were to be revealed. These latter were connected
with the Messianic Manifestation and the Oblation. Though
these were directly related to themselves and the Houses of
Ya-akob-El and Judah, yet they were to be of a Cosmic Order.
Greatly honoured was Israel to have such Revelation.

⁶ The vision of hope was theirs, so should their Song be one
of gladness. They had reason to rejoice though as yet captives
in a strange and weary land. They were of those who had
fathomed something of the Great Deeps; and surely they
should sing of the glory of these. They were of GOD's Isles
amid the Great Deep; for in HIS Argosies they had voyaged
from Isle to Isle. For had they not visited many spheres and
learnt of HIS manifestations there? There were great ages
during which their dwelling was amid the Isles.

⁷ Divine Song has power to make wilderness conditions give
place to those of fruitfulness. It can make even the dusky and
dark places become scenes of light and beauty.

⁸ Great is the burden of responsibility upon Israel, whose
service is to be the means of accomplishing so much for this
world and all its children.

XX

The Restoration of Zion

Arise, O Zion!
Shine! for thy Light is come.
The Glory of the Lord is again upon thee.
Behold thou, and know Him in His coming!
Though the darkness still covereth the Earth, and the
people remain amid its grossness, yet the Radiant One has
arisen within thee to shine; for His Glory is to be seen
upon thee.[1]

All the Gentile lands shall bathe in His Light; all
ruling powers shall share in the Glory of His arising
within thee.

*   *   *   *   *   *

Behold, O Zion!
See with thine own eyes!
Look around thee and witness the coming together of all
thy sons and thy daughters from the far countries to dwell
at thy side.

The vision of their coming will move thee till thy streams
flow together; for the motion of thy Heart shall be intensified
in its outgoing and incoming.[2]

Thy sons and thy daughters shall bring with them the
wealth of the Gentiles.[3]

Those rescued from the Great Sea shall turn unto thee.[4]

The Camels and Dromedaries of Midian and Ephah
shall again work within thy land;[5]

Those travelling from Sheba shall come unto thee bringing
Gold and Incense with them for worship and praise.[6]

Even the flocks of the wilderness of Kedar shall be gathered
together and brought unto thee that thou mayest minister unto
them, as the Rams of Nebaioth minister unto thee.[7]

They shall come up unto My Altar with acceptable sacrifices;

In the House of My Dwelling I will glorify them; and the Dove from out the Cloud shall fly to their windows bearing messages from Me.[8]

*　　*　　*　　*　　*　　*

Assuredly, the Isles await the coming of Mine Anointed One![9]

Those of Tarshish shall be the first to receive from Me.

They shall bring of their gold and silver impressed with the image of the Eternal, and bearing the insignia of the Holy One of Israel who hath glorified thee.[10]

My sons who have been in strange lands, shall again build up thy walls; as the Ancient Kings, they shall minister unto thee and through thee.[11]

In that Day thy Gates shall never be shut; for night shall be no more.[12]

All who desire to come unto thee shall find entrance through thy Gates; for these shall be continuously open.

The sons of those who afflicted thee shall come unto thee, to bend the knee in service unto Me;

And those who have despised thee in thine affliction shall bow down before Me, and acknowledge thee to be the City of the Lord which He hath named, "Zion of the Holy One of Israel."[13]

Even as thou wast so stricken and forsaken that none had regard unto thee, so shalt thou be clothed with the Glory of the Eternal, and become once more a joy throughout all the generations.[14]

Thy walls shall be salvation unto those who seek unto thee; and thy Gates shall be full of Praise.[15]

The Sun shall not set again within thee, nor shall thy Moon be veiled any more; for the Radiance of thy Lord shall be thy Light everlastingly, and the long night of sorrowful travail shall be ended.[16]

The Glory of Lebanon shall be restored unto thee; the place of thy dwelling shall indeed be glorious. [17]

I who am thy Lord will hasten the Day of its coming unto thee.

XX

NOTES ON TEXT

[1] This is a clarion call by the Servant unto the Sons of GOD who once formed the City of Zion. The term was related to the Solar Christhood. These Sons of GOD were the ancient Christs who came to this Earth as Divine Manifestors and Interpreters. It was to them all Divine Messengers were sent. It was for them the Prophets and Seers arose. Unto them did the true Prophets appeal and all Messages from the Heavens were directed. Of all the Souls who dwelt upon the Earth they alone could apprehend the meaning of and understand truly the Celestial Mysteries and Divine communications. Hence the frequent appeal to them to arise and come back into the realms of Light, and be once more the channels of the Light of GOD upon the Earth.

Here the promised resultant of their return is world-wide redemption. All Souls would share in the radiance shed by them.

[2] Zion is here addressed as if quite separate from though related to Israel. But it is always the Christhood that is meant, in individual state and corporate manifestation. What rejoicing there will be (and there even now is) as the Sons of GOD return to their Ancient estate.

Here also is indicated the great mystery of the Heart's part in the Return. Its systolic and diastolic action becomes intensified as the result of the ascension of the Being into higher realm experiences. For in the degree that the Body or Soul-vehicle which through the Divine Ætheria is fashioned, is affected from the Inner Worlds, so is the Heart. And as this becomes an experience of the individual, in like manner it is made manifest in and through the corporate Body of the Christhood.

[3] The wealth of the Gentiles is a mystical term signifying that which is gathered out of experience on the outer spheres of Life. For the Court of the Gentiles is the more outward

manifestation and service. It is analogous to the term the riches of Egypt, and the Wisdom of Egypt.

⁴ The great Astral Sea. The rescue was effected by means of the Oblation. The changing of that sea made it give up the dead who were in it. So lacking was it in spiritual conditions and vital breaths, that no Soul could live in it. In it all went down into spiritual death. By means of the Oblation the elements were purified and new conditions created.

⁵ The fallen celestial minds whose pride had brought them down, and who perpetuated strife and spiritual darkness. For Midian means strife and Ephah the darkness, whilst Camels and Dromedaries represent supercilious minds in bondage. There is a world of history hidden in the Camel and Dromedary. That secret is part of the Story of *the Spirits in Prison*. But all these shall be healed and redeemed, and shall return to their former estate, and work in the Land.

⁶ Sheba was the Land of the Seven Wells. These latter were Divine Fountains. They represented the ELOHIM. The Queen of Sheba is a Mystery of profound order, and belonged to the Solar regnancy. Those from such a country would naturally bring Gold and Incense—the Divine Love in Auric Splendour, and the Spirit of Worship and Adoration.

⁷ The flocks of Kedar and the Rams of Nebaioth refer to earthly and divine races. The former relates to those Children of the Earth whom once the Sons of GOD taught. They were to be gathered together again to learn from the true Israel of the ETERNAL GOD. And during that ministry the Messengers would minister unto The House of Israel.

⁸ In the Redemption and the Regeneration, all who were of the Children of the Adoption would be brought together again—*those who fell asleep in Jesus on their way to the Christhood;* and they would share in the great deliverance and the new revelation, and be once more taught the sacred Mysteries. And their Soul evolution towards the Christhood would begin again and they would attain to high Angelic estate and become dwellers within the Sanctuary of the Presence as HE is manifest there, and receive the Holy Guest in greater fulness through the window of their Inner Life being open, even the Dove from out the Cloud.

⁹ The Isles represent the various spiritual, Celestial and Divine Estates amid the Great Deep. They too looked out for the resultant of the Advent and the Oblation. Because the coming of the One Anointed would be the herald of the Redemption, and the liberation of all the Sons of God who were bound by the fallen conditions.

¹⁰ The Isles of Tarshish are often thought to have had reference to Great Britain. But the name is mystical. Any significance in its application to these Isles would arise from incidental reasons. The Cryptic meaning will be found in Celestial interpretaticn. Yet it is likewise true that in these Isles in these latter days, vast numbers of the Ancient House of Israel have sought incarnation and ministry. In this there was surely Divine Purpose, for the last lives of the Oblation had to be lived on these Isles, and the Recovered Messages of the Prophets and the Christhood, together with the Oblation, have been given back to Israel in these days.

The Gold and the Silver impressed with the insignia of the Eternal—Love and Faith—are significant avowals.

¹¹ The Holy City of Zion or the Corporate Christhood had its walls and buttresses thrown down during the great spiritual earthquake that shook•the Earth to her Divine foundation. The sacred story of the Christhood was changed and Messengers became local deities. The Divine Messianic idea was made to give place to the coming in a personal way of a deliverer for Jewry, and a regnancy whose seat would be in the Jerusalem of Palestine. To rebuild the walls and buttresses of Zion meant the restoration of the Life and Service by which Christhood is made manifest. And such a work, none but the Ancient Sons of God could accomplish. Hence the prophecy as Message of the Eternal unto Israel.

¹² The Prophet made the outlook glorious. Zion was to be so fully restored that night would be no more. The Gates—or ways of ingress for those seeking Christhoood and egress for those who were appointed unto the Christhood—would never more be shut. There would be no night there.

¹³ This was indeed a great promise. The Lives of the Saints or Sons of God in all ages have revealed the effects of persecution. They have passed through deep waters and been made to pass through fires of suffering, because of their fidelity to the Vision and Service they most loved. Often have their Lives

been made unendurable. The promise here anticipates a great event when the Divine worth of the Life of a Son of GOD will be recognized, and those who have scorned it and oppressed those who embodied it shall come to those who make it manifest that they may learn the way of Christ, and what it signifies to be a dweller in Zion.

¹⁴ In the day of the great resilience as the result of the Oblation, those who have so greatly suffered shall in like measure partake of the Glory that shall follow. For they shall all come back to Zion clothed in the Glory of the LORD, and their Divine Sonship written upon them.

¹⁶ The manifestation of the Christhood by Israel is to be the instrumental force for the bringing of Salvation unto all the Earth and filling her children with the spirit of Thanksgiving and Praise. For all the Gates or Avenues of the Christhood shall resound with the Songs of Zion.

¹⁶ The Sun and Moon are mystical terms. Zion is no mere earthly city requiring external light; Zion is a City of Sol in his Divine Estate. Thence let it be understood that the Sun is the LORD ADONAI Who illumines the Being of the Christhood, individual, corporate and cosmic; whilst the Moon is the illumined Understanding. When the Divine Light for ever shines, and there is no more night in the Mind, then the Soul shall travail no more as it has done for long ages upon the Earth, for such pain and sorrow shall cease, and even the whole Earth shall take on the Glory of the LORD in the degree in which its children can receive that radiance.

¹⁷ The restoration of the Christhood to the heights signified by the Glory of Lebanon, implies tremendous things for the whole Household of Zion. Lebanon is the Great White Mountain of LORD-consciousness altitude. Only those in Divine Christhood can abide there; but the Celestial States named Zion are flooded with the Divine Glory of Lebanon. So the restoration of all Israel to the Zion-hood of such a glorious overshadowing will be realized by every member of the Holy City, and made manifest upon the Earth as auric and resplendent atmosphere.

XXI
The Servant unto Zion

For Zion's sake I would enter into the Silence; and because of Ierusalem I would find His Rest.[1]

But the Word of the Lord I must speak till His Righteousness doth become the Radiance of Zion, and His Salvation the Lamp that burneth as the Sacred Flame within Ierusalem.[2]

Thus wise shall all the Kings of His Orient behold once more His Glory, and reveal Him until the Gentiles have their share therein.

For, by the Lord shall Zion be called a Crown of Glory, and wear the royal Diadem given her from God.[3]

* * * * * *

O Zion, most Holy City of God!

Then shalt thou no more be accounted as one forsaken, nor thine estate as that of the Desolated;

For again shalt thou be known as Hephzibah, and thine estate as the land of Beulah;

For the Delight of the Lord shall be within thee, and thou shalt be in union with Him, as one who is in Joy and Unity in the Marriage Bond.[4]

* * * * * *

Even as those in virgin state do marry and the Bridegroom rejoiceth in his Bride;

So shall thou be married unto Yahweh, and He shall have Joy in overshadowing thee.[5]

* * * * * *

O Ierusalem!

Hear ye this message from the Lord![6]

The Watchmen proclaim it upon thy walls!

394

For these are the Remembrancers of the Lord who serve Him day and night, though they be dwellers in the Silence:
These rest not in the motion of their Being; for they would establish His Glory within thee, and make His Praise to be perfected throughout thy Land.

*   *   *   *   *   *

Prepare ye the Way of the Lord, O Zion!
Raise up the Highway of God for the people, that, through thy Gates they may go into the Holy City.
Gather ye them (as the precious stones within Ierusalem) for the re-building of His Holy Sanctuary within Zion:
Unfurl the Banner of Yahweh before them that they may see the coming of His Salvation, and inherit the Recompense which He doth bring![7]

*   *   *   *   *   *

Then shall the Children of Zion be called a Holy People; the Redeemed of the Lord; a People not forsaken, but sought after and found again.[8]

XXI

NOTES ON TEXT

[1] Here the Prophet revealed the deep yearning of his Being. Incidentally he unmasks his relationship to the House of Israel, and the profound motion of his own Spirit. The Silence to him is something more than being silent. To find the Silence is to enter into a realm where all Soul experiences are most Divinely intimate. The Silence may be expressed as the profoundly reverent vibrant atmosphere that enshrouds a Soul who takes flight to the Presence. In such an instance the Silence is inexpressible.

[2] The Divine Rest is the Sabbath of GOD. It expresses perfect Divine Repose. From it perfect equilibrium proceeds. It is the Rest that remaineth for the People of GOD. In its possession there is found perfect functioning and the Eternal Peace. The Prophet longed for the highest realization of it that he might so affect Zion by the Message, that Ierusalem—

or the whole House of the Earth spiritually considered—should henceforth come to know the blessing of GOD's Love and Wisdom shed through Zion's Children as they ministered and manifested.

³ The Crown of Glory expressed the Life and Service of the Christhood, and the Diadem the regnancy expressed in the Theocracy. For every member was to be bejewelled with all the precious Gems of Zion. The Cosmic Diadem was to be glorious.

It shall yet be glorious, for the promise is being fulfilled.

⁴ The Most Holy City of GOD does not imply that there is nothing higher than Zion in relation to the House of Israel. For even in the Solar constitution there were those who belonged to Zion in the Divine Kingdom as well as the Celestial Zion. But whether Celestial or Divine, the estate signified is always most holy and most consecrate.

There is much that is beautifully intimate here. The desolated one is to be restored to the estate of Hephzibah, and enter into the delights of Beulah. Hephzibah represents the joy of the LORD in HIS restored Zion, and Beulah expresses the delight of the Soul entering into union with the LORD. Such are in the Joy and Unity of a Divine Marriage bond.

⁵ The promise is pregnant with the most vital experience a Soul could know. To be married to the Eternal Mystery whose Name we speak of as JEHOVAH, and be overshadowed by HIS Presence, is one of the most profound parts of a Soul's history as it rises into high Cosmic Consciousness and becomes one with the Eternal. It enters the atmospheric circulus of the Tetragammaton seen and understood from *the Within*. It is in the stream of the Divine Electric Force. It is empowered directly from the Divine World.

If such be the experience of a Son of GOD, what must be the resultant of a community of such Souls rising to the like estate? Yet it is such an exaltation and empowerment of the House of Israel that is promised. For Zion, the Solar Cosmic Christhood, to be directly overshadowed from the Divine World, would mean the rehabilitation of the Cosmic Christhood upon the Earth, and the manifestation of the Eternal through that concrete Body of Sons of GOD.

⁶ The Prophet's appeal is unto all who are able to hear his

Message, that the Ancient Sons of God are again to appear within Ierusalem, the Household of Judah. The Watchmen of Zion are to proclaim it upon the planes of the Earth, and reveal it in the streets or avenues of service. And from the Towers of the middle-kingdom named Samaria, the Remembrancers are sounding forth the Messages. Such Watchmen are dwellers in the Silence and minister for the LORD of Being. They work to redeem Ierusalem and recover for her the resplendence she once possessed. For, in such a restoration, the whole motion of Life upon the Planet would reveal the Divine Wisdom and be expressive of perfect Praise.

7 There is great pathos as well as command in this appeal of the Prophet. To him the full restoration of Zion is everything. He knew the Life and Service the state implied, and what it would mean for the Children of the Planet to have such a manifestation. Hence his appeal. To prepare the Way of the LORD, is to bring every redeeming and purifying influence upon life. To raise up the Highway of God for the people, is to make manifest and teach the Jesus Life; for Jesushood is the Gateway into everything Immortal. To gather the precious stones within the Planet's spheres of service for the rebuilding of the Temple within Zion, is a call to the Sons of God to establish upon the Earth through service and manifestation, all that Zion stands for, and thus to cause the Tribes of Judah to become in soul experience, even as·the Tribes of Israel. To unfurl the Banner of YAHWEH, is assuredly nothing less than the embodiment of the Life that reveals the true nature and auric splendour of Divine Incarnation; such an interpretation of Life will at last have heavenly recompense in world salvation such as the LORD of Being brings.

8 In such a revelation of Divine Life and Service, Zion shall again become the Glory of the Heavens upon the Earth, and the Joy of all who come to know her and share her manifestation and service.

XXII

Yahweh Unto Zion

Thus saith Yahweh, the Eternal One:[1]

*"Awake! Awake! O Zion! In the strength of your Lord,
arise ye! Put on once more the beautiful garments, the robes
ye wore within the Holy City.*[2]

*Arise ye! Shake yourselves free from the bondage ye have
known within fallen Ierusalem: the bands of the oppressors
are broken.*[3]

*In your arising, shake from your garments even the dust
scattered upon them in the day of your great humiliation.*[4]

*Know once more that the Lord God, even I AM the Eternal
One, reigneth within you."*

* * * * * *

*The Watchmen shall again lift up the voice in Praise
of Him; they shall be as one Band.*

*They shall see with open Vision when Yahweh bringeth
them unto Zion.*[5]

*And the places that were laid waste by the enemy shall
burst forth into songs of joy, because the Lord Himself hath
comforted His People Israel, and is accomplishing the
Redemption of Ierusalem.*

*Then shall His Holiness be made manifest, until all
peoples shall behold it; and His Israel shall He gather from
amongst the nations, when He bringeth them all back to
Zion.*

* * * * * *

Thus saith Yahweh unto Israel:—

"O my People! Depart ye not from Me!

*Separate yourselves from all the unclean things found in
Ierusalem.*[6]

Be free from bondage to her fallen ways; for ye are the

chosen vessels of your Lord, separated to dwell within the Holy City.

Therefore, haste ye unto Zion!

Let your flight thither be as of those before whom Yahweh goeth."[7]

*   *   *   *   *   *

How beautiful are the feet of the Messenger who appeareth upon the Mountains of God![8]

He bringeth the Glad Tidings that Yahweh doth bestow His Peace upon all.

Unto Israel is he the bearer of great joy; for His Message proclaims the restoration of Zion, and reveals the Mystery of the Salvation wrought out for her by the Hand of the Eternal God.

XXII

NOTES ON TEXT

[1] The Prophet had received the Message to give to Israel. It was from the ETERNAL. How could the Sons of GOD know that the Message was from the LORD? By the internal evidence of the Message. Those who have known the Truth will recognize it again when they hear it. That which the Prophet was commanded to proclaim unto them, the whole House of Israel had known.

[2] The Voice of the ETERNAL is irresistible. "Awake! Awake O Zion!" The vibrations produced by the utterance of that Call, are immeasurable. One *feels* these touching the Being in the deepest places. And to hear the Call again opens up a world of history. Unless the reader has at some time heard *that Voice*, he could not realize the power and significance of it.

[3] The Prophet speaks as if the bands of the oppression were actually broken. But he was experiencing in vision that day. Then they were broken in the Divine Purpose; now they are broken in fact. The Oblation brought this to pass. They were broken during the Travail of ADONAI in the Divine Passion in which the Sin-Offering was made.

⁴ In nothing is Israel to fall short. The awakening and arising must be completed by shaking from the Life all the effects of the bondage experienced in this world. Only thus could it be possible for them to realize once more the regnancy of the ETERNAL ONE. The process of such a purification is that of the Regeneration.

⁵ The Watchmen of Zion are those who look for the Dawn. They are the early awakened ones looking out for the signs of the Divine appearing. Often they are alone, separated from their brethren. Oft-times their vision is under great limitation, and they cannot see afar in the Dawn. But they are *the real workers* for the healing of Life upon the Earth. Often they become so absorbed in their limited service, that they mistake it for the larger vision of Life and Service for Zion. These are all to be brought into the fuller vision and the realization of the Christhood. They will yet arise and share the Glory of Zion through this Message, and again unite themselves to the Sons of GOD who are to form the Solar Cosmic Christhood. YAHWEH is in this Message, and all HIS Sons shall return to HIM.

⁶ This is not a call from the Divine World to the Sons of GOD to be anxious to leave this world; for they are sorely needed. But it is a call to them which they may not disregard, to separate themselves from the unclean ways of the commercial, social and national life of the people. A Son of GOD may not—he could not—be involved in the awful traffic of the Creature-lives for food and clothing, nor take part in the corrupted social and national politics. He may not be a man of self-seeking parties, but a man of Righteousness and Equity, Compassion and Pity. He must separate himself from all forms of evil policies, and be guarded from the Heavens that he does not become ensnared by those who are out to mislead and betray for power and self-aggrandizement. The Sons of GOD must be separated in their lives, from everything that hurts and destroys, all that is unjust and unlovely, whatsoever casts a shadow upon Life and the Sacred Name; for the state of Zion is holy.

⁷ This is the thought that should dominate the consciousness of every son of Israel. Life should be lived in the vision of YAHWEH. In such a state the Son walks with the LORD. Pursuing such a path there is no looking back and longing

after the City of the plains. The unredeemed ways of the
Children of this world must be absolutely left; they must not
have any power over the Son of God. When the prince or
Zeitgeist of this world comes to Israel, he must find no response;
YAHWEH alone must reign.

⁸ The Mountains relate to Celestial and Divine Altitudes.
All Divine Messages are given from those heights. The
Messenger is one who dwells upon them. He is able to stand
upon their summits. His feet are most beautiful; for the feet
signify *the Understanding* in its dual function. It is a reflector
of the Divine Glory and an interpreter of the Divine Mystery.

XXIII

A Song of Israel

*In that day shall this song be sung throughout
the Land of Judah:—*
Behold, the City of God is ours!
It is Inheritance of Himself He giveth unto us.
Its Walls and Bulwarks speak of His Salvation.
We will enter through its Gates;
*For all who love His Righteousness and whom His
Truth holds fast, may enter in.*[1]

* * * * * *

O Israel! Trust in the Lord for evermore;
For in Jehovah is your Eternal Strength.

*O Lord, Thou keepest in Thy Peace all Thy
children when they put their trust in Thee and hold their
Mind in equipoise from Thee.*[2]

XXIII

Notes on Text

[1] When this Song can be truly sung in this Planet, then to
incarnate upon its Planes will not mean for the Sons of God
who come to minister, a life of pain, sorrow, and deep travail.
Those who love the Divine Truth, and would ever live to
make manifest God's Righteousness, shall be able to enter its
Gates with Joy. For in that Day Eden will have come back
again, and all Life will be full of the Light and Gladness of
the Heavens.

[2] In the Regenerate Life the Mind is in true balance. So
are all the Planes. They are equipoised in God. They have
found their place of *rest*. In this state the Great Peace is a
possession. And though there will be no deflection in polarity,
the Mind and the Planes will have power to move in any
direction when so commanded for service.

Thus God giveth His Peace unto His Children.

XXIV

THE CITIES OF EGYPT

Behold, O Israel!

The Lord of Hosts cometh swiftly, riding upon the Chariot of the Heavens;[1]

Into Egypt doth His Presence come, to move her Heart with streams of Life from out His Cloud, and cause to be removed the idols she hath bowed before and served.[2]

*   *   *   *   *   *

In that day shall five cities which are within the land of Egypt, speak again the ancient tongue of Canaan;[3]

And Heres shall once more be lit up with the full radiance of the Adonai.[4]

And in the centre of the land shall rise the Altar of the Lord for Sacrifice;[5]

And on her borders shall be reared again, to be most manifest, the Pillars of the Lord.[6]

These shall be as sign of and as witness to God's over-shadowing Cloud, from out whose Glory shall come forth His Anointed One, Who shall, through the great power of Yahweh, restore to Israel, the Law of ancient Egypt redeemed.[7]

*   *   *   *   *   *

In that day shall Egypt know the Lord:

Unto Him shall she make sacrifice of all her powers, and in sweet oblation give the Life's forces to fulfil His Law in perfect service.

Then shall His Name be written over all the land.[8]

*   *   *   *   *   *

In His coming He shall touch and heal the many wounds of Egypt, and cause these so to return in full response to His entreaty, that all the Powers shall be restored to Equity.

*And in that day there shall be built God's Highway,
whose length shall stretch across the land and reach unto
Assyria;*[9]

*O'er it shall all Assyrians pass to commerce with the
Egyptian Powers;*

For these shall rise into the service of Assyria.

* * * * * *

*And in that day shall Israel be crown of both and o'er
them reign, outpouring blessing;*[10]

For the Lord of the Heavens shall bless them all:

*The Powers of Egypt are His people, the Assyrian Land
the fashion of His Hands, and Israel the Royal Household
whose Sons hold heritage from the Gods, even the Lord's
Inheritance, for embodiment.*[11]

*And in that day, the waters of God's Nile shall flow
again, to heal the wounded land, and bring back treasures
which have been long lost to all her children.*[12]

*Then shall the Delta be restored; the channels of the
Seven-fold Stream be purified and opened, receiving the rich
flow of Yahweh's waters whose coming will give Life to all,
enriching Egypt as she receives the Assyrian commerce, and
returns enhanced unto the Assyrians, the age-long riches of
her land.*[13]

*Then too shall Fisher-Argosies of Israel pass through her
waters, bearing wealth from the Eternal shores of Yahweh;
thus crowning Egypt with Assyrian glory, even as Assyria
becomes enshrined with Israel, in Yahweh's Radiance.*[14]

XXIV

NOTES ON TEXT

[1] The Chariot of YAHWEH is the Eternal Fire whose cloud is
said to have borne Eli-jah into Heaven. The Mystery of
JEHOVAH is expressed as Love and Wisdom, Life and Light,
Energy as Force or Power, and transmutory Energy, Fire or
Energy. These special Attributes are revealed in the Celestial

embodiments and motions; and empirically, every Soul becomes conscious of them, for all glorious attributes of the Eternal Mystery we speak of as the FATHER-MOTHER, are felt by the Soul because it has the correspondences of them in its constitution.

2 Egypt is mystical, representing a state of manifestation even in an unfallen world as well as a fallen state. In some of the cryptic references to Egypt, the outer Body is meant and the experiences gathered out of it. Originally the term belonged to the Mysteries. Something of this may be discerned in the Nile with its White and Blue streams having been accounted a Sacred river. This is emphasized in the Delta.

3 The five Cities are states and attributes. They represent the five senses; but the senses are attributes and powers. In their origin and source they are of the Soul. The senses of the Body are only avenues through which the real senses operate. Sight, hearing, smelling, tasting and feeling are of the inner Life. The outer avenues may see, hear, smell, taste, and feel without understanding anything, relating to objects, correlating the various objects. The Cities are, therefore, Soul attributes which are intimately related to all the planes of the Being, and can express themselves in and through every vehicle as the need arises. And they are likewise states of experience which, elsewhere in this volume, the reader will find unveiled as Courts of the Temple of Life.

4 Heres is the City of Light. Therefore the restored Vision is meant. The term was used as synonymous with the Sun. The Vision will be full of Divine Radiance that will interpret everything to the Understanding. In the resplendence of ADONAI it will recover the ancient mystery-tongue of Canaan.

5 The magnetic centre of the Body shall be so responsive to the inner Life that it shall be one with it. The solar-plexus, the centre of relationship between the inner and the outer Life, and pivot of contact of the Soul with the vehicle, shall so respond to the Being's Will as to become an Altar for GOD whereon the Life-Forces are laid in sacrifice.

6 The Pillars of the LORD upon the borders express the restored ministry of Boaz and Joachim—the two guardians at the porch of the Temple of Solomon. These represent Divine strength and fidelity, and also the Divine Love and Wisdom

carried through to support the portico or arch of the porch at the entrance to the Temple of Being. Here it is shown that the redeemed and regenerate Life will be complete from the centre of Being to the circumference of experience.

⁷ Love and Wisdom, Divine Fidelity and Strength, are the sure evidences that the Soul has been with GOD, and dwells within HIS Cloud of overshadowing Radiance. And where such an experience is realized, the Messiah or Christ comes forth from the Cloud, for the Soul becomes one with the Anointed. And when all Israel enters into such a realization, as the Cosmic Christhood they shall again be the vehicle of YAHWEH for the manifestation of HIS Anointed One, revealing HIS Eternal Law.

⁸ What profound significance is hidden here! For the sacred Name of YAHWEH to be written over all the land, means that, in that Day, HIS Presence will be felt by all Israel throughout each Tribe and community, and that in the Life of Israel, from the central Altar of Being to the full circumference of the manifested Life within the Earth's realms of service for the Sons of GOD, the Divine Glory shall be revealed.

⁹ The Highway of GOD is one of Righteousness and Equity, Love in its majesty, justice and mercy. From the outer life the way must show the Presence of GOD, as it passes towards and into the heart of Assyria, the Mind. Assyria is midway between Egypt and Syria, or the Land of the Soul. It was and is a great country. All the creations of Art are expressed within and through it. And it represents the regnant administrative attributes of both Soul and Christhood. The Assyrians are the powers of the Mind used by the Soul in the creative and administrative realms, and through into the realms of the outer manifestation, named Egypt. When these realms are in unison, the powers of Egypt become servants unto Assyria; and the creative forces of the latter can express themselves through Egypt, the realm of the Body.

¹⁰ When such a unifying event takes place, Israel shall be the crown of both and have regal sway over them. For Israel represents the Divine Man in the Divine Kingdom of the Soul, the ruling Presence in the Soul system to whom Assyria and Egypt both pay tribute, and whose lands are placed at the Service of the Divine LORD. The relationship of all Israel

to Assyria and Egypt, is mystical. And the bondage of Israel in Egypt, and captivity in Assyria, are to be understood as the Spiritual Being in bondage to the ambition of the Mind and desires of the Body.

11 How slow men and women are to recognize that all the powers of Body and Mind—Egypt and Assyria, are GOD's. They are HIS creations and given endowments. There is a very real sense in which the powers of the Body and Mind are HIS people. All the forces of Egypt are HIS own creations, all the land of Assyria—the realm of the Mind, the fashion of HIS own Hands. If the children of men could be brought to recognize and acknowledge this in all their conduct, how different the world would become! Israel will assuredly acknowledge it, for Israel belongs to the Royal Household of the Gods, for whom the supreme end of Life and Service must ever be unity in the Divine, and the exposition of the LORD of Love and Wisdom in embodiment.

12 The Nile, as stated above, is a Mystical river. Its dual streams are the channels through which the Divine Love flows to water the Land and make it fruitful. The sources of the Nile are far above the Land of Egypt, and flow down, even as the physical plane Nile, through a great tract of Divine and Celestial country. When the land is healed of its wounds, the Divine Stream will be able to accomplish great things for all HIS children.

13 A world of spiritual history, past and yet to be again, is expressed here. For the Delta of the Nile has a more profound meaning. In its mystical significance it is related to the ELOHIM; for the Streams of the sacred Seven flow through the whole Being, even unto and through the land of the outer life manifestation.

14 The Fisher-Argosies of Israel indicate what the Cosmic Christhood will become in ministry unto all the Children of Assyria and Egypt. They will transmit GOD's wealth.

XXV

The Coming of The Sons of God

In that day the Earth's wilderness shall be changed,
and the solitary places turned into scenes of joy.

The desert shall even be rejoiced for their coming, and
the Rose shall blossom in the midst of it.[1]

Abundant shall be the blooms within its borders, and
gladness shall be expressed in Songs of Joy.

Unto it may come the glory of great Lebanon; for
the excellency of Carmel and Sharon shall return.[2]

In them shall be beheld the Glory of the Lord; through
them shall be revealed the Excellency of God.[3]

* * * * * *

Be ye strong again, ye whose hands have been weakened.

Stand upright, ye whose powers have been enfeebled,
whose hearts have been smitten by the shadow of fear!

Behold ye, how God doth come to give you recompense!
In His coming He will save you.

* * * * * *

Then shall the veiled Eyes be opened and enlightened;
the long lost power of Audience once more be restored.

Then shall the maimed and halting leap as the hart,
and those who have been silent, sing songs of joy.

For, through the Wilderness shall flow the Living Waters
whose streams shall reach unto the desert land:

Then all the parched ground shall be refreshed when
heavenly dews have filled the empty pools.[4]

* * * * * *

From out the hidden places where the dragons dwelt
shall spring forth reeds and rushes of pure thought and
feeling whose motion shall make music in their response to
heavenly Breaths, as these pass through them.[5]

408

*The Zion-Highway shall then be built, paved with the
precious stones of Truth and Love.*[6]
Upon its walls there shall be writ in Gold,
THE SACRED WAY
*Over its stones the unclean shall not pass, nor foolish men
who are but wayfarers;*
It shall not be for those:[7]
*Nor shall the lion astral-forces be found there, nor ravenous
desire attain to walk therein—these shall find no place of
action there.*[8]

*　　*　　*　　*　　*　　*

*That Way shall be for those who are the Lord's redeemed;
His ransomed ones; they shall walk therein as they return
to Zion, now no longer captives held hostage to prevent the
day of their Redemption; but free men who once knew the
freedom of God's City, and now return again to that estate,
singing the Songs of Joy Eternal and glad Praise, in which
the ebb and flow of sorrow have no place.*[9]

XXV

NOTES ON TEXT

[1] The one-time spiritual planes of the Earth have long been
in the confusion of a wilderness and the barrenness of a desert.
The coming of the Sons of GOD will effect great changes. It is
the Rose of Sharon that is referred to. It is the flower of the
Christhood. It will bloom in every true Son of Israel. The
manifestation of Christ shall be in the midst of the desert, and
the places that have been made spiritually solitary.

[2] Lebanon has already been explained as a cryptic term for
the Divine Kingdom—the Great White Mountain. Carmel is
the Mount of the Intellect, the vehicle of our Divine Intelligence. Sharon is the Angelic state of Love revealed in the
Christhood manifestation. Carmel is a state in the middle

court of the Temple of Being, Sharon is a state in the realm of the Soul, Lebanon is a state in the sanctuary of Being in which the Sublime Mystery-Presence has become realized.

³ When the Sons of GOD return to their ancient inheritance, the Glory of Lebanon shall shine through them, making the realm of Sharon blossom with the Rose of Christhood, and Carmel take on the radiance of the Divine Splendour, and reveal GOD as the LORD of Being, and High Excellency in all the Earth.

⁴ The empty pools may be expressed as the Mind, Understanding, Heart, Intuition, Perception and Realization. How empty of true vision, right understanding, Soul-interpretation, and the empiricism of Divine realities, these pools have been throughout great ages, the state of the world reveals to-day in every realm. Even within supposed spiritual gardens, believed to be well-watered from the Heavens, the drought and impoverishment have been unspeakable.

⁵ The hidden places of dragons is a mystical expression. The dragon is the unredeemed Mind. An evil Mind is indeed a ravenous beast. It lies in wait for its prey. It is subtle, cunning, and destructive. It makes captive the whole spiritual man, and ravishes the unsuspecting Soul. It is the destroyer of the peace of all the world, and opposes itself to everything that is of GOD. It is breathing *fire* from its nostrils now in the ravishing spirit of war.

In the Redemption to be accomplished by the Sons of GOD through their manifestation of Christ, the dragon will be destroyed; for the Mind of the world shall be healed. And in the places of thought, purpose, ambition, envy and hatred where the dragon lay in wait, shall grow up all those qualities that are the children of harmony, goodness, truth, compassion, pity and Love.

⁶ Over such conditions of redeemed state the Highway to Zion may be built. That is, the sacred Mysteries associated with the Christhood may once more be unveiled and revealed to all who would make processional to higher degrees of Life. It will be possible, then, to have established upon the Earth, the Sacred Temple of the Christhood as Solomon's Masonic Temple.

⁷ Gradually the wayfarers and foolish will cease to walk the

Earth, for the time will come when no place will be found for such. The merely curious, the unattached to Divine Ideas, the insincere, the modern sophist and mere experimentalist, could not possibly walk over the High-way of Zion. All such are mere wayfarers.

⁸ The materialistic systems which have devastated the Earth, socially, commercially, and religiously.

⁹ The Zion-Highway, which is now being built by the restoration of the Christhood and all that such implies, is for those Souls who desire unutterably to attain again to be in estate and service, the Sons of GOD.

XXVI
Divine Counsels

This is the Inheritance of the Servants of the Lord,[1] *even
that Righteousness which is of Me, saith the Lord God.*

* * * * * *

*Oh come to the Living Streams, all ye who are athirst;
and drink ye of His Waters of Life!*[2]

*Oh come to His Table of Shew-bread, all ye who through
the way of your going, have been impoverished in your
gifts;*[3] *and eat ye once more of the Bread of His Sanctuary!*

*Oh come, all ye who are athirst for the milk of His
Word, that ye may again drink of the Wine of His Love!*[4]

* * * * * *

*Be ye not of those who expend their strength for naught,
and who toil for the bread and wine which satisfy not!*

*Buy ye from your Lord those priceless gifts of the Bread
of His glorious Substance, and the Wine from the Chalice
of His Heart.*

*Buy ye these, O Servants of the Lord, of Him who selleth
not His treasures for earthly gain, but who doth gift the
priceless riches of Bread and Wine unto all who seek His
Presence within the Sanctuary.*[5]

* * * * * *

Thus saith the Lord, the God of Sabaoth:
"Hearken unto Me, My people!

*I will restore unto you again those riches wherewith you
were enriched when you dwelt in the land of your ancient
Inheritance.*[6]

Therefore, incline to Me.

*Come with opened ears that being quickened, ye may
remember the ancient covenant of the Eternal One.*

*Remember again the tender mercies revealed unto you
through My Servant David,* THE BELOVED ONE,[7] *whom I*

have anointed to be your Shepherd-King; for he is once more to witness of Me, and lead many into the paths of My commandments."

* * * * * *

"The peoples that yet know Me not, shall be called; through the witness of My beloved Servant shall thy Lord, the God of Israel, become manifested.

Then shall the nations come to know that the Lord of Sabaoth is with you, because My Glory shall rest upon the Sanctuary, and shall be revealed through you.[8]

For ye shall be the channels through which My Life-giving streams shall flow unto them.

Then it shall come to pass that ye shall be able to speak unto the people as those who know Me, and say to them:—

Seek ye the Lord, for He may be found;

Let your prayer be unto Him, for He is ever nigh;

Forsake the path of the wicked, and give no place to the ways of the unrighteous.

Turn ye to the Lord who bestoweth compassion, whose blessings are multiplied unto the healing of all afflictions.

Thus saith the Eternal One, the Lord of all the Heavens:—

"My thoughts are not as the thoughts of men; neither are the ways of My Love and Wisdom like those revealed in the way of their going.

Even as the Heavens of My Dwelling are higher than those of the Earth, so are My thoughts high above the thoughts of men, and My ways other than their ways.

As the rain falling upon the Earth doth refresh it and make it bring forth life unto manifestation through leaf and bud, and provide bread for man's need and wine for his refreshment, even so shall it be when My Word goeth forth to accomplish My Will.

It shall fructify and enrich all things whereon it alighteth;

The wickedness of man it shall make void;

It shall clothe the Earth with her ancient glory, and fill the hearts of all her children with joy and peace;

In its proceeding it will unveil the Hills of Zion, making them resonant with joy and gladness, revealing the Glory of My Presence;

For the Hills of Zion shall once more vibrate to the motion of Praise, as that is offered continually upon My high Mountains.[9]

All the Cedars of Lebanon shall see the work of My hand; as they spread forth their branches in ministry for Me, they shall have joy and gladness.[10]

Through the Trees of My planting My Word shall once more be made manifest;

For these shall be the ensign of My Presence upon the Earth.[11]

XXVI

NOTES ON TEXT

[1] The Divine Inheritance embraced the Christhood. The riches of Grace are found in the realization of the Divine Love and Wisdom. These form the Righteousness and Equity of the Eternal. All who are GOD's Servants possess as Inheritance these Divine qualities, and make them manifest.

[2] This appeal is unto Israel. They were always the Souls who felt great spiritual thirst. For them, the Waters of Life were absolutely necessary. They were vital elements without which they could not live the inner Life, nor even endure the life of existence. For the Being requires oxygen, hydrogen and nitrogen, as these are found in their primal state in the Divine World, before they are reduced and changed in order to be accommodated to such a world as this is, as water.

[3] The Table of Shewbread was in the Middle-court of the Temple. It represents the nourishment that comes to the Being through Revelation and corresponds in the realm of the

Intuition and Understanding, with the Manna or Ambrosia of the Gods in the realm of Realization. The Shewbread comforts and sustains on the way, the Priests of GOD; the Manna nourishes the Being, and keeps the whole of the Soul system in the fashion of and in unison with the ETERNAL LORD.

4 The Wine is more than the Water. The latter has added to it the Life-Stream of the Divine Passion.

5 The Divine Substance and Life-stream are gifts of GOD. They are of HIS Own inner Mystery. Those who imagine they can barter with GOD, or have these added to their life like something purchasable, are truly children of the night; Souls who cannot have known the holy Mystery of GOD. Eternal Life is Divine realization. It is gifted to us; yet it is won. It is gifted by the FATHER-MOTHER in HIS endowment of us, it is won through our natural growth and true response.

6 The measure of the power of the House of Israel to reveal through interpretation and make manifest in embodiment, the ETERNAL ONE, will be equal to the measure in which the priceless treasures have become again realized in Christhood. For that high estate is won by the Soul as it appropriates the Divine Substance and Life stream.

7 David, the son of Jesse, becomes the Shepherd-King-Prophet. He is a mythical personage, in many ways, very different in character from the Jewish story of King David. David is the Beloved One. He is the Divine Beloved One. He is the Soul's Beloved. He is the LORD's Servant, the Christ in the Heavens and within the Soul, the Herd of Israel in one of the Messengers of the FATHER-MOTHER. As ADONAI He becomes the progenitor of Christ; as the Divine Regal Principle in the Soul, He becomes the Manifestor. He is the Principal or Head of the Divine System, and is chief Singer and Instructor. He Herds, or gathers and guides the whole flock of the Soul's emotions, affections and thoughts.

8 The Cloud upon the Sanctuary is a realizable sublime Mystery. It is the Aura of the Presence of the ETERNAL. It has its representations in the Aura of Stars and Souls, for every Star has its own glory. So has every Soul. And each one is, in the degree of its manifestation and service, an individuation of the Sublime Mystery.

⁹ The Hills of Zion refer to exalted spiritual states, and the High Mountains to still greater altitudes. All the states of Zion are in harmony with the Divine Will, and respond to the Praise sung upon the great realms.

¹⁰ The Cedars of Lebanon are the Christs of GOD. They grow upon the slopes of the Great White Mountain. Symbolically, Cedar-wood was most precious. The Ark of the Covenant was built of it (which is the Presence within). And it was used for Incense, the symbol of the Prayers of GOD's Christs.

The Cedars of Lebanon, trees of great ages and mighty branches, fittingly symbolize the most holy Mystery of the Christhood. They are the Children of the Divine Cross, Trees of GOD's planting, the vehicles of the LORD for HIS manifestation.

¹¹ Such Souls upon the Earth are, through their manifestation, the surest possible sign that GOD draws near to reveal HIMSELF as the Eternal Love and Wisdom; and as the LORD, full of compassion and graciousness.

JEHOVAH

COMETH AS

THE EARTHQUAKE, WHIRLWIND AND FIRE

THEN THE GREAT PEACE